As Miss Beelzebub Likes

Volume 4

matoba

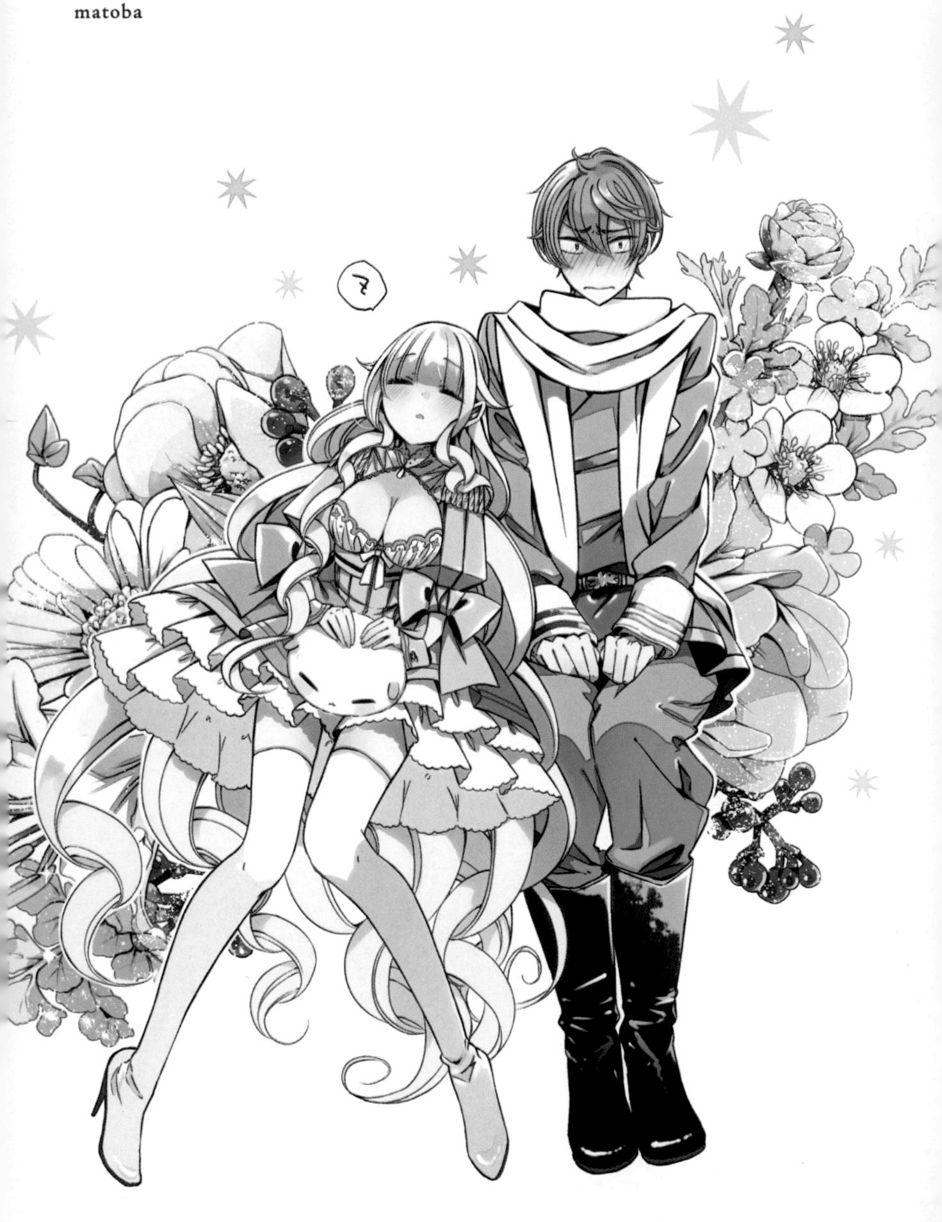

contents

As Miss
Beelzebub
Likes

THE USUAL LIBRARY DUO

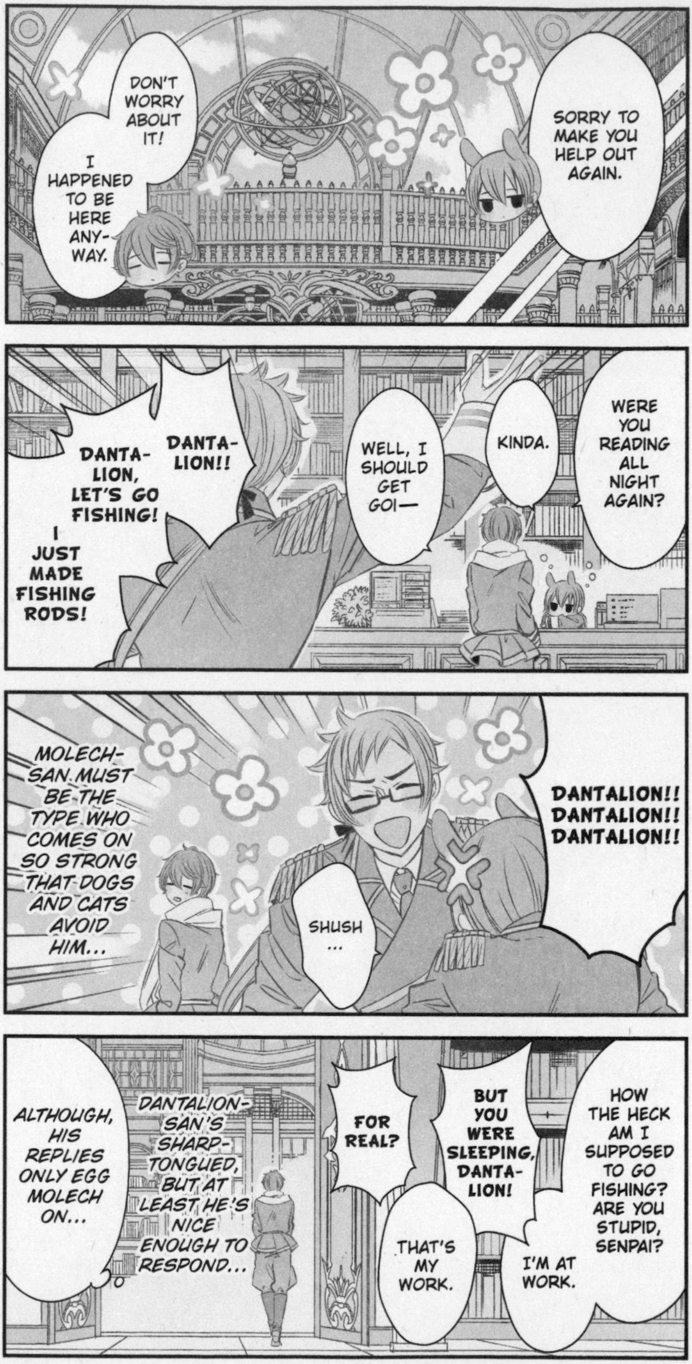
SORRY TO MAKE YOU HELP OUT AGAIN.
DON'T WORRY ABOUT IT!
I HAPPENED TO BE HERE ANYWAY.
WERE YOU READING ALL NIGHT AGAIN?
KINDA.
WELL, I SHOULD GET GOI—
DANTALION!!
DANTALION, LET'S GO FISHING!
I JUST MADE FISHING RODS!
DANTALION!! DANTALION!! DANTALION!!
SHUSH...
MOLECH-SAN MUST BE THE TYPE WHO COMES ON SO STRONG THAT DOGS AND CATS AVOID HIM...
HOW THE HECK AM I SUPPOSED TO GO FISHING? ARE YOU STUPID, SENPAI?
I'M AT WORK.
BUT YOU WERE SLEEPING, DANTALION!
THAT'S MY WORK.
FOR REAL?
DANTALION-SAN'S SHARP-TONGUED, BUT AT LEAST HE'S NICE ENOUGH TO RESPOND...
ALTHOUGH, HIS REPLIES ONLY EGG MOLECH ON...

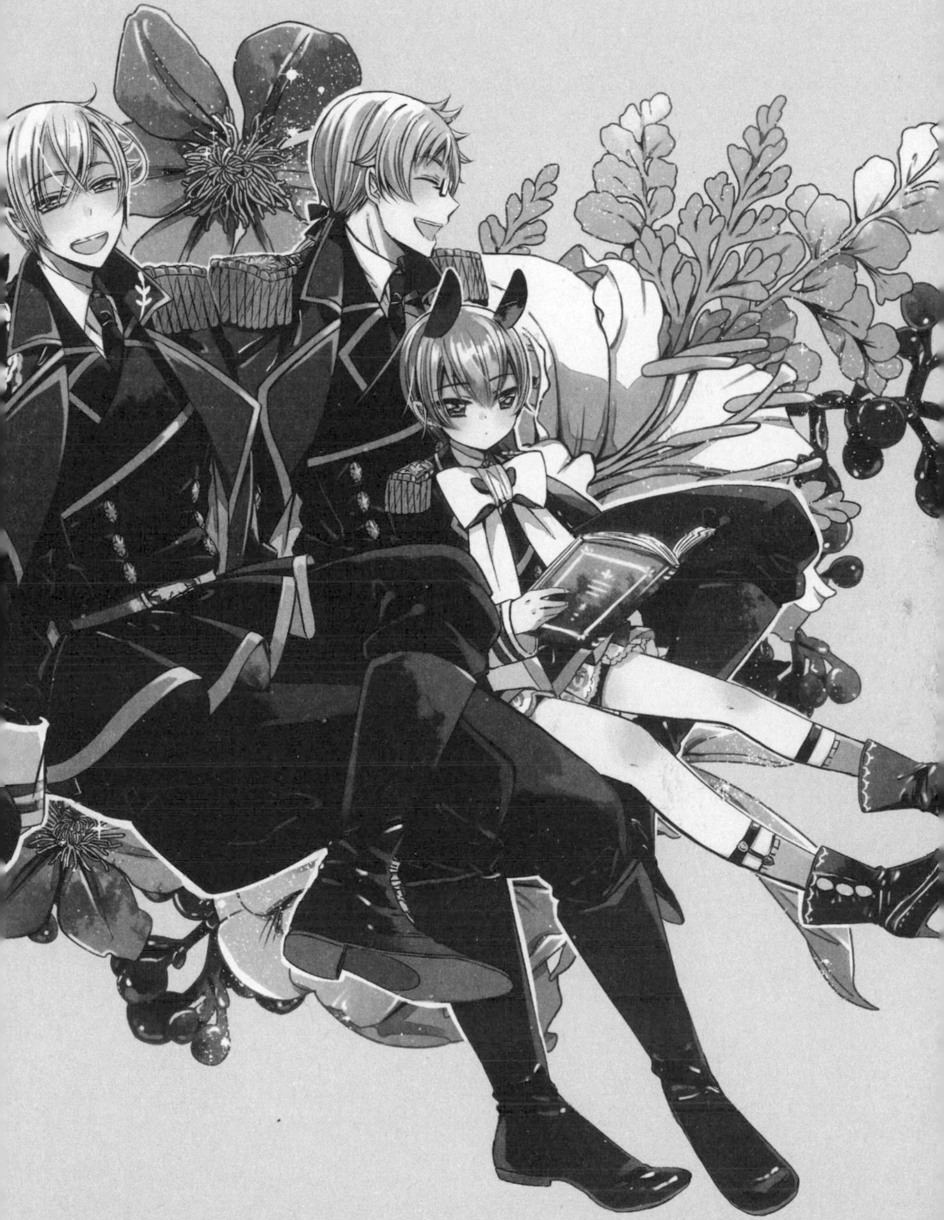

CHAPTER 23

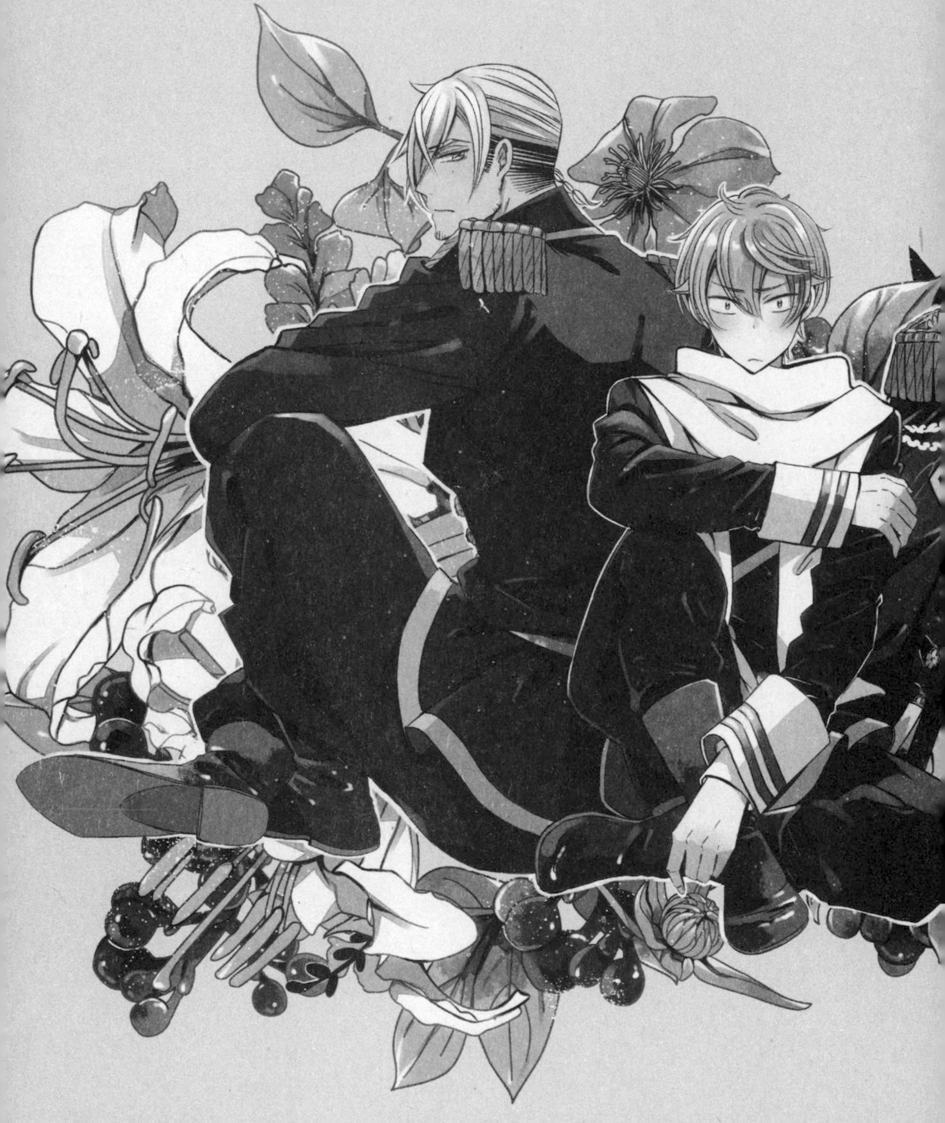

As Miss Beelzebub Likes

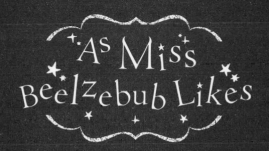

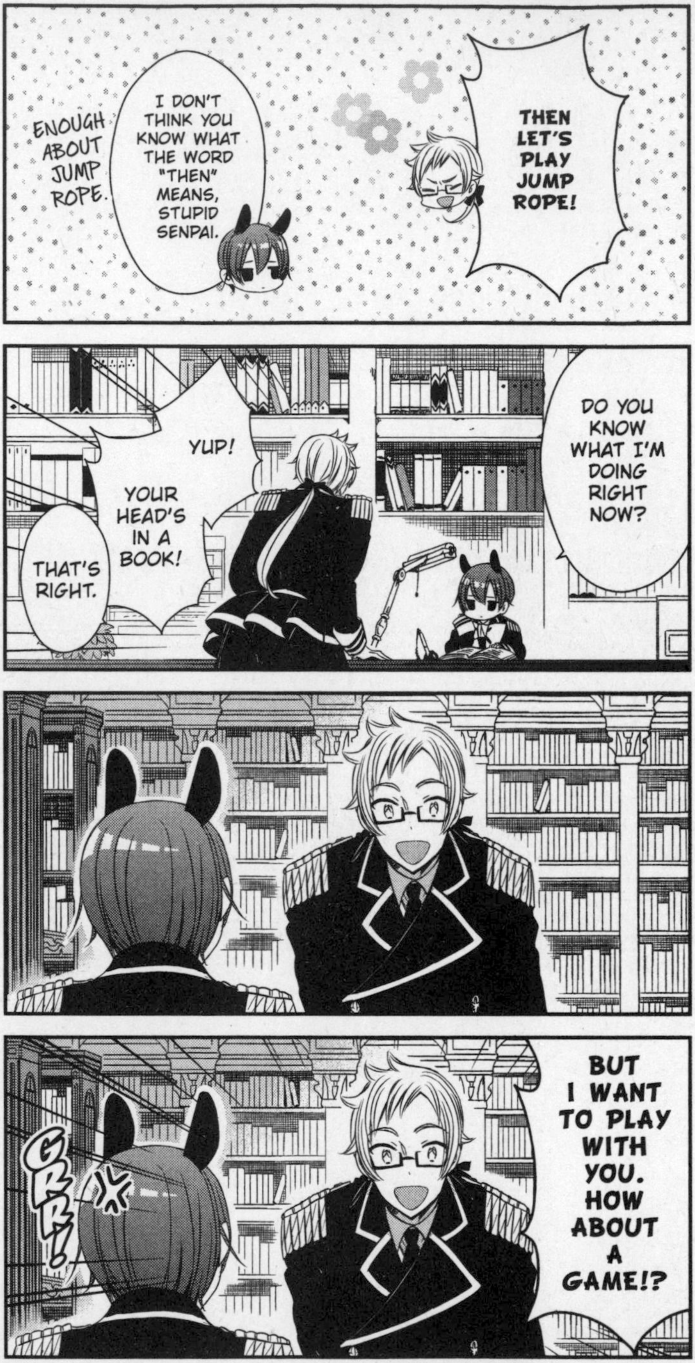
THEN LET'S PLAY JUMP ROPE!
I DON'T THINK YOU KNOW WHAT THE WORD "THEN" MEANS, STUPID SENPAI.
ENOUGH ABOUT JUMP ROPE.
DO YOU KNOW WHAT I'M DOING RIGHT NOW?
YUP!
YOUR HEAD'S IN A BOOK!
THAT'S RIGHT.
BUT I WANT TO PLAY WITH YOU. HOW ABOUT A GAME!?
GRR!

WHAT THE HECK IS HE SAYING?

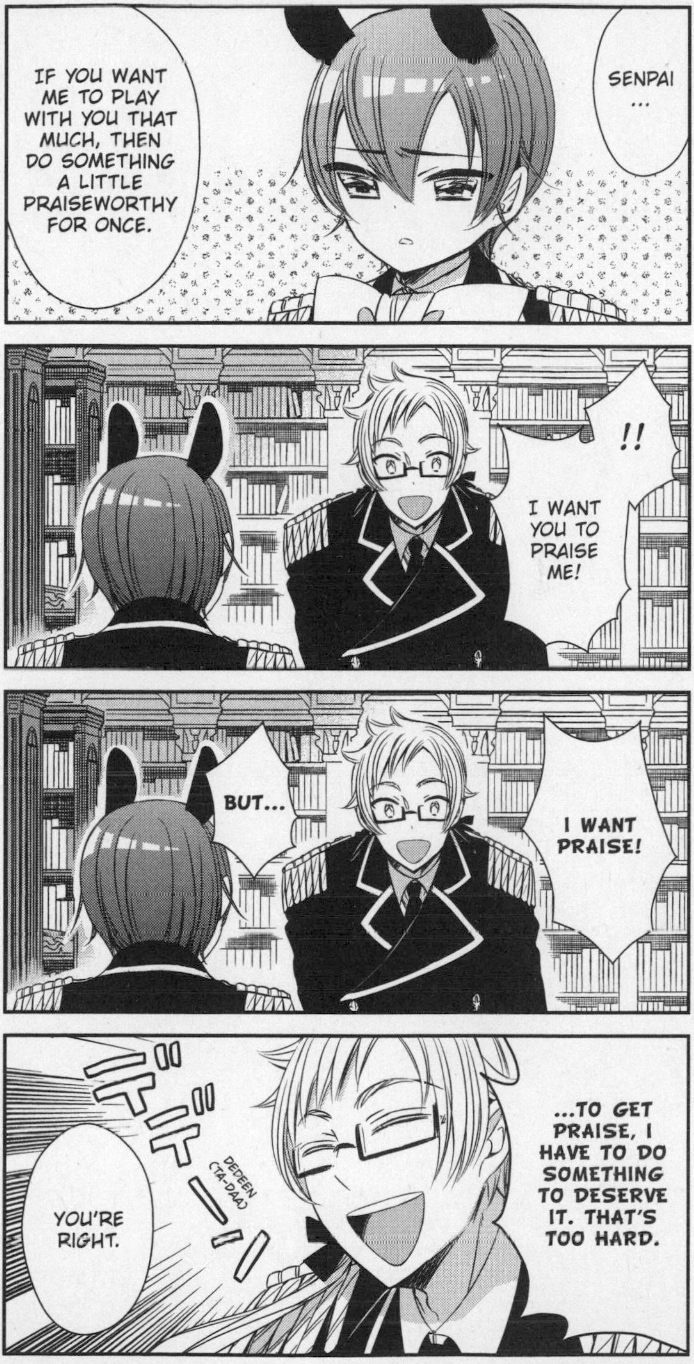
SENPAI ...
IF YOU WANT ME TO PLAY WITH YOU THAT MUCH, THEN DO SOMETHING A LITTLE PRAISEWORTHY FOR ONCE.
!!
I WANT YOU TO PRAISE ME!
I WANT PRAISE!
BUT...
...TO GET PRAISE, I HAVE TO DO SOMETHING TO DESERVE IT. THAT'S TOO HARD.
DEDEEN (TA-DAA)
YOU'RE RIGHT.

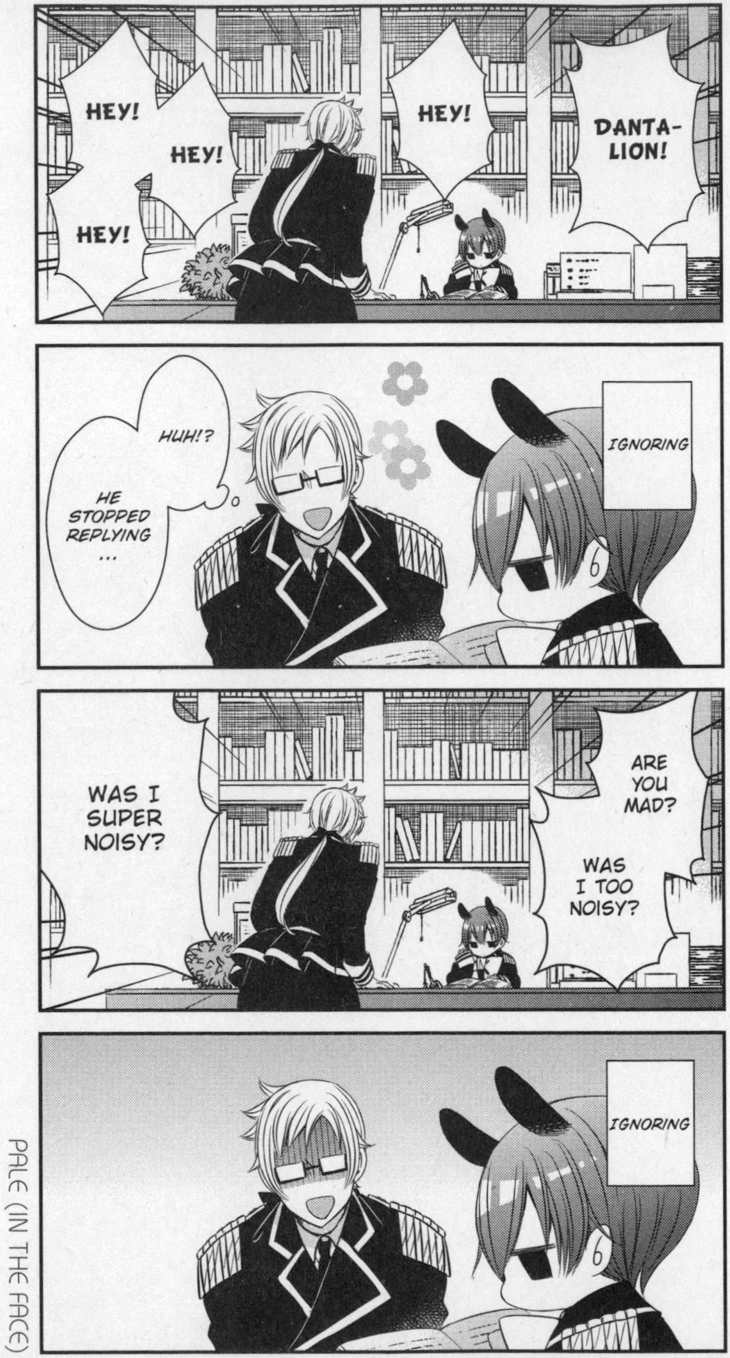
DANTA-
LION!
HEY!
HEY!
HEY!
HEY!
IGNORING
HUH!?
HE STOPPED REPLYING...
ARE YOU MAD?
WAS I TOO NOISY?
WAS I SUPER NOISY?
IGNORING
PALE (IN THE FACE)

TOTALLY IGNORED

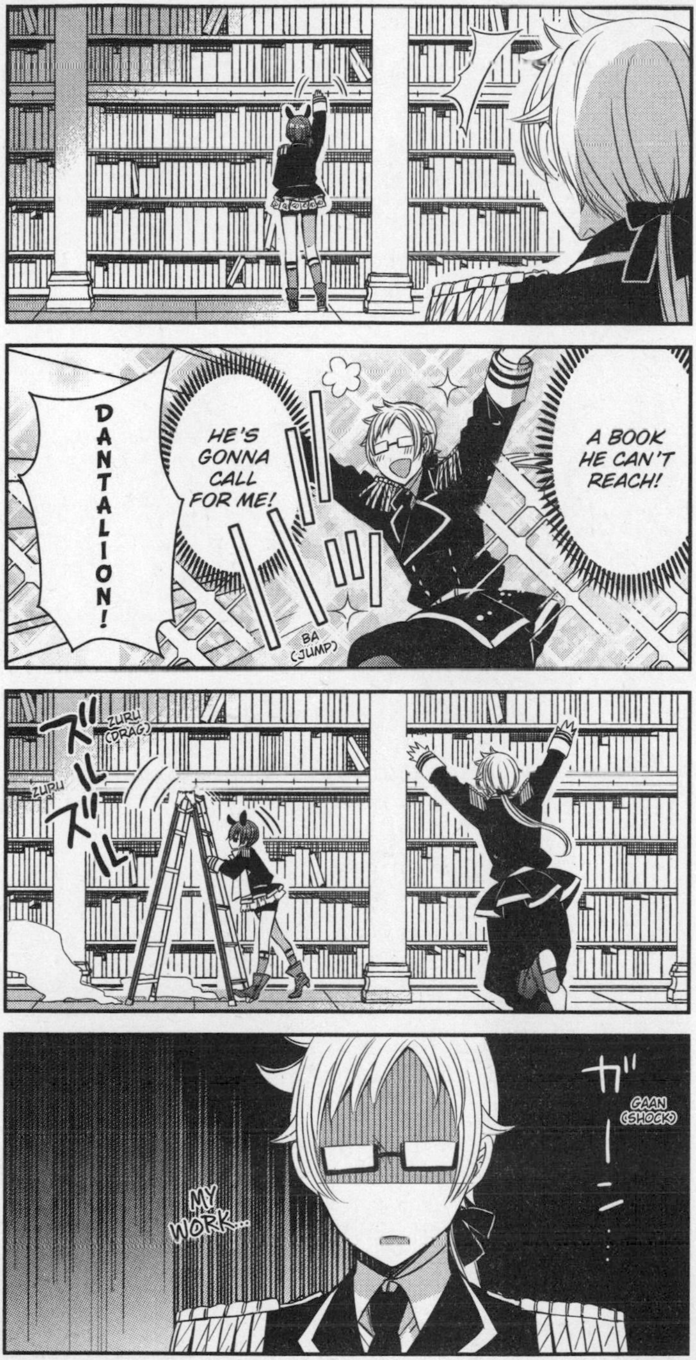
A BOOK HE CAN'T REACH!
HE'S GONNA CALL FOR ME!
DANTALION!
BA (JUMP)
ZURU (DRAG)
ZURU
ズルズル
ガーン
GAAN (SHOCK)
MY WORK...

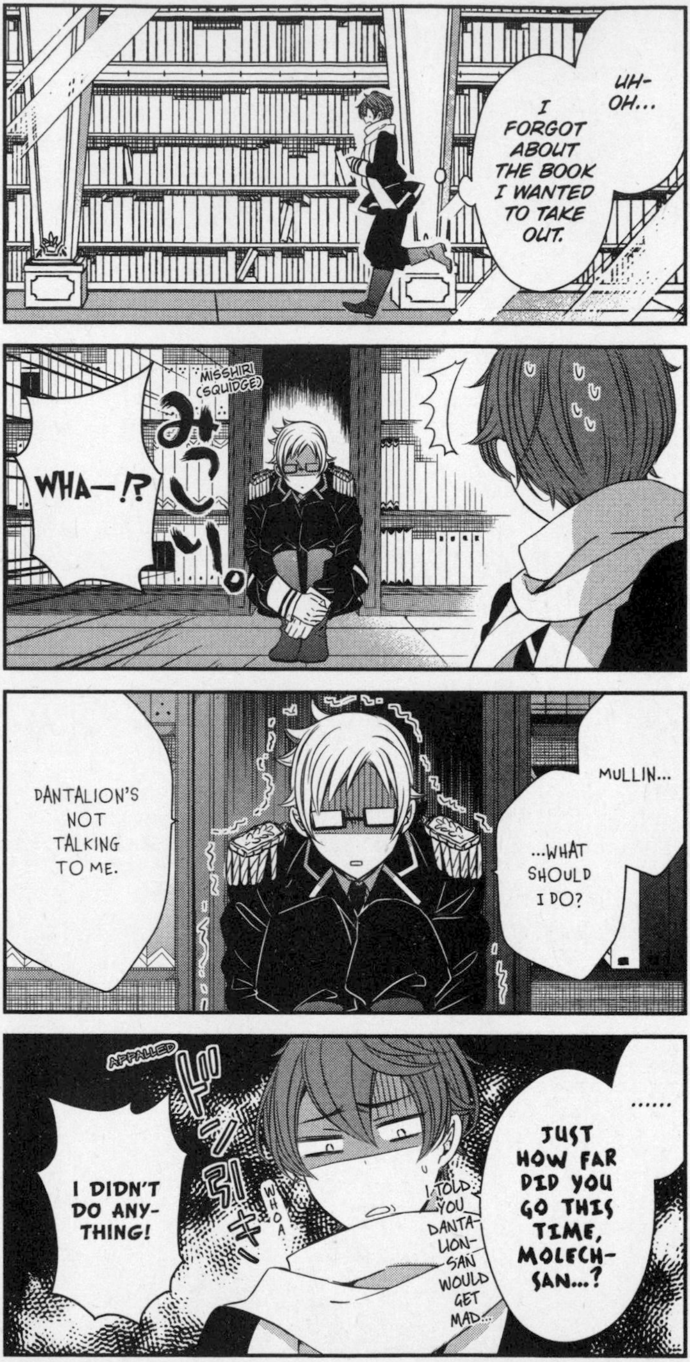
UH-OH... I FORGOT ABOUT THE BOOK I WANTED TO TAKE OUT.
MISSHIRI (SQUIDGE)
WHA—!?
MULLIN... ...WHAT SHOULD I DO?
DANTALION'S NOT TALKING TO ME.
......
JUST HOW FAR DID YOU GO THIS TIME, MOLECH-SAN...?
I TOLD YOU DANTALION-SAN WOULD GET MAD...
WHOA
APPALLED
I DIDN'T DO ANYTHING!

(I THINK!!)

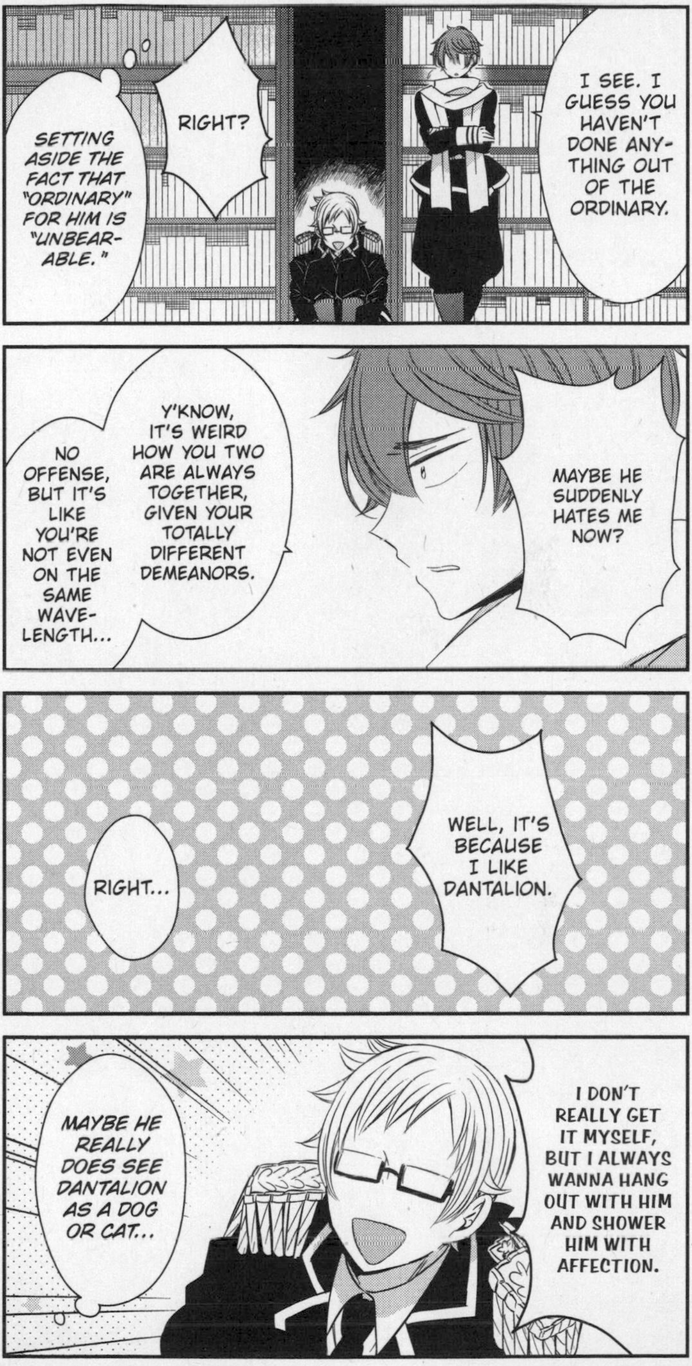
I SEE. I GUESS YOU HAVEN'T DONE ANYTHING OUT OF THE ORDINARY.
RIGHT?
SETTING ASIDE THE FACT THAT "ORDINARY" FOR HIM IS "UNBEARABLE."
MAYBE HE SUDDENLY HATES ME NOW?
Y'KNOW, IT'S WEIRD HOW YOU TWO ARE ALWAYS TOGETHER, GIVEN YOUR TOTALLY DIFFERENT DEMEANORS.
NO OFFENSE, BUT IT'S LIKE YOU'RE NOT EVEN ON THE SAME WAVELENGTH...
WELL, IT'S BECAUSE I LIKE DANTALION.
RIGHT...
I DON'T REALLY GET IT MYSELF, BUT I ALWAYS WANNA HANG OUT WITH HIM AND SHOWER HIM WITH AFFECTION.
MAYBE HE REALLY DOES SEE DANTALION AS A DOG OR CAT...

HE HAS BUNNY EARS, THOUGH

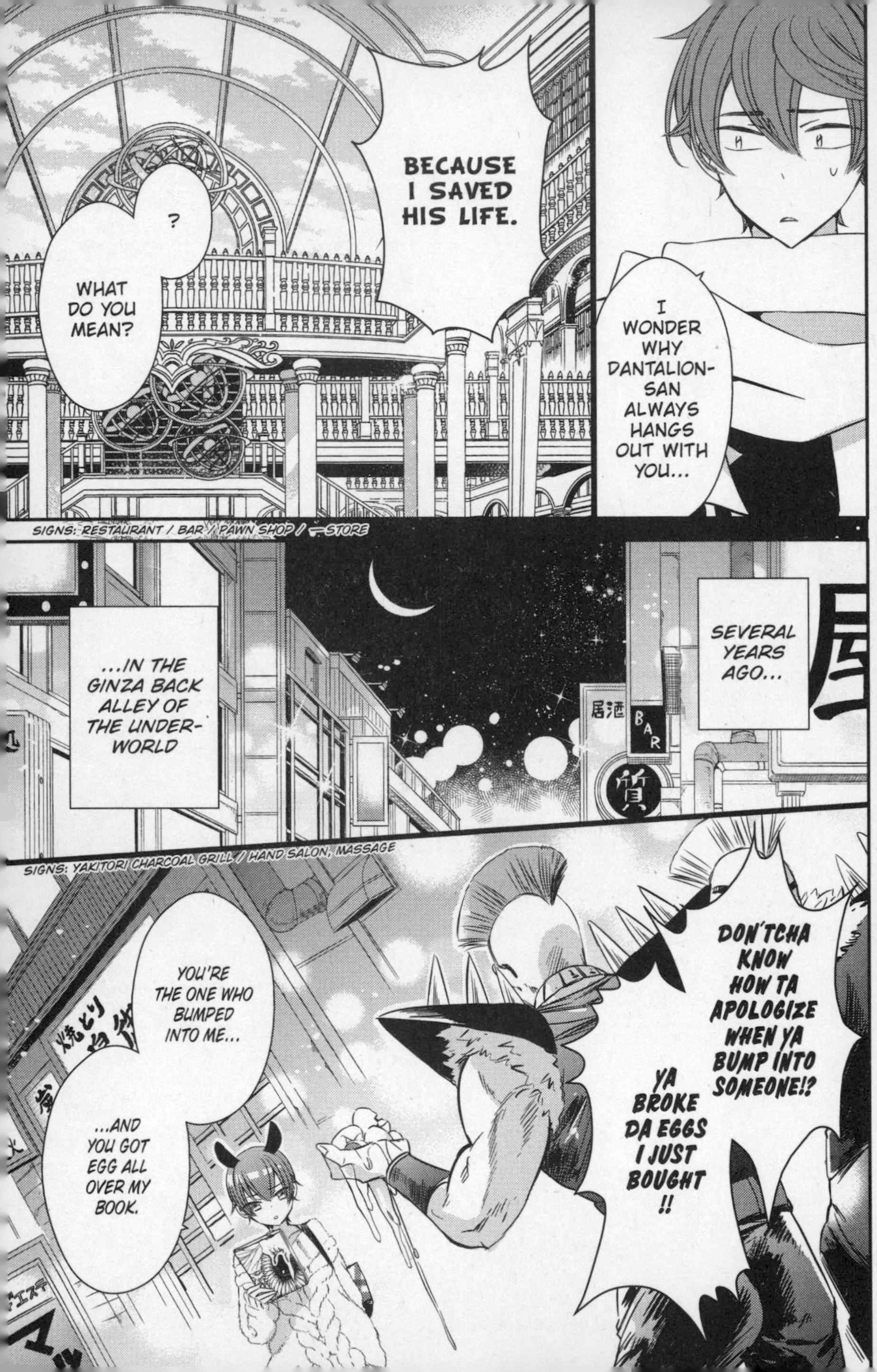
I WONDER WHY DANTALION-SAN ALWAYS HANGS OUT WITH YOU...
BECAUSE I SAVED HIS LIFE.
?
WHAT DO YOU MEAN?
SIGNS: RESTAURANT / BAR / PAWN SHOP / —STORE
SEVERAL YEARS AGO...
居酒
BAR
質
...IN THE GINZA BACK ALLEY OF THE UNDER-WORLD
SIGNS: YAKITORI CHARCOAL GRILL / HAND SALON, MASSAGE
DON'TCHA KNOW HOW TA APOLOGIZE WHEN YA BUMP INTO SOMEONE!?
YA BROKE DA EGGS I JUST BOUGHT!!
YOU'RE THE ONE WHO BUMPED INTO ME...
...AND YOU GOT EGG ALL OVER MY BOOK.
焼とり

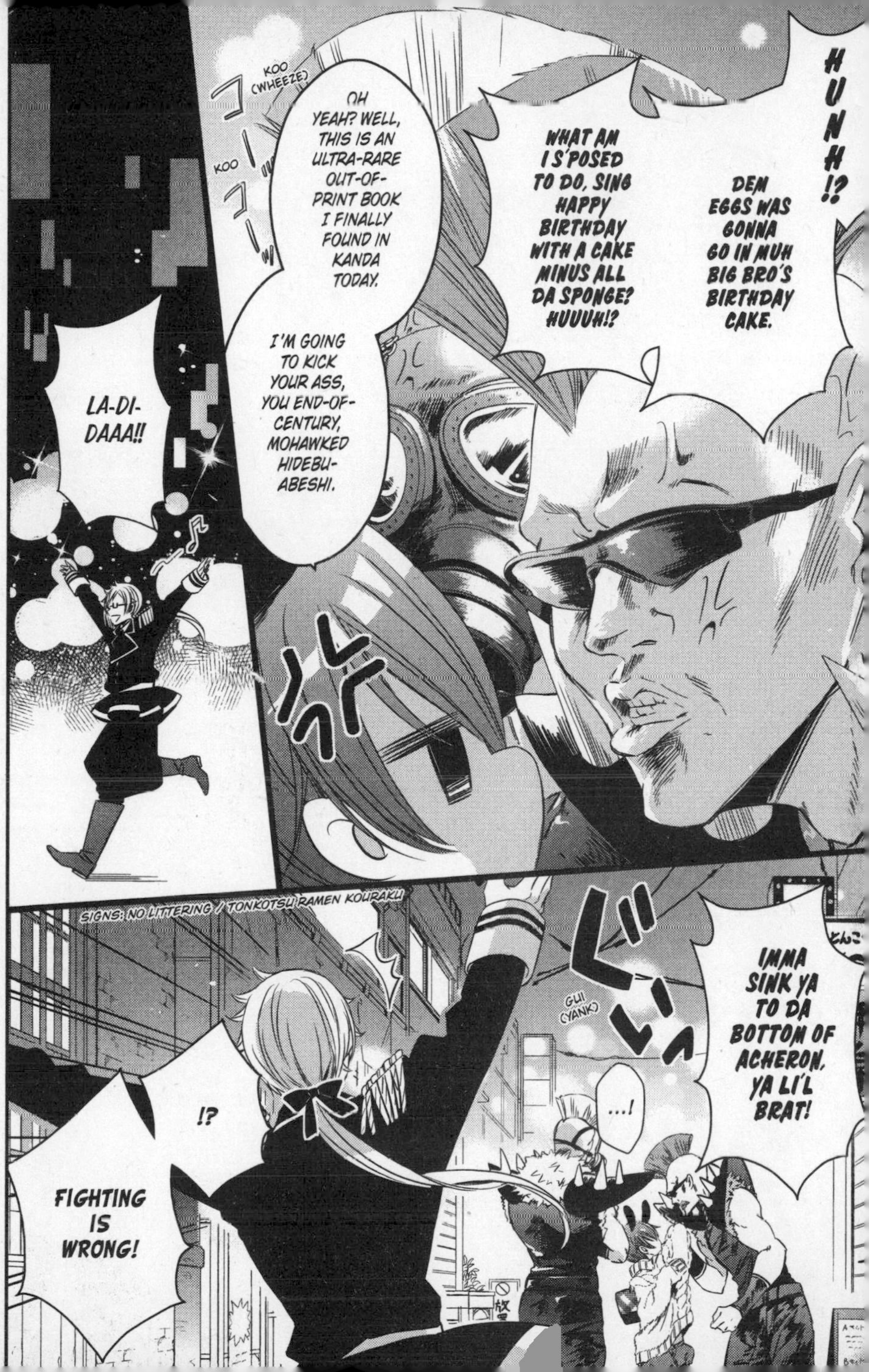
HUNH!?
DEM EGGS WAS GONNA GO IN MUH BIG BRO'S BIRTHDAY CAKE.
WHAT AM I S'POSED TO DO, SING HAPPY BIRTHDAY WITH A CAKE MINUS ALL DA SPONGE? HUUUH!?
KOO (WHEEZE)
KOO
OH YEAH? WELL, THIS IS AN ULTRA-RARE OUT-OF-PRINT BOOK I FINALLY FOUND IN KANDA TODAY.
I'M GOING TO KICK YOUR ASS, YOU END-OF-CENTURY, MOHAWKED HIDEBU-ABESHI.
LA-DI-DAAA!!
SIGNS: NO LITTERING / TONKOTSU RAMEN KOURAKU
IMMA SINK YA TO DA BOTTOM OF ACHERON, YA LI'L BRAT!
GUI (YANK)
...!
!?
FIGHTING IS WRONG!

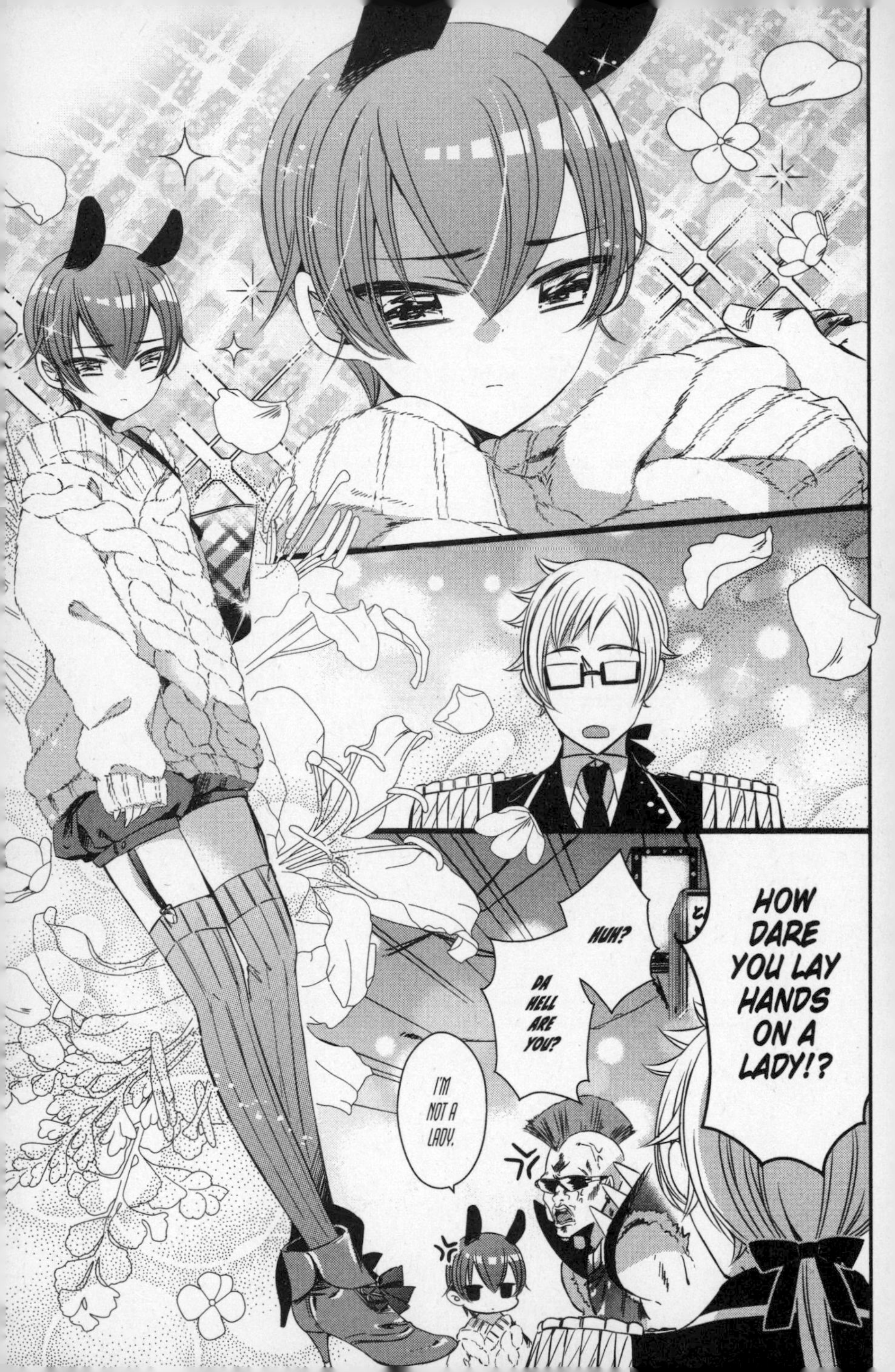
HOW DARE YOU LAY HANDS ON A LADY!?
HUH?
DA HELL ARE YOU?
I'M NOT A LADY.

AIN'T NO PLOY

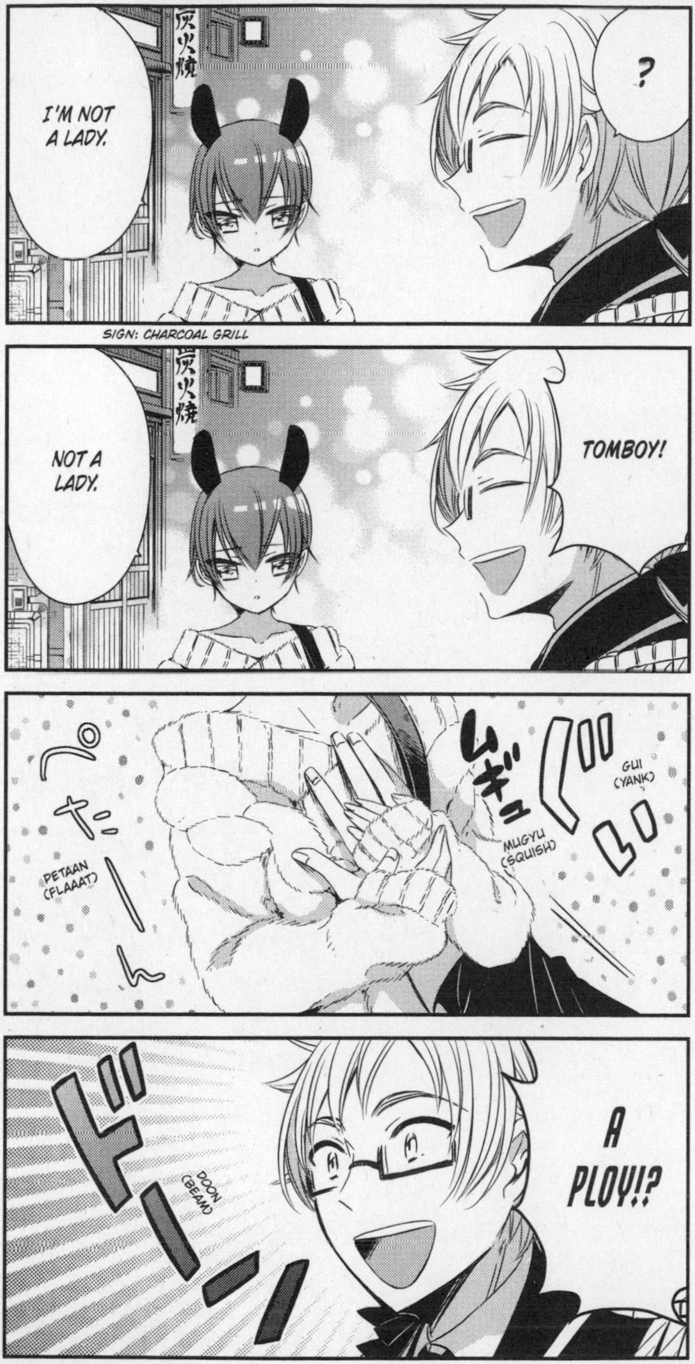
?
I'M NOT A LADY.
炭火焼
SIGN: CHARCOAL GRILL
TOMBOY!
NOT A LADY.
炭火焼
ぐいっ
GUI (YANK)
ムギュ
MUGYU (SQUISH)
ぺたーん
PETAAN (FLAAAT)
A PLOY!?
ドーン
DOON (BEAM)

COUNTERATTACK

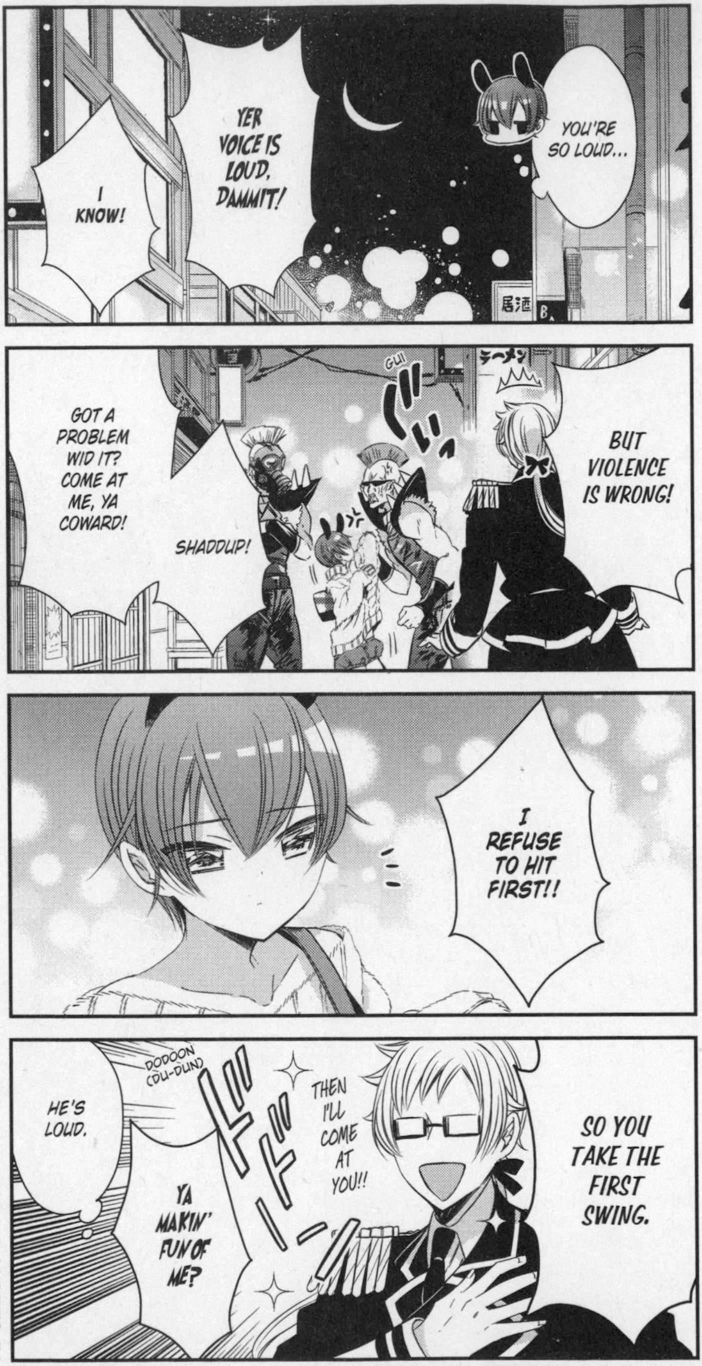
YOU'RE SO LOUD...
YER VOICE IS LOUD, DAMMIT!
I KNOW!
BUT VIOLENCE IS WRONG!
GUI
GOT A PROBLEM WID IT? COME AT ME, YA COWARD!
SHADDUP!
I REFUSE TO HIT FIRST!!
SO YOU TAKE THE FIRST SWING.
THEN I'LL COME AT YOU!!
DODOON (DU-DUN)
YA MAKIN' FUN OF ME?
HE'S LOUD.

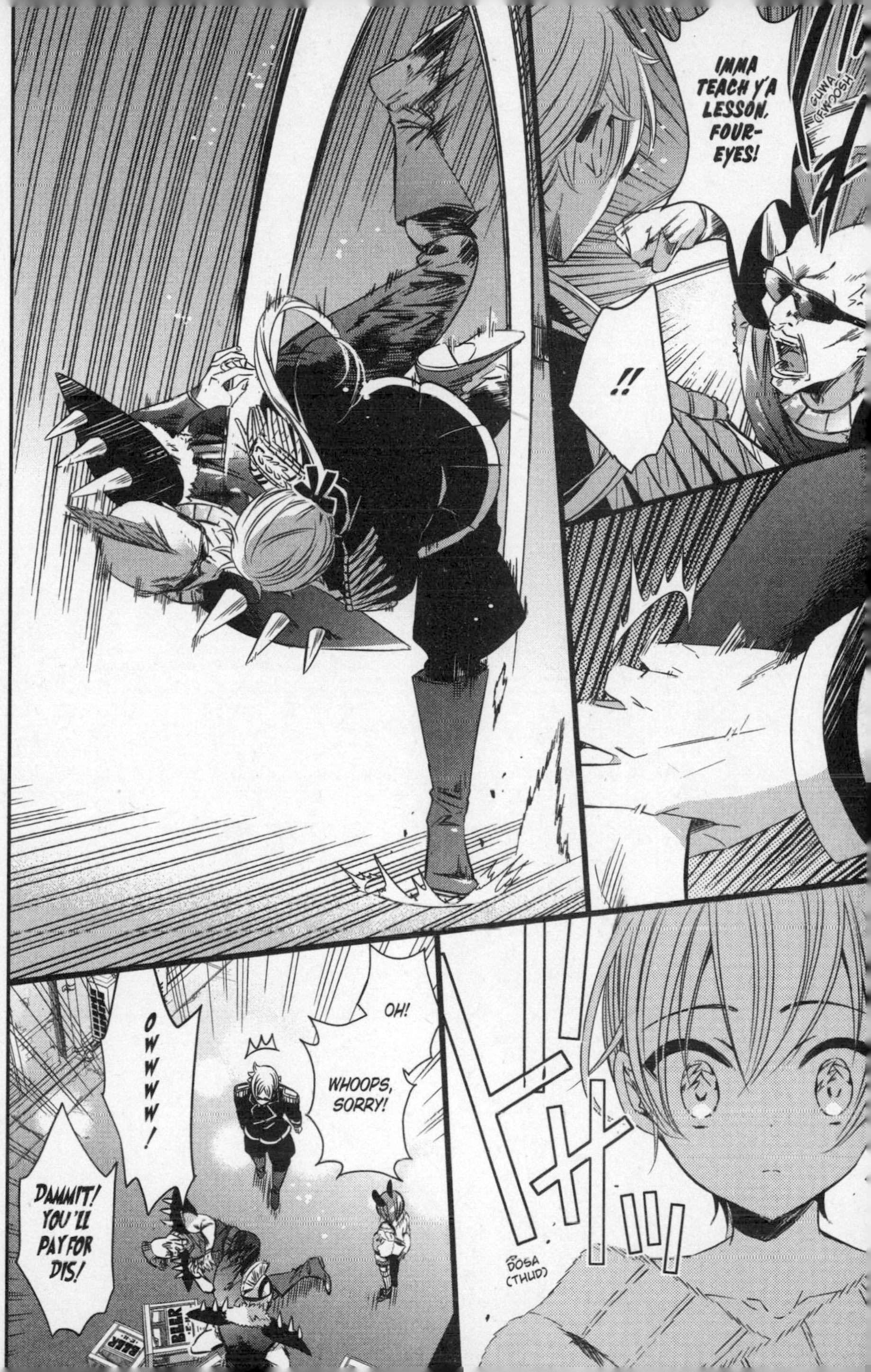
IMMA TEACH Y'A LESSON, FOUR-EYES!
GUWA (FWOOSH)
!!
DOSA (THUD)
OH!
WHOOPS, SORRY!
OWWWWW!
DAMMIT! YOU'LL PAY FOR DIS!
BEER

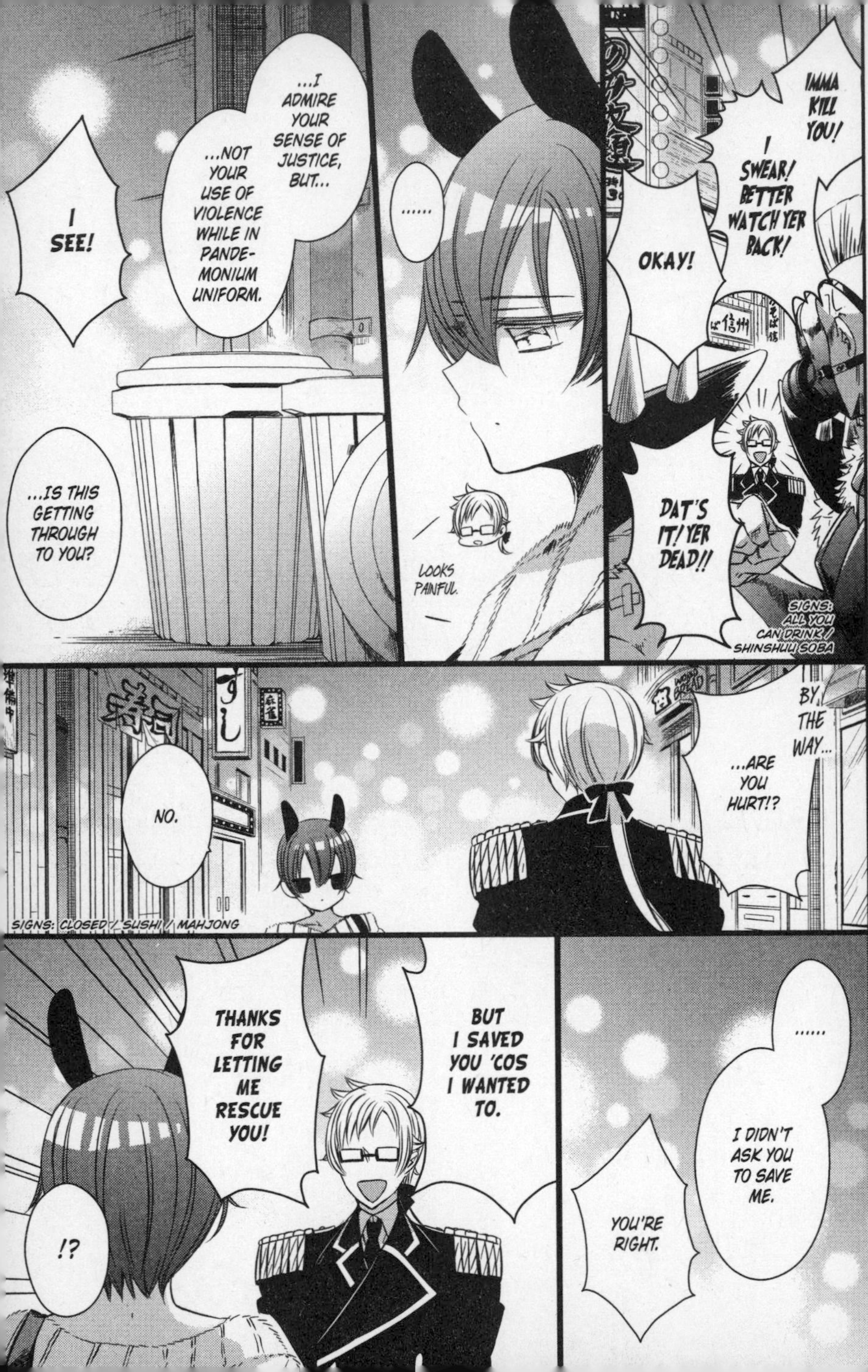
IMMA KILL YOU!
I SWEAR! BETTER WATCH YER BACK!
OKAY!
DAT'S IT! YER DEAD!!
SIGNS: ALL YOU CAN DRINK / SHINSHUU SOBA
......
LOOKS PAINFUL.
...I ADMIRE YOUR SENSE OF JUSTICE, BUT...
...NOT YOUR USE OF VIOLENCE WHILE IN PANDE-MONIUM UNIFORM.
I SEE!
...IS THIS GETTING THROUGH TO YOU?
BY THE WAY...
...ARE YOU HURT!?
NO.
SIGNS: CLOSED / SUSHI / MAHJONG
......
I DIDN'T ASK YOU TO SAVE ME.
YOU'RE RIGHT.
BUT I SAVED YOU 'COS I WANTED TO.
THANKS FOR LETTING ME RESCUE YOU!
!?

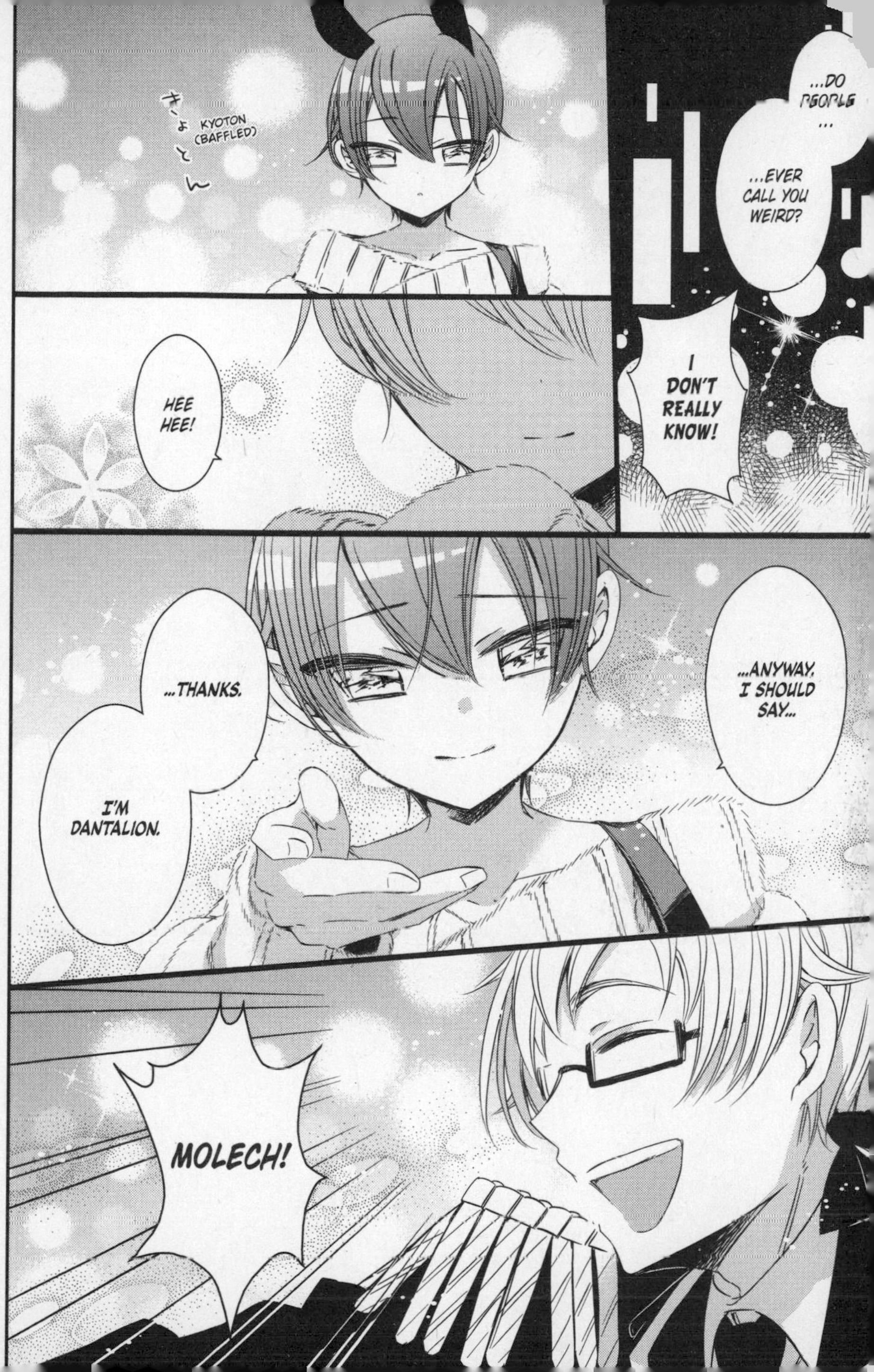
...DO PEOPLE ...
...EVER CALL YOU WEIRD?
I DON'T REALLY KNOW!
きょとん
KYOTON (BAFFLED)
HEE HEE!
...ANYWAY, I SHOULD SAY...
...THANKS.
I'M DANTALION.
MOLECH!

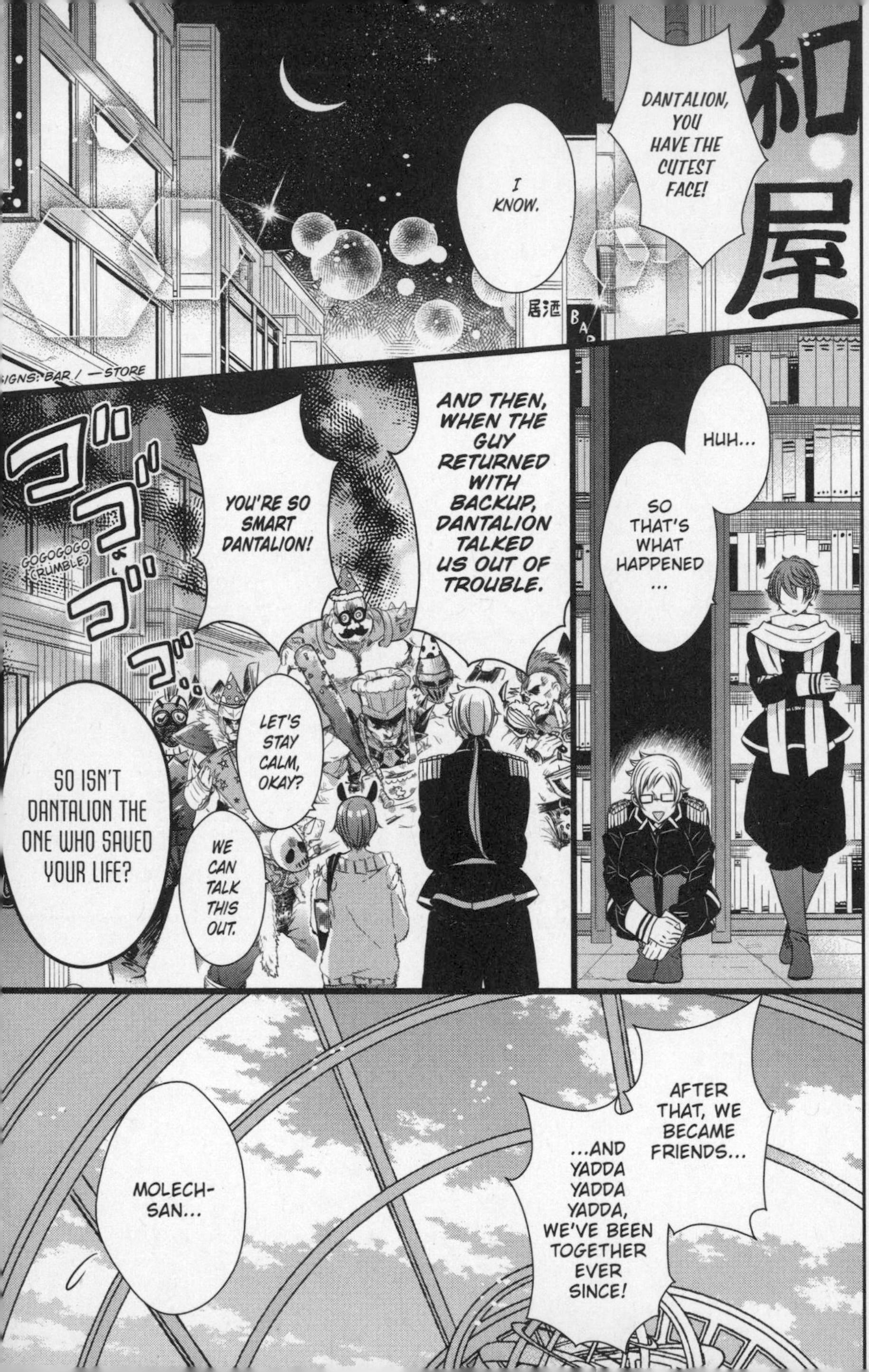
DANTALION, YOU HAVE THE CUTEST FACE!
I KNOW.
和屋
居酒
BAR
SIGNS: BAR / —STORE
HUH...
SO THAT'S WHAT HAPPENED...
AND THEN, WHEN THE GUY RETURNED WITH BACKUP, DANTALION TALKED US OUT OF TROUBLE.
YOU'RE SO SMART DANTALION!
ゴゴゴゴ
GOGOGOGO (RUMBLE)
LET'S STAY CALM, OKAY?
WE CAN TALK THIS OUT.
SO ISN'T DANTALION THE ONE WHO SAVED YOUR LIFE?
AFTER THAT, WE BECAME FRIENDS...
...AND YADDA YADDA YADDA, WE'VE BEEN TOGETHER EVER SINCE!
MOLECH-SAN...

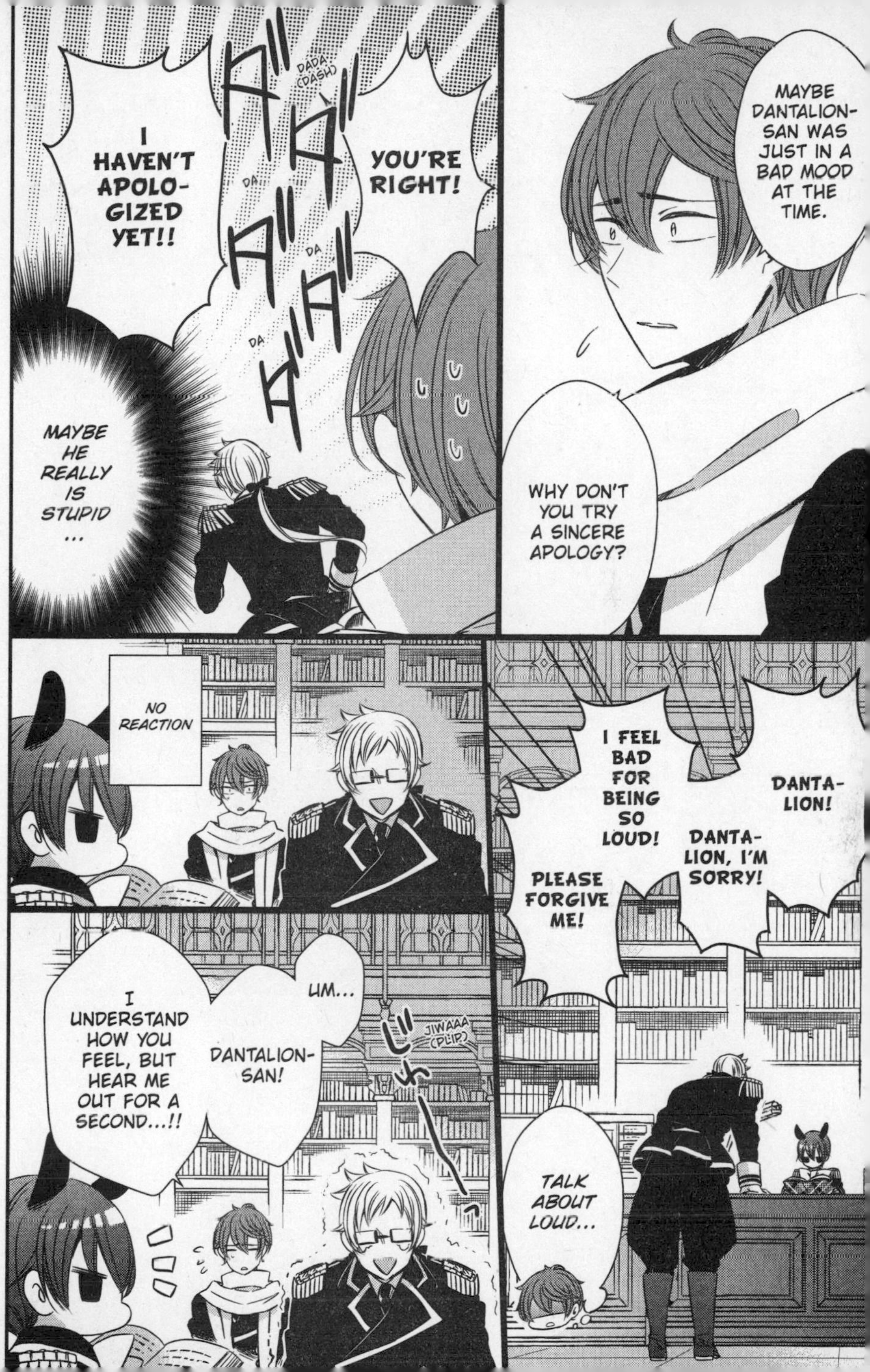
MAYBE DANTALION-SAN WAS JUST IN A BAD MOOD AT THE TIME.
WHY DON'T YOU TRY A SINCERE APOLOGY?
YOU'RE RIGHT!
DADA (DASH)
DA
DA
DA
I HAVEN'T APOLOGIZED YET!!
MAYBE HE REALLY IS STUPID...
DANTALION!
DANTALION, I'M SORRY!
I FEEL BAD FOR BEING SO LOUD!
PLEASE FORGIVE ME!
TALK ABOUT LOUD...
NO REACTION
UM...
DANTALION-SAN!
I UNDERSTAND HOW YOU FEEL, BUT HEAR ME OUT FOR A SECOND...!!
JIWAAA (PLIP)

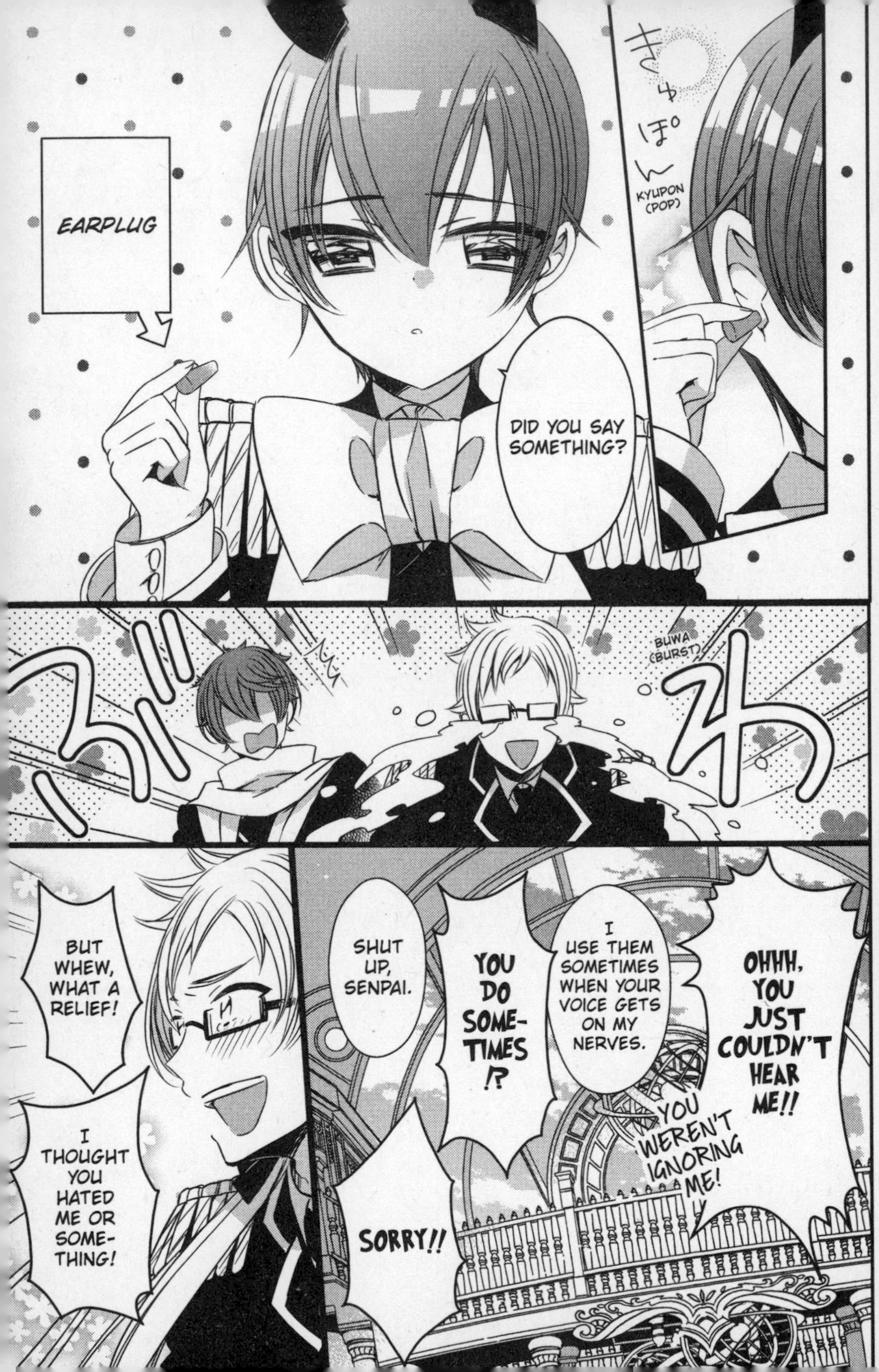
きゅぽん
KYUPON (POP)
EARPLUG
DID YOU SAY SOMETHING?
BUWA (BURST)
ぶわっ
OHHH, YOU JUST COULDN'T HEAR ME!!
YOU WEREN'T IGNORING ME!
I USE THEM SOMETIMES WHEN YOUR VOICE GETS ON MY NERVES.
YOU DO SOME-TIMES!?
SHUT UP, SENPAI.
SORRY!!
BUT WHEW, WHAT A RELIEF!
I THOUGHT YOU HATED ME OR SOME-THING!

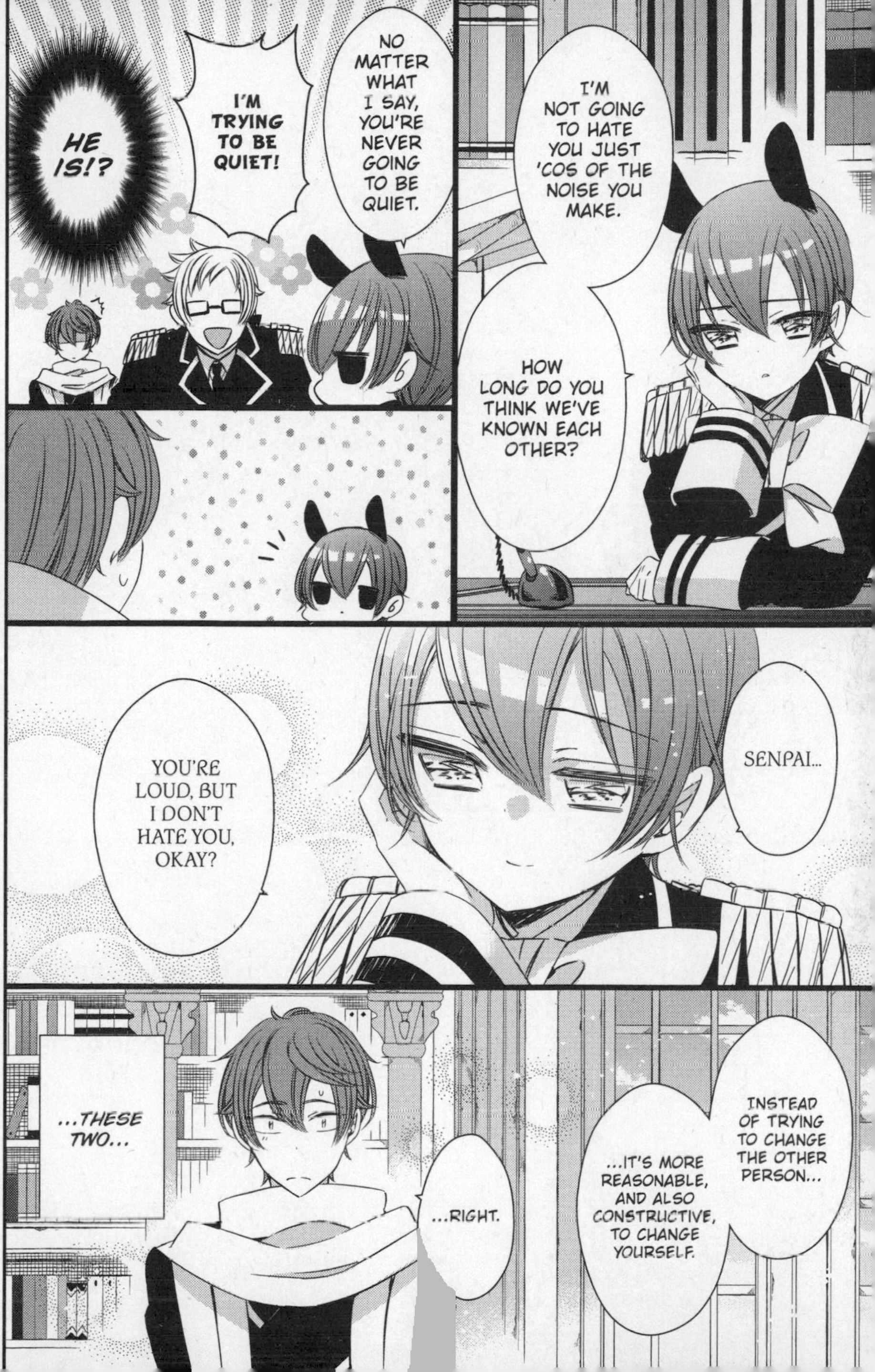
I'M NOT GOING TO HATE YOU JUST 'COS OF THE NOISE YOU MAKE.
HOW LONG DO YOU THINK WE'VE KNOWN EACH OTHER?
NO MATTER WHAT I SAY, YOU'RE NEVER GOING TO BE QUIET.
I'M TRYING TO BE QUIET!
HE IS!?
SENPAI...
YOU'RE LOUD, BUT I DON'T HATE YOU, OKAY?
INSTEAD OF TRYING TO CHANGE THE OTHER PERSON...
...IT'S MORE REASONABLE, AND ALSO CONSTRUCTIVE, TO CHANGE YOURSELF.
...RIGHT.
...THESE TWO...

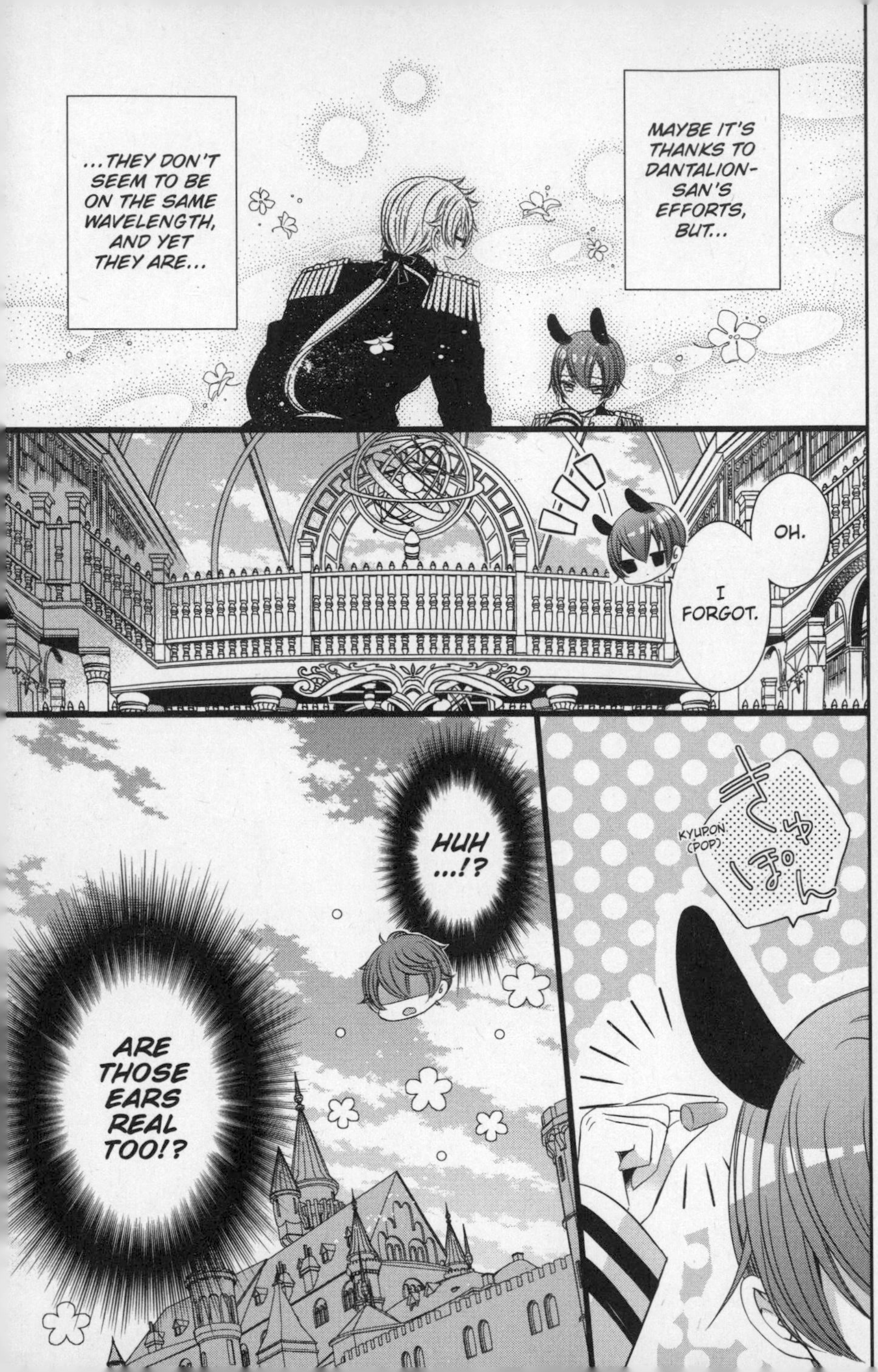
MAYBE IT'S THANKS TO DANTALION-SAN'S EFFORTS, BUT...
...THEY DON'T SEEM TO BE ON THE SAME WAVELENGTH, AND YET THEY ARE...
OH.
I FORGOT.
KYUPON (POP)
HUH ...!?
ARE THOSE EARS REAL TOO!?

As Miss Beelzebub Likes

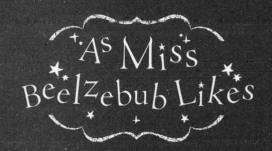

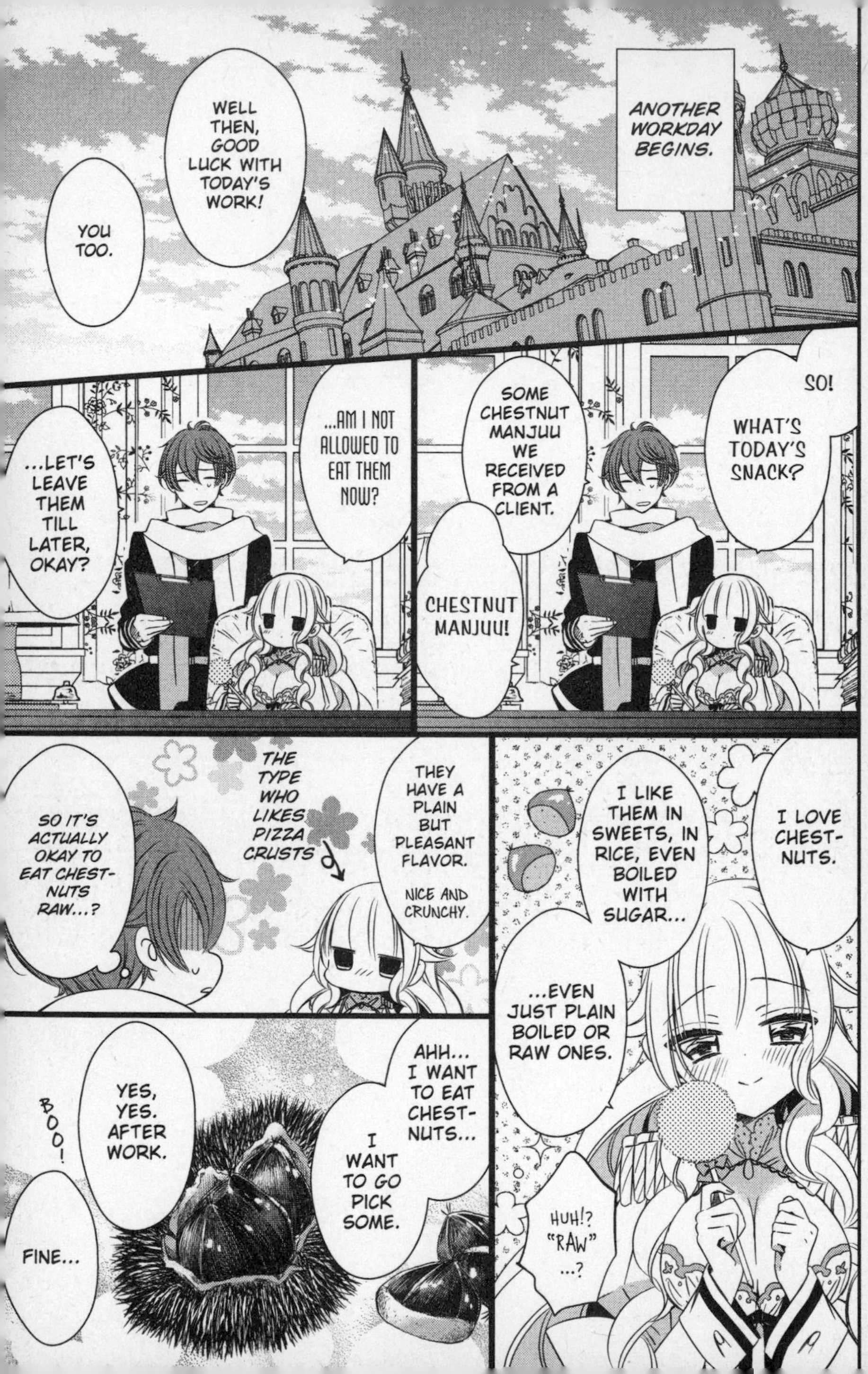
ANOTHER WORKDAY BEGINS.
WELL THEN, GOOD LUCK WITH TODAY'S WORK!
YOU TOO.
SO!
WHAT'S TODAY'S SNACK?
SOME CHESTNUT MANJUU WE RECEIVED FROM A CLIENT.
CHESTNUT MANJUU!
...AM I NOT ALLOWED TO EAT THEM NOW?
...LET'S LEAVE THEM TILL LATER, OKAY?
I LOVE CHEST-NUTS.
I LIKE THEM IN SWEETS, IN RICE, EVEN BOILED WITH SUGAR...
...EVEN JUST PLAIN BOILED OR RAW ONES.
HUH!? "RAW" ...?
THEY HAVE A PLAIN BUT PLEASANT FLAVOR.
NICE AND CRUNCHY.
THE TYPE WHO LIKES PIZZA CRUSTS
SO IT'S ACTUALLY OKAY TO EAT CHEST-NUTS RAW...?
AHH... I WANT TO EAT CHEST-NUTS...
I WANT TO GO PICK SOME.
YES, YES. AFTER WORK.
BOO!
FINE...

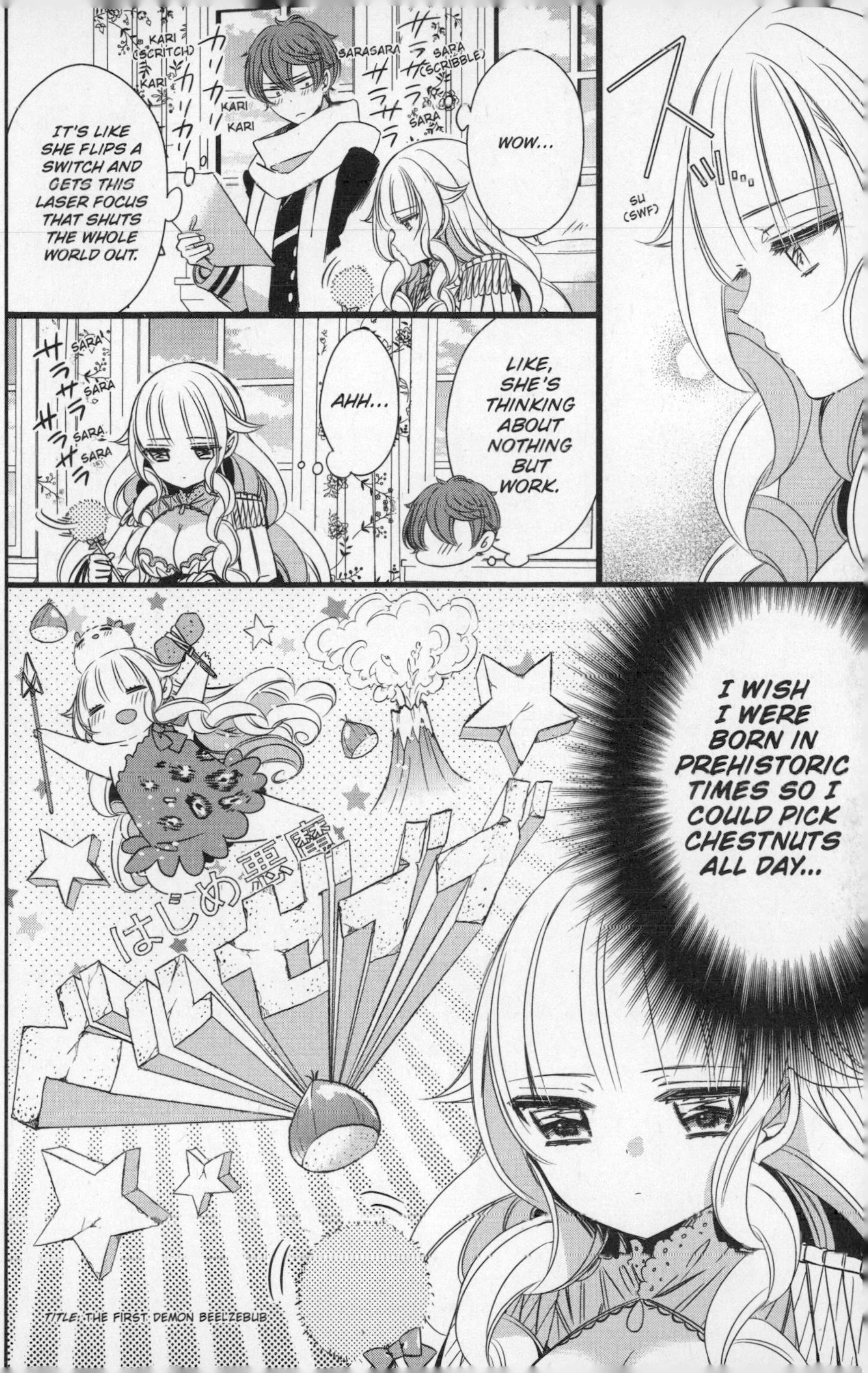
SU (SWF)
WOW...
SARASARA
SARA (SCRIBBLE)
SARA
KARI (SCRITCH)
KARI
KARI
KARI
IT'S LIKE SHE FLIPS A SWITCH AND GETS THIS LASER FOCUS THAT SHUTS THE WHOLE WORLD OUT.
LIKE, SHE'S THINKING ABOUT NOTHING BUT WORK.
AHH...
SARA
SARA
SARA
SARA
I WISH I WERE BORN IN PREHISTORIC TIMES SO I COULD PICK CHESTNUTS ALL DAY...
はじめ悪魔
TITLE: THE FIRST DEMON BEELZEBUB

CHAPTER 24

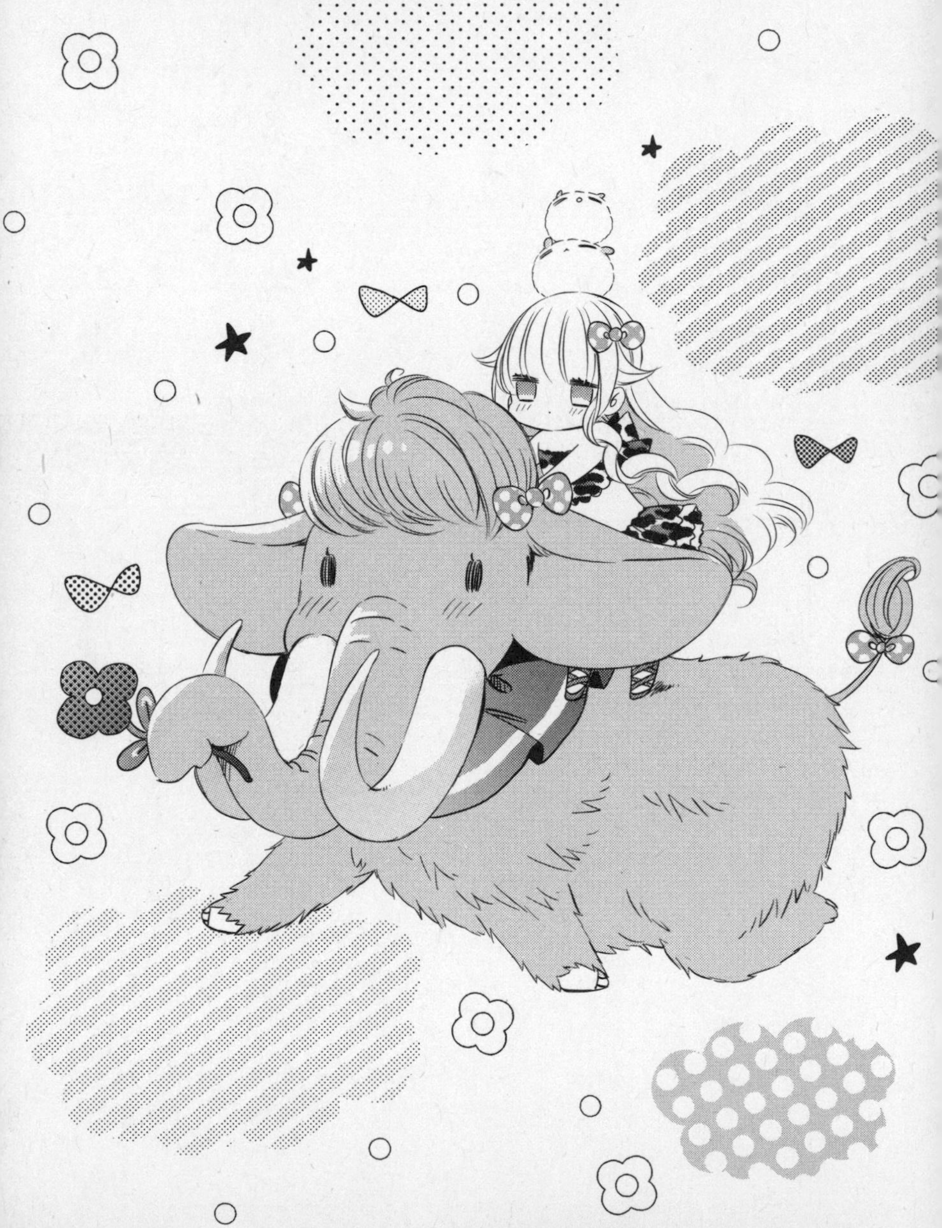

PREHISTORIC UNDIES

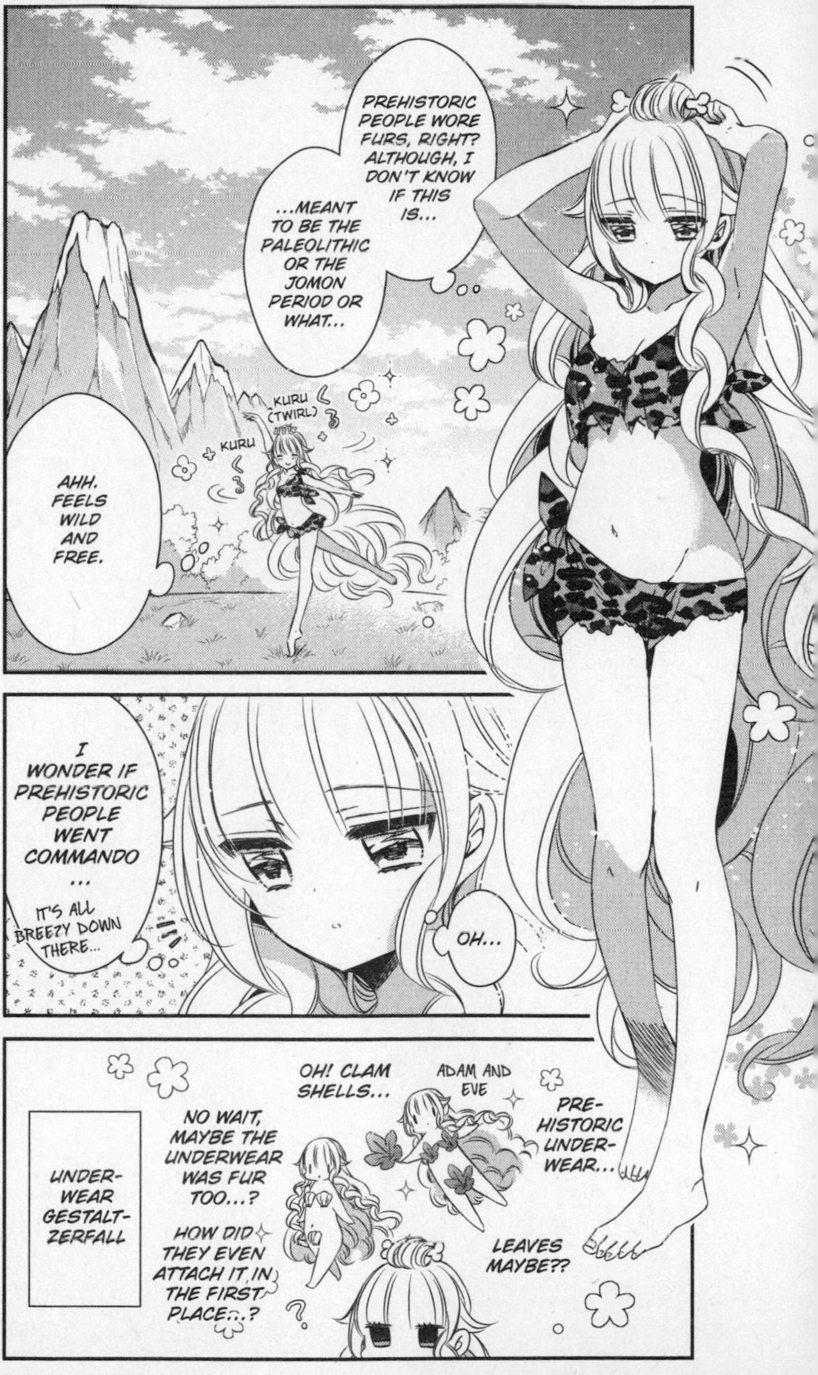
PREHISTORIC PEOPLE WORE FURS, RIGHT? ALTHOUGH, I DON'T KNOW IF THIS IS...
...MEANT TO BE THE PALEOLITHIC OR THE JOMON PERIOD OR WHAT...
KURU (TWIRL)
KURU
AHH. FEELS WILD AND FREE.
OH...
I WONDER IF PREHISTORIC PEOPLE WENT COMMANDO...
IT'S ALL BREEZY DOWN THERE...
PRE-HISTORIC UNDER-WEAR...
ADAM AND EVE
OH! CLAM SHELLS...
LEAVES MAYBE??
NO WAIT, MAYBE THE UNDERWEAR WAS FUR TOO...?
HOW DID THEY EVEN ATTACH IT IN THE FIRST PLACE...?
UNDER-WEAR GESTALT-ZERFALL

THE TYPE WHO COMPLETELY DISSOCIATES AT WORK

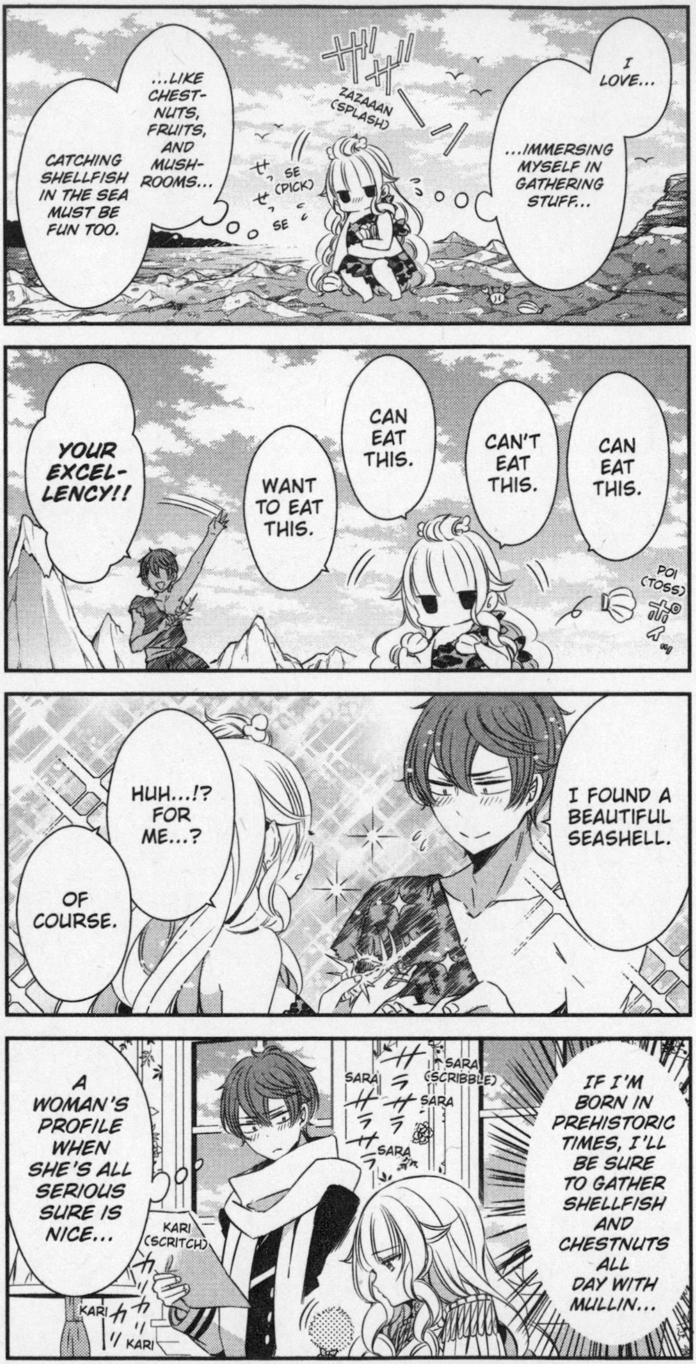
I LOVE...
...IMMERSING MYSELF IN GATHERING STUFF...
ZAZAAAN (SPLASH)
SE (PICK)
SE
...LIKE CHESTNUTS, FRUITS, AND MUSHROOMS...
CATCHING SHELLFISH IN THE SEA MUST BE FUN TOO.
POI (TOSS)
CAN EAT THIS.
CAN'T EAT THIS.
CAN EAT THIS.
WANT TO EAT THIS.
YOUR EXCELLENCY!!
I FOUND A BEAUTIFUL SEASHELL.
HUH...!? FOR ME...?
OF COURSE.
IF I'M BORN IN PREHISTORIC TIMES, I'LL BE SURE TO GATHER SHELLFISH AND CHESTNUTS ALL DAY WITH MULLIN...
SARA (SCRIBBLE)
SARA
SARA
SARA
KARI (SCRITCH)
KARI
KARI
A WOMAN'S PROFILE WHEN SHE'S ALL SERIOUS SURE IS NICE...

TRULY THE GREAT AGE OF MUSCLE

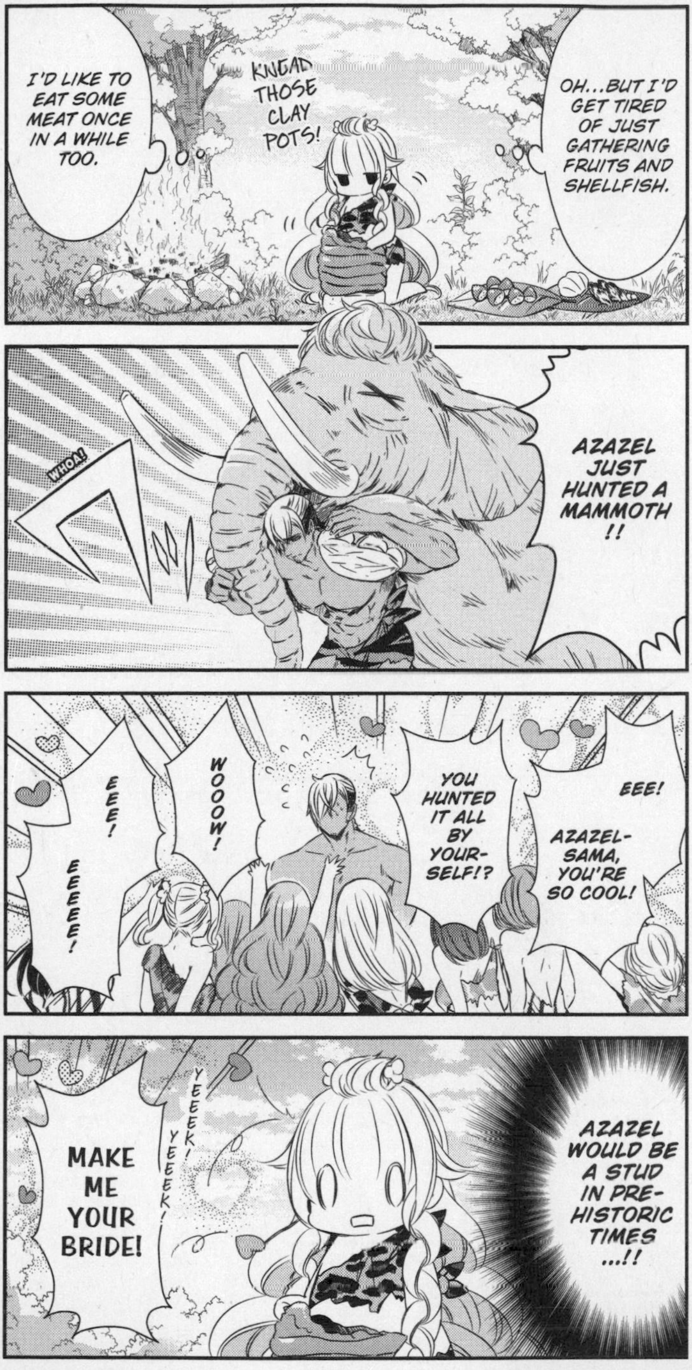
OH...BUT I'D GET TIRED OF JUST GATHERING FRUITS AND SHELLFISH.
KNEAD THOSE CLAY POTS!
I'D LIKE TO EAT SOME MEAT ONCE IN A WHILE TOO.
AZAZEL JUST HUNTED A MAMMOTH!!
WHOA!
EEE!
AZAZEL-SAMA, YOU'RE SO COOL!
YOU HUNTED IT ALL BY YOUR-SELF!?
WOOOOW!
EEE! EEEEEE!
AZAZEL WOULD BE A STUD IN PRE-HISTORIC TIMES ...!!
YEEEK! YEEEK!
MAKE ME YOUR BRIDE!

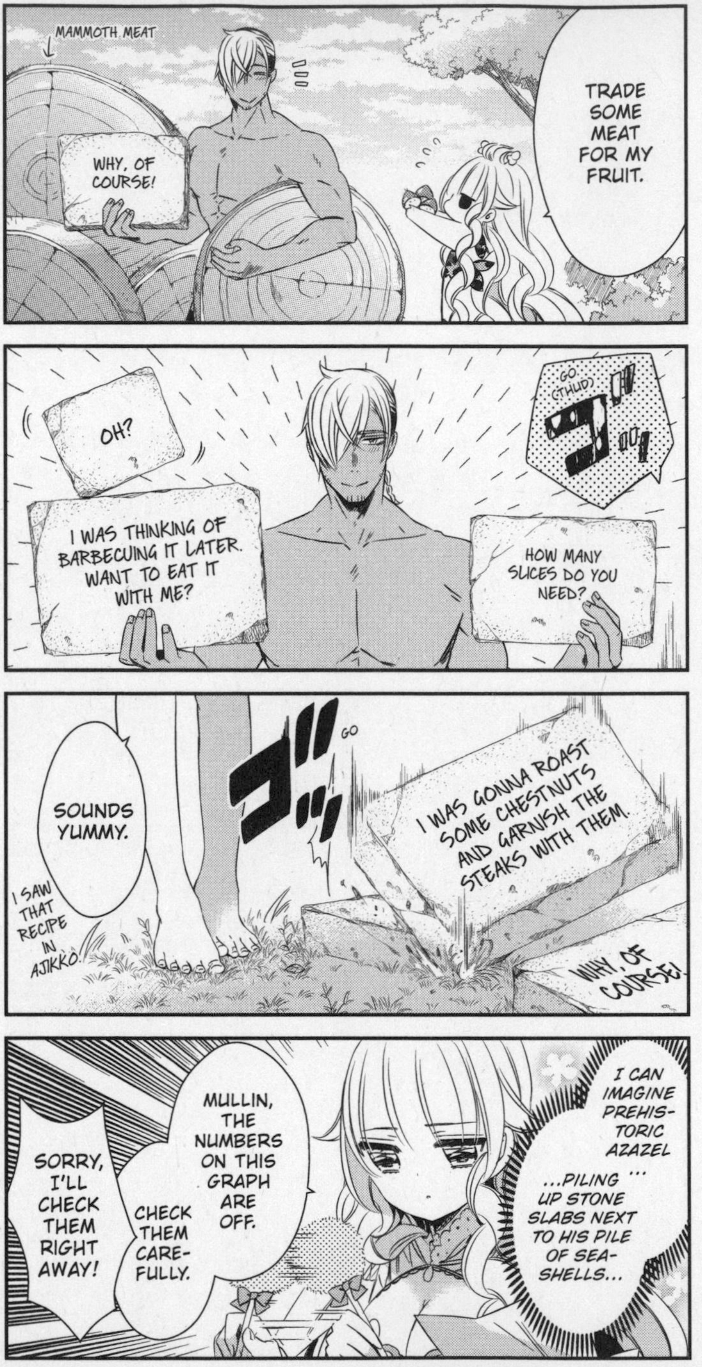
TRADE SOME MEAT FOR MY FRUIT.
WHY, OF COURSE!
MAMMOTH MEAT
GO (THUD)
HOW MANY SLICES DO YOU NEED?
OH?
I WAS THINKING OF BARBECUING IT LATER. WANT TO EAT IT WITH ME?
GO
I WAS GONNA ROAST SOME CHESTNUTS AND GARNISH THE STEAKS WITH THEM.
WHY, OF COURSE!
SOUNDS YUMMY.
I SAW THAT RECIPE IN AJIKKO.
I CAN IMAGINE PREHISTORIC AZAZEL...
...PILING UP STONE SLABS NEXT TO HIS PILE OF SEA-SHELLS...
MULLIN, THE NUMBERS ON THIS GRAPH ARE OFF.
CHECK THEM CAREFULLY.
SORRY, I'LL CHECK THEM RIGHT AWAY!

CRAZY-CUMBERSOME

WHAT'S GOING ON?

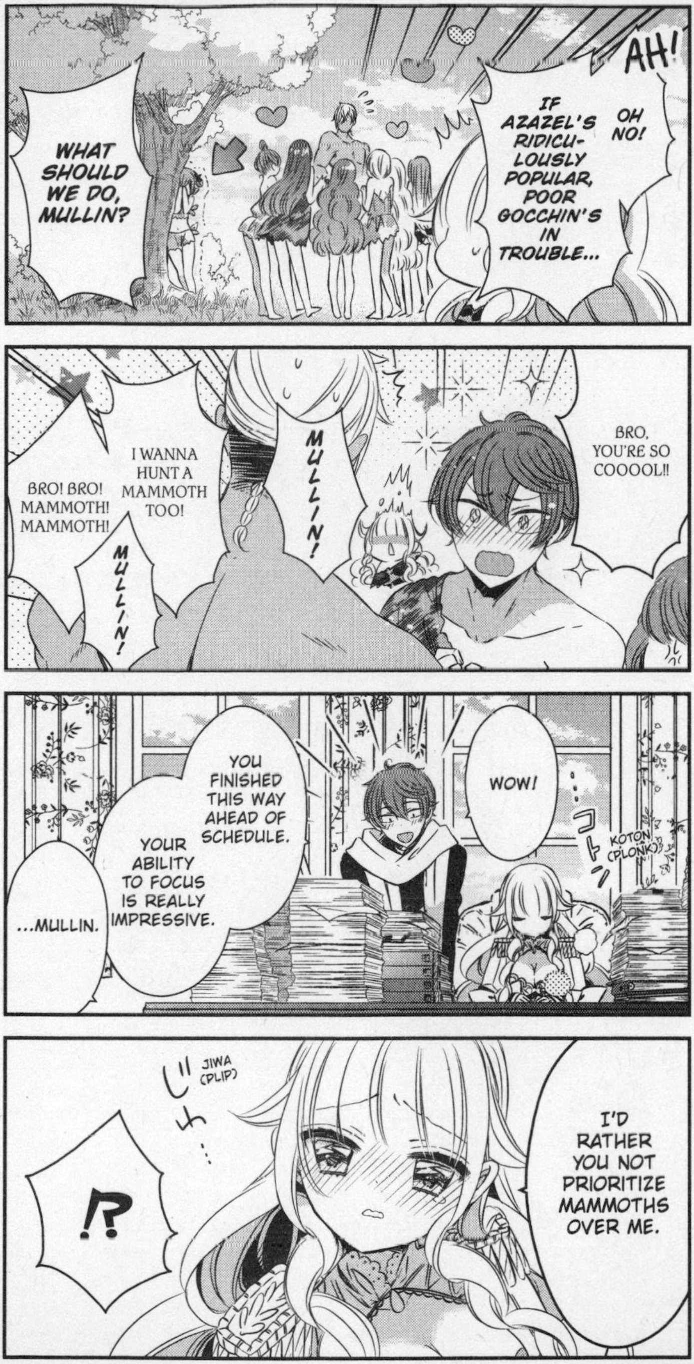
AH!
OH NO!
IF AZAZEL'S RIDICU-LOUSLY POPULAR, POOR GOCCHIN'S IN TROUBLE...
WHAT SHOULD WE DO, MULLIN?
BRO, YOU'RE SO COOOOL!!
MULLIN!
I WANNA HUNT A MAMMOTH TOO!
MULLIN!
BRO! BRO! MAMMOTH! MAMMOTH!
KOTON (PLONK)
...
WOW!
YOU FINISHED THIS WAY AHEAD OF SCHEDULE.
YOUR ABILITY TO FOCUS IS REALLY IMPRESSIVE.
...MULLIN.
I'D RATHER YOU NOT PRIORITIZE MAMMOTHS OVER ME.
JIWA (PLIP)
!?

A PREHISTORIC DANTALION-KYUN! THIS NEW BOYISH ATTRACTION OF COMBINED INTELLIGENCE AND SAVAGERY WHISKS ME AWAY, INTO A SENSUALITY OVERFLOWING WITH RUSTIC SPLENDOR—A WORLD OF ECSTASY, AS IF TO OPEN PANDORA'S BOX BEFORE MY VERY EYES!

OHHH!

A PRE-HISTORIC DANTALION, DEPRIVED OF BOOKS, WOULD BE BORN INTO DESPAIR...

WHAT AN "ORIGINAL SIN"...

As Miss Beelzebub Likes

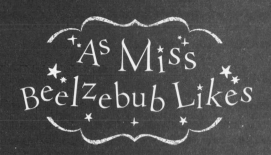

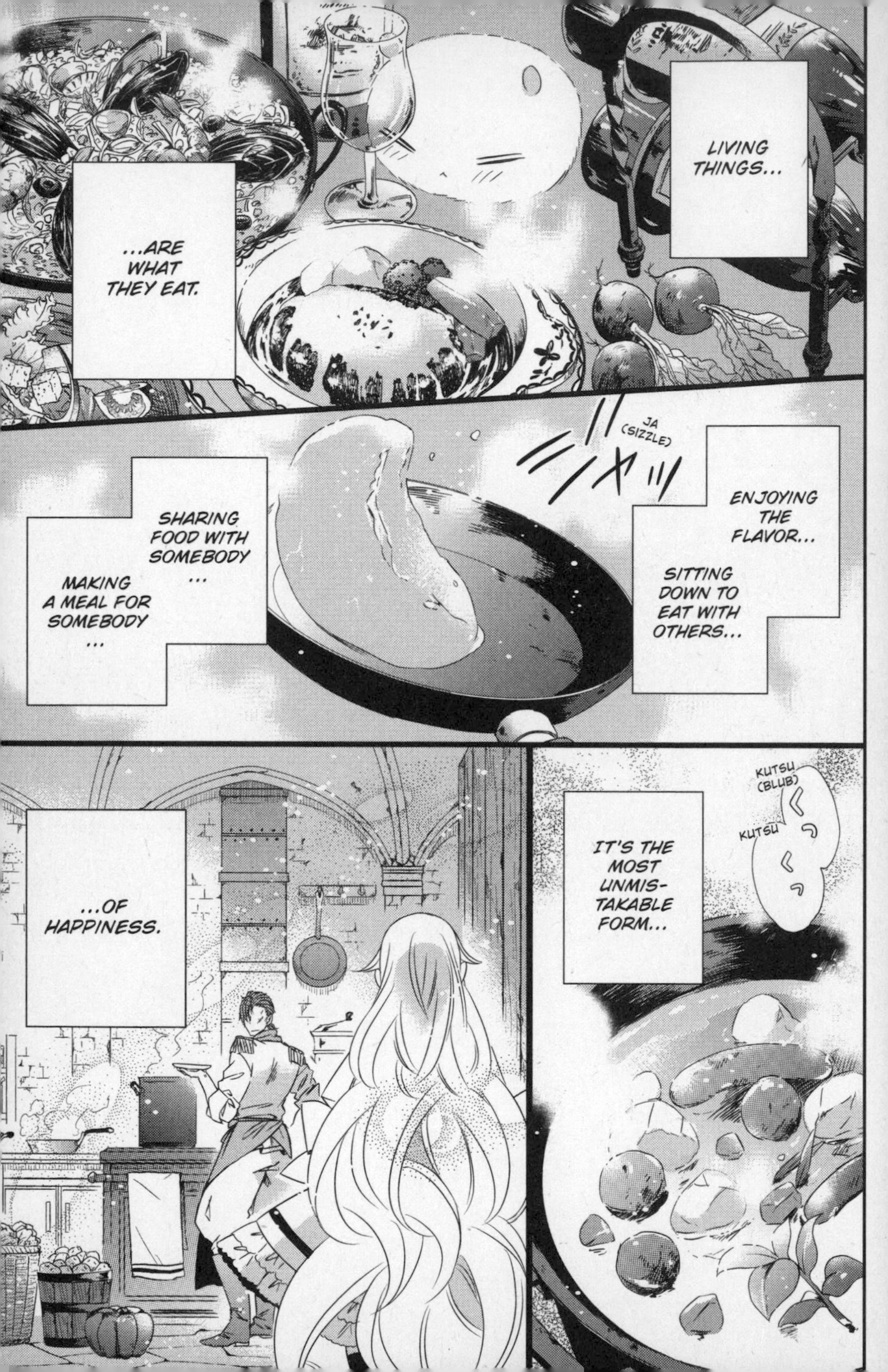
LIVING THINGS...
...ARE WHAT THEY EAT.
JA (SIZZLE)
ENJOYING THE FLAVOR...
SITTING DOWN TO EAT WITH OTHERS...
SHARING FOOD WITH SOMEBODY ...
MAKING A MEAL FOR SOMEBODY ...
KUTSU (BLUB)
KUTSU
IT'S THE MOST UNMIS-TAKABLE FORM...
...OF HAPPINESS.

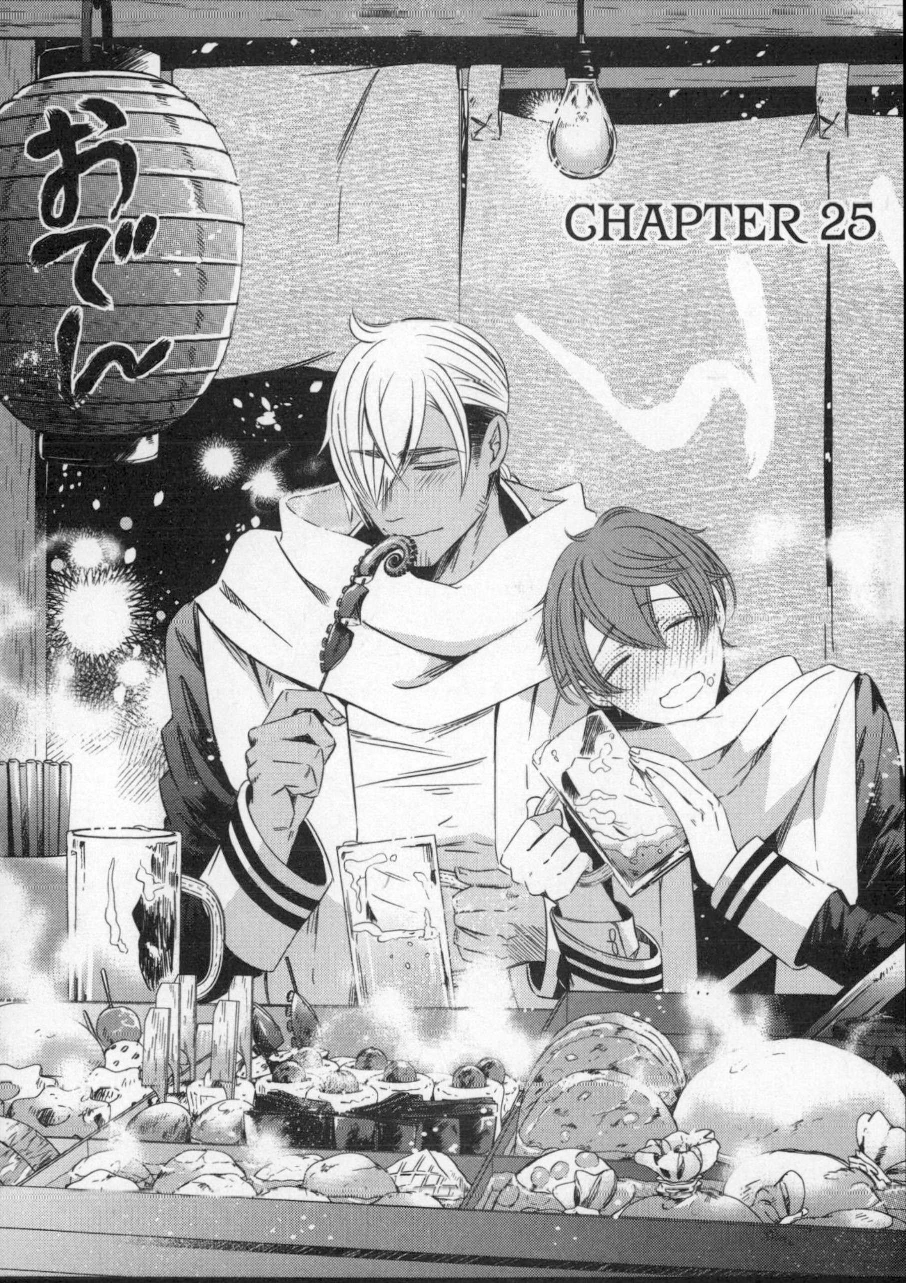
CHAPTER 25
おでん
LANTERN: ODEN

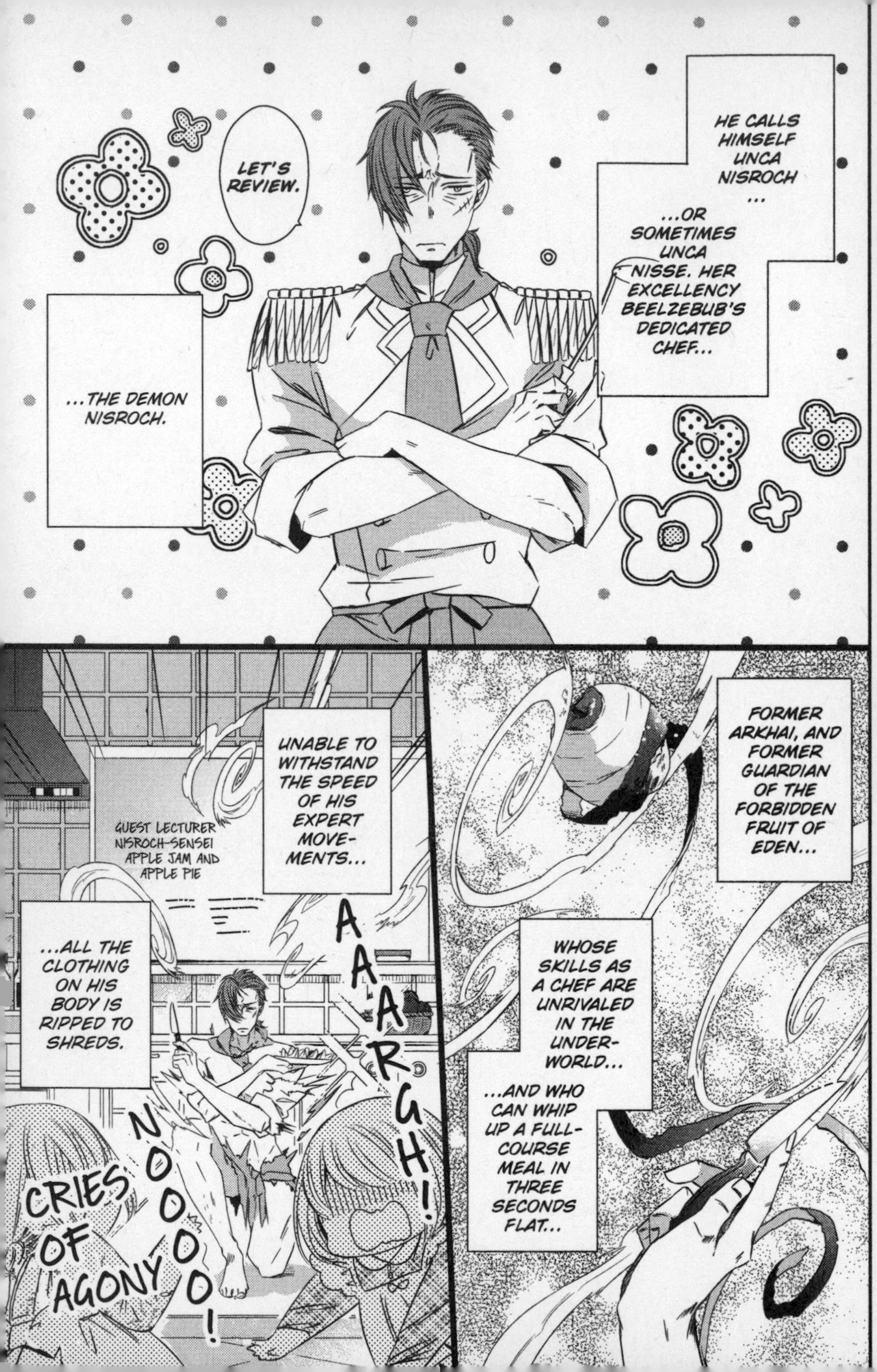
HE CALLS HIMSELF UNCA NISROCH ...
...OR SOMETIMES UNCA NISSE. HER EXCELLENCY BEELZEBUB'S DEDICATED CHEF...
LET'S REVIEW.
...THE DEMON NISROCH.
FORMER ARKHAI, AND FORMER GUARDIAN OF THE FORBIDDEN FRUIT OF EDEN...
WHOSE SKILLS AS A CHEF ARE UNRIVALED IN THE UNDER-WORLD...
...AND WHO CAN WHIP UP A FULL-COURSE MEAL IN THREE SECONDS FLAT...
UNABLE TO WITHSTAND THE SPEED OF HIS EXPERT MOVE-MENTS...
GUEST LECTURER NISROCH-SENSEI APPLE JAM AND APPLE PIE
AAAARGH!
...ALL THE CLOTHING ON HIS BODY IS RIPPED TO SHREDS.
NOOOOOO!
CRIES OF AGONY

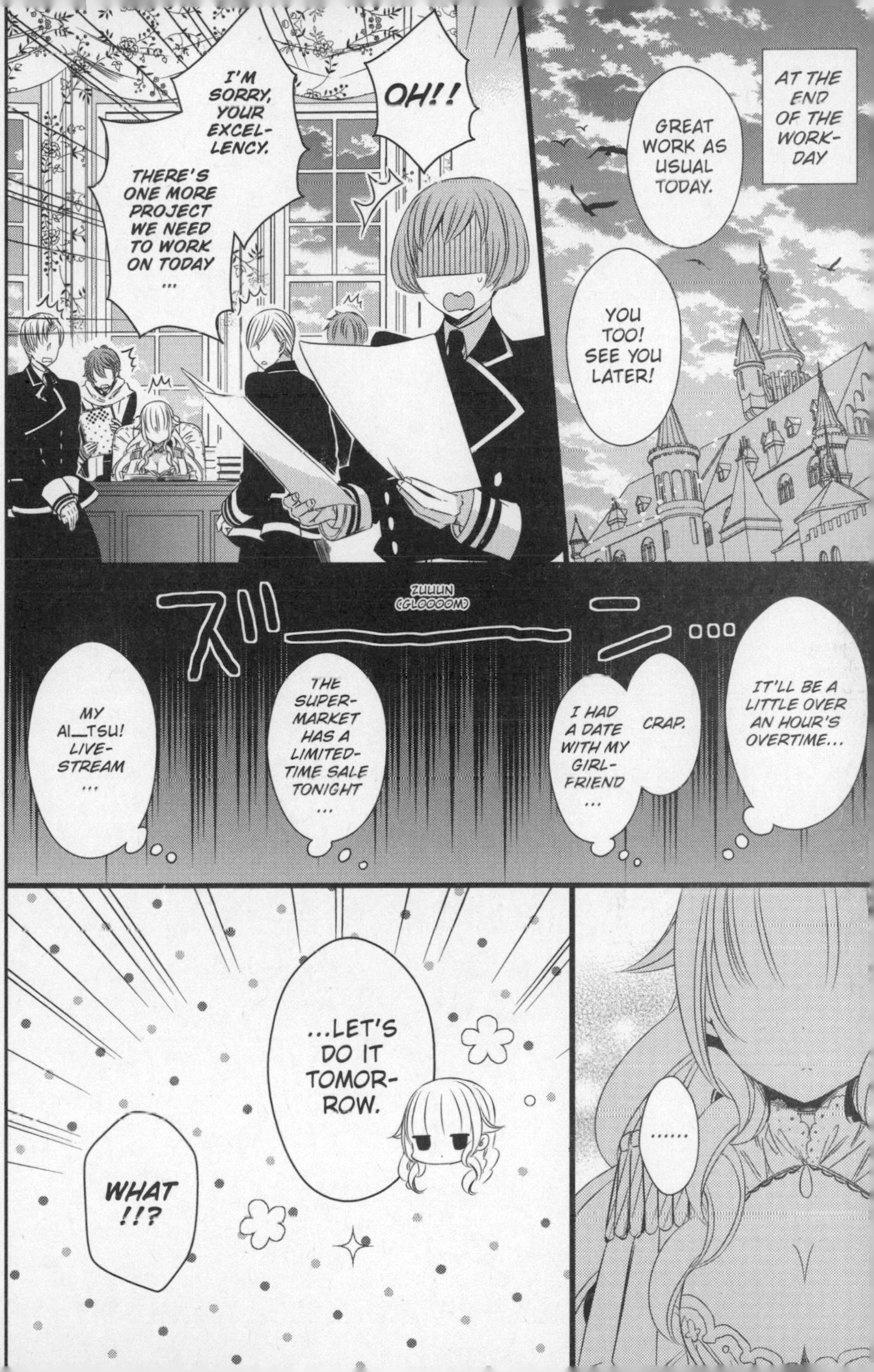
AT THE END OF THE WORKDAY
GREAT WORK AS USUAL TODAY.
YOU TOO! SEE YOU LATER!
OH!!
I'M SORRY, YOUR EXCELLENCY.
THERE'S ONE MORE PROJECT WE NEED TO WORK ON TODAY...
ZUUUN (GLOOOOOM)
IT'LL BE A LITTLE OVER AN HOUR'S OVERTIME...
CRAP.
I HAD A DATE WITH MY GIRLFRIEND...
THE SUPERMARKET HAS A LIMITED-TIME SALE TONIGHT...
MY AI_TSU! LIVESTREAM...
......
...LET'S DO IT TOMORROW.
WHAT!!?

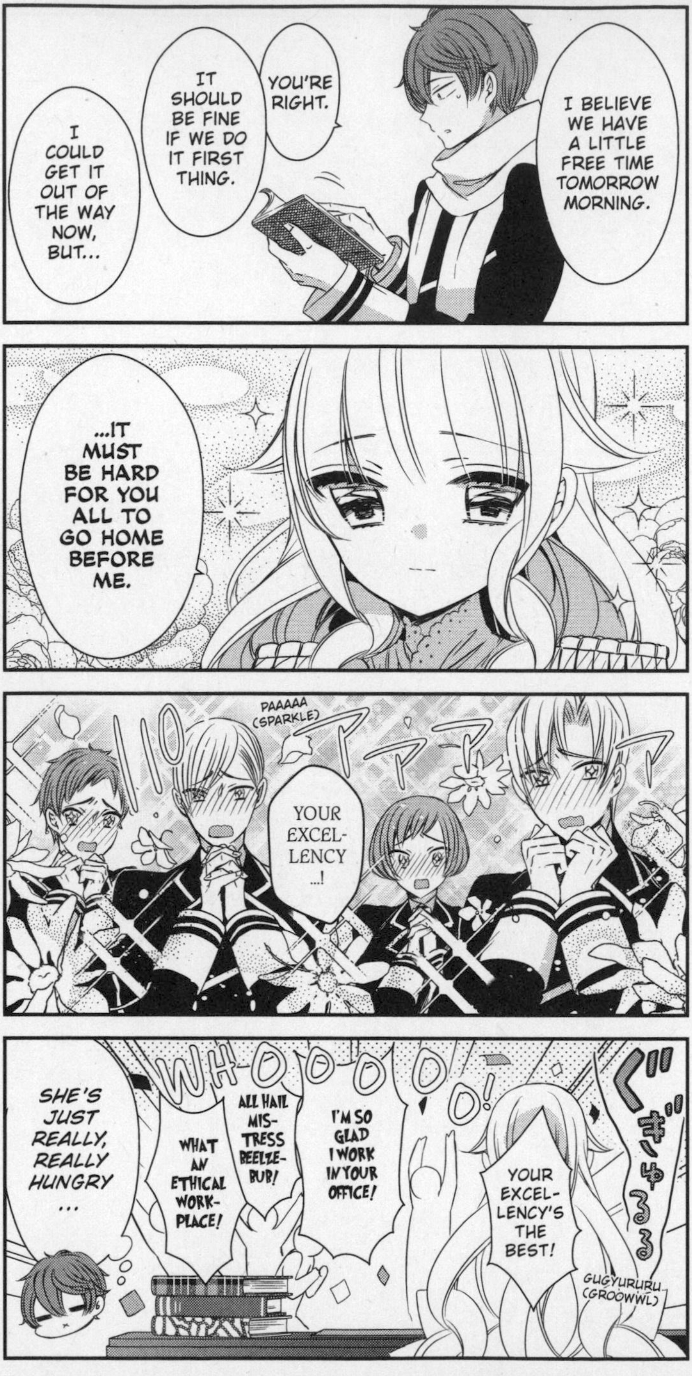

I BELIEVE WE HAVE A LITTLE FREE TIME TOMORROW MORNING.
YOU'RE RIGHT.
IT SHOULD BE FINE IF WE DO IT FIRST THING.
I COULD GET IT OUT OF THE WAY NOW, BUT...
...IT MUST BE HARD FOR YOU ALL TO GO HOME BEFORE ME.
PAAAAA (SPARKLE)
YOUR EXCEL-LENCY ...!
WHOOOOOO!
ぐぎゅるる
GUGYURURU (GROOWWL)
YOUR EXCEL-LENCY'S THE BEST!
I'M SO GLAD I WORK IN YOUR OFFICE!
ALL HAIL MIS-TRESS BEELZE-BUB!
WHAT AN ETHICAL WORK-PLACE!
SHE'S JUST REALLY, REALLY HUNGRY ...

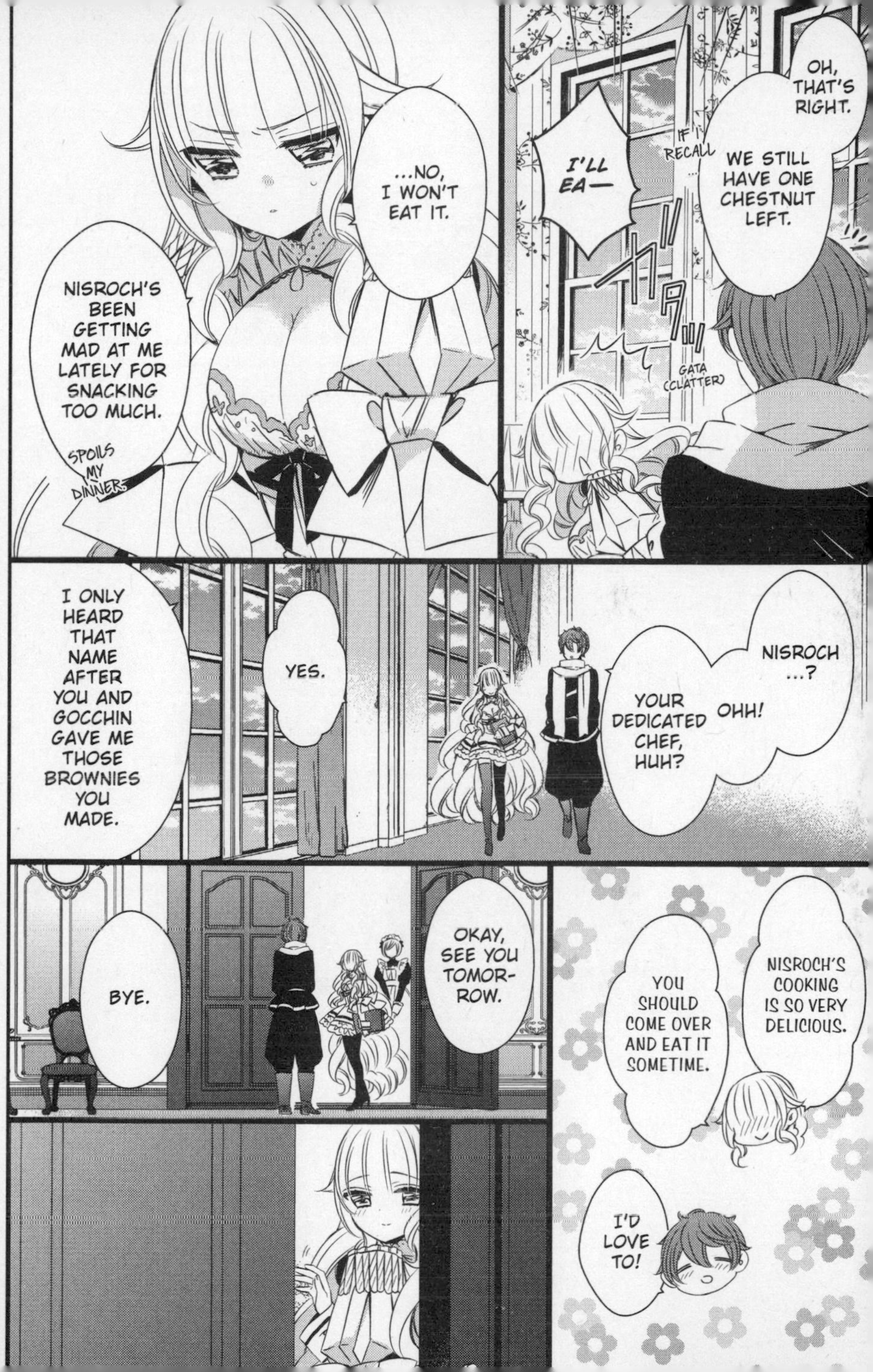
OH, THAT'S RIGHT.
WE STILL HAVE ONE CHESTNUT LEFT.
IF I RECALL...
I'LL EA—
GATA (CLATTER)
...NO, I WON'T EAT IT.
NISROCH'S BEEN GETTING MAD AT ME LATELY FOR SNACKING TOO MUCH.
SPOILS MY DINNER.
NISROCH...?
OHH!
YOUR DEDICATED CHEF, HUH?
YES.
I ONLY HEARD THAT NAME AFTER YOU AND GOCCHIN GAVE ME THOSE BROWNIES YOU MADE.
NISROCH'S COOKING IS SO VERY DELICIOUS.
YOU SHOULD COME OVER AND EAT IT SOMETIME.
I'D LOVE TO!
OKAY, SEE YOU TOMORROW.
BYE.

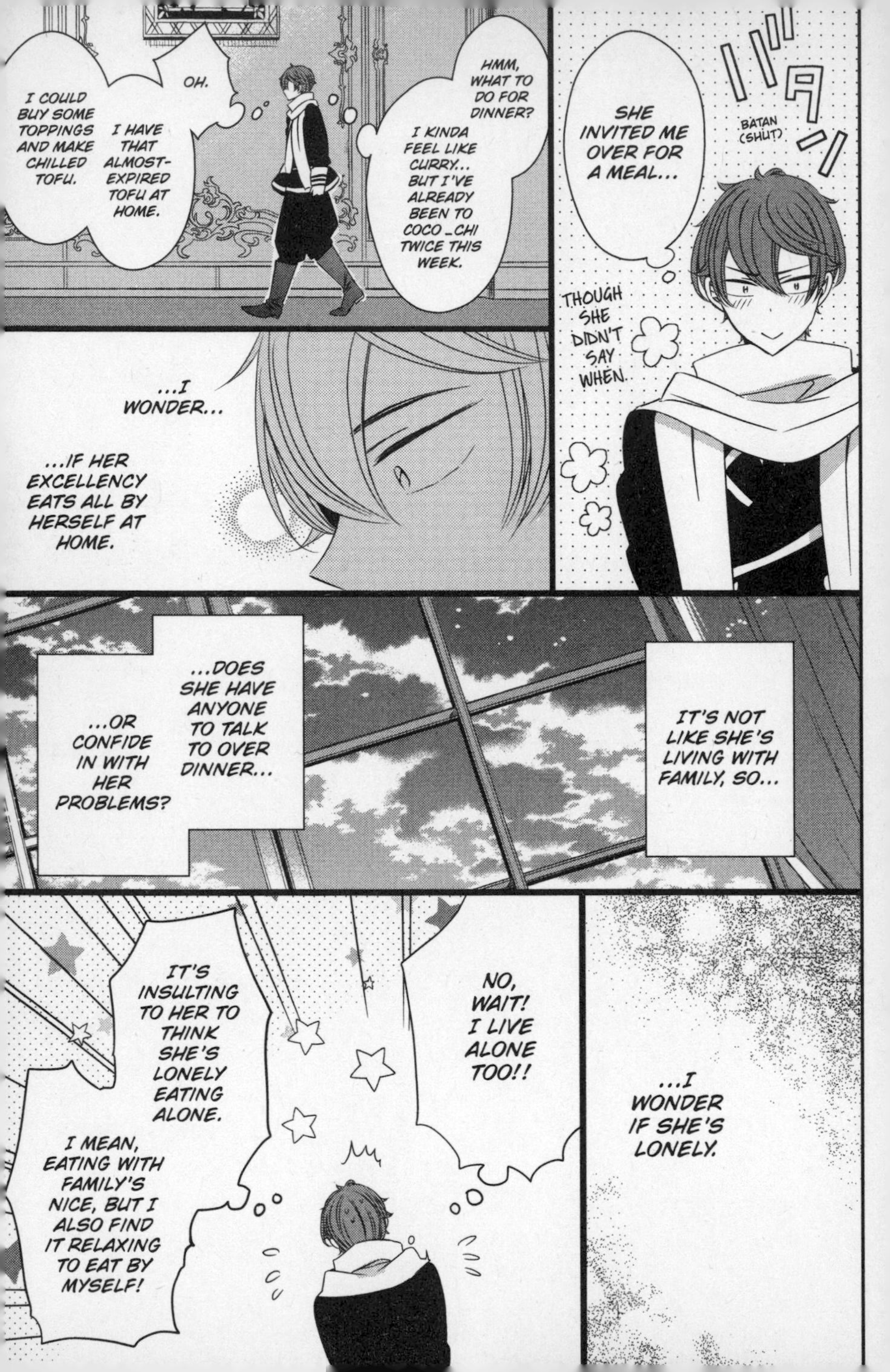

BATAN (SHUT)
SHE INVITED ME OVER FOR A MEAL...
THOUGH SHE DIDN'T SAY WHEN.
HMM, WHAT TO DO FOR DINNER?
I KINDA FEEL LIKE CURRY... BUT I'VE ALREADY BEEN TO COCO-CHI TWICE THIS WEEK.
OH.
I HAVE THAT ALMOST-EXPIRED TOFU AT HOME.
I COULD BUY SOME TOPPINGS AND MAKE CHILLED TOFU.
...I WONDER...
...IF HER EXCELLENCY EATS ALL BY HERSELF AT HOME.
IT'S NOT LIKE SHE'S LIVING WITH FAMILY, SO...
...DOES SHE HAVE ANYONE TO TALK TO OVER DINNER...
...OR CONFIDE IN WITH HER PROBLEMS?
...I WONDER IF SHE'S LONELY.
NO, WAIT! I LIVE ALONE TOO!!
IT'S INSULTING TO HER TO THINK SHE'S LONELY EATING ALONE.
I MEAN, EATING WITH FAMILY'S NICE, BUT I ALSO FIND IT RELAXING TO EAT BY MYSELF!

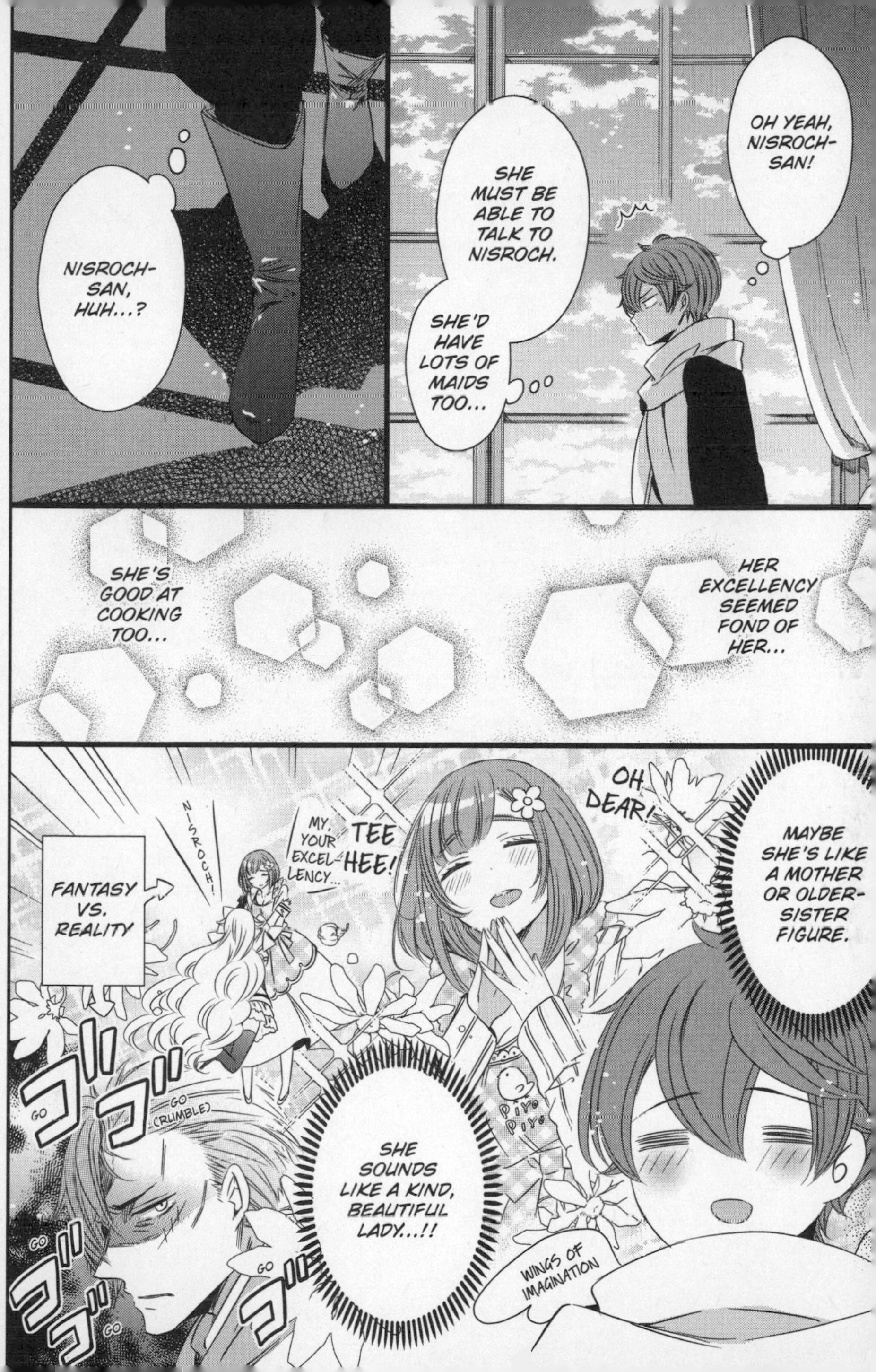
OH YEAH, NISROCH-SAN!
SHE MUST BE ABLE TO TALK TO NISROCH.
SHE'D HAVE LOTS OF MAIDS TOO...
NISROCH-SAN, HUH...?
HER EXCELLENCY SEEMED FOND OF HER...
SHE'S GOOD AT COOKING TOO...
MAYBE SHE'S LIKE A MOTHER OR OLDER-SISTER FIGURE.
OH DEAR!
TEE HEE!
MY, YOUR EXCELLENCY...
NISROCH!
FANTASY VS. REALITY
SHE SOUNDS LIKE A KIND, BEAUTIFUL LADY...!!
WINGS OF IMAGINATION
PIYO PIYO
GO (RUMBLE)
GO
GO
GO
GO

NO ULTERIOR MOTIVE

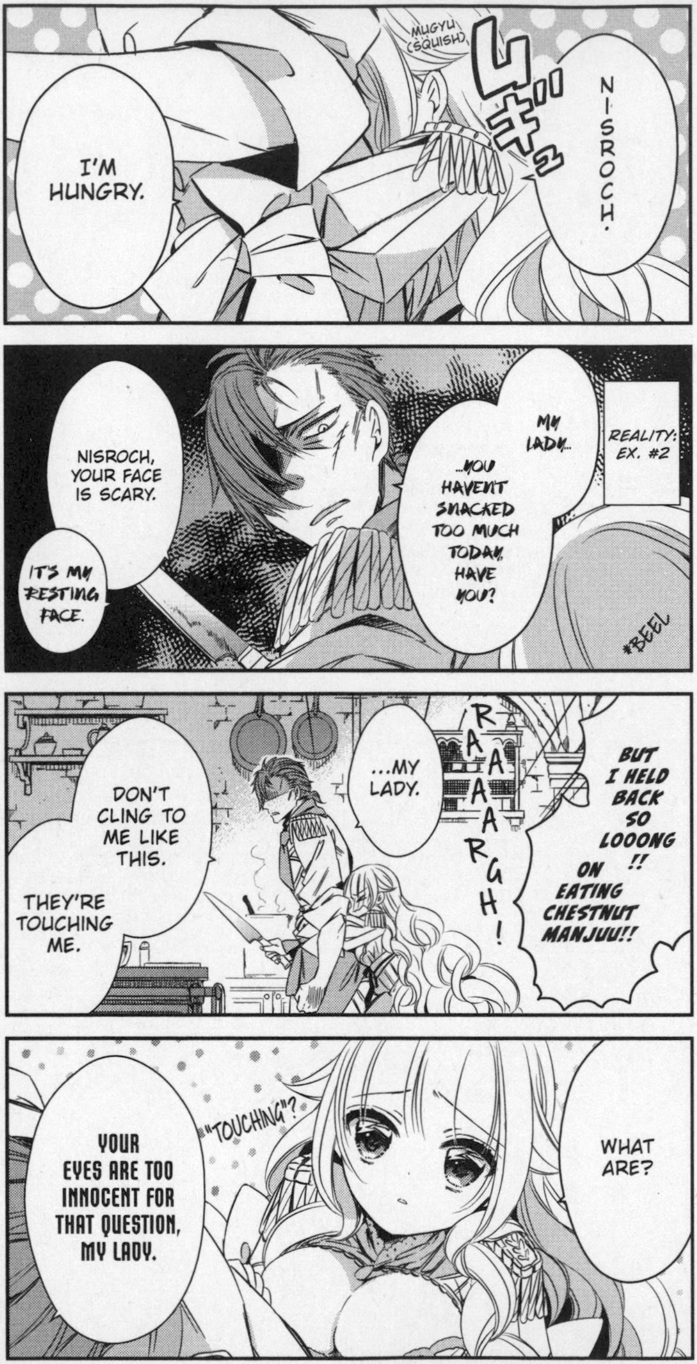

NISROCH.
ムギュ
MUGYU (SQUISH)
I'M HUNGRY.
REALITY: EX. #2
*BEEL
MY LADY...
...YOU HAVEN'T SNACKED TOO MUCH TODAY, HAVE YOU?
NISROCH, YOUR FACE IS SCARY.
IT'S MY RESTING FACE.
BUT I HELD BACK SO LOOONG!! ON EATING CHESTNUT MANJUU!!
RAAAARGH!
...MY LADY.
DON'T CLING TO ME LIKE THIS.
THEY'RE TOUCHING ME.
WHAT ARE?
"TOUCHING"?
YOUR EYES ARE TOO INNOCENT FOR THAT QUESTION, MY LADY.

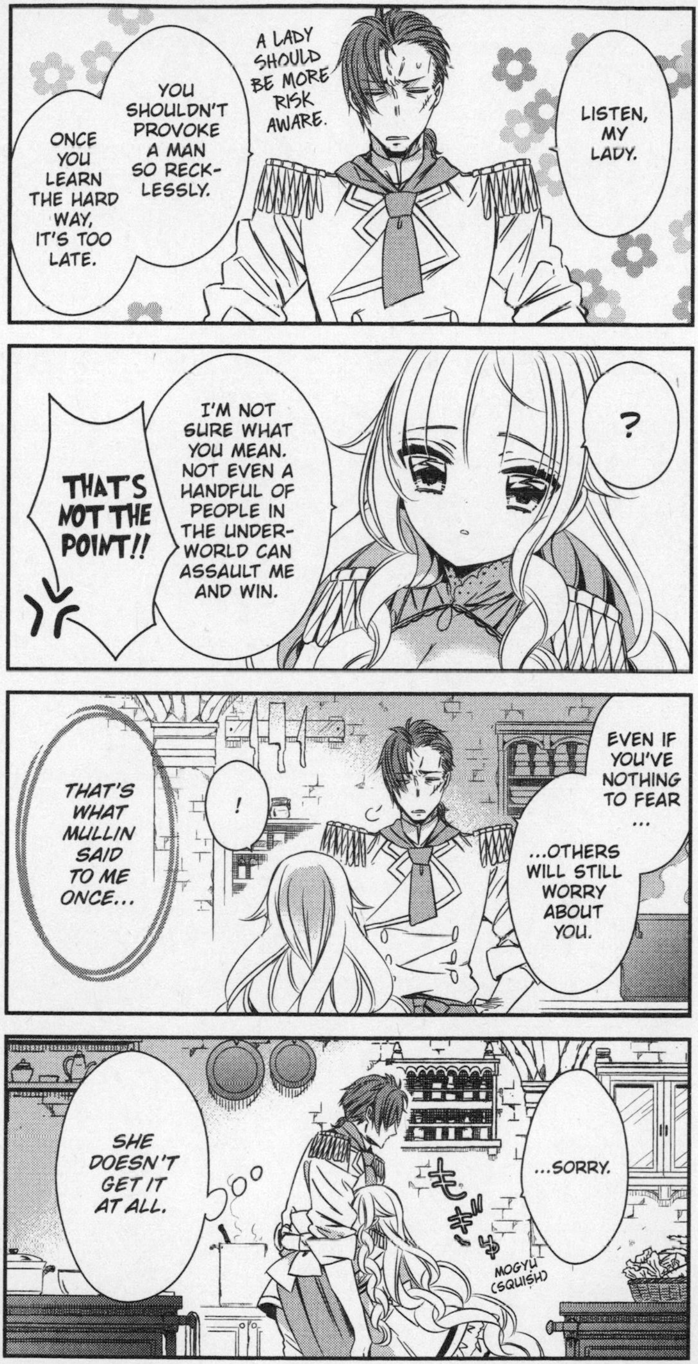
LISTEN, MY LADY.
A LADY SHOULD BE MORE RISK AWARE.
YOU SHOULDN'T PROVOKE A MAN SO RECK-LESSLY.
ONCE YOU LEARN THE HARD WAY, IT'S TOO LATE.
?
I'M NOT SURE WHAT YOU MEAN. NOT EVEN A HANDFUL OF PEOPLE IN THE UNDER-WORLD CAN ASSAULT ME AND WIN.
THAT'S NOT THE POINT!!
EVEN IF YOU'VE NOTHING TO FEAR ...
...OTHERS WILL STILL WORRY ABOUT YOU.
!
THAT'S WHAT MULLIN SAID TO ME ONCE...
...SORRY.
MOGYU (SQUISH)
SHE DOESN'T GET IT AT ALL.

SELF-REFLECTION

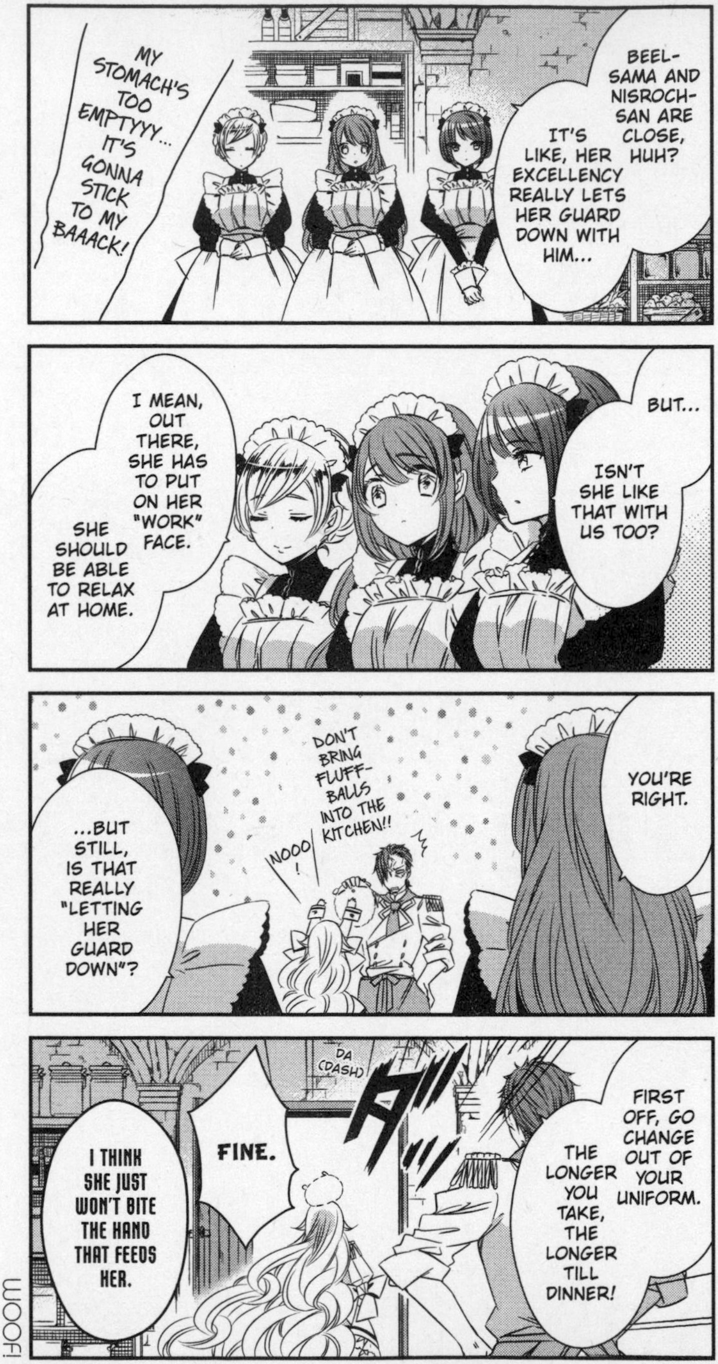
BEEL-SAMA AND NISROCH-SAN ARE CLOSE, HUH?
IT'S LIKE, HER EXCELLENCY REALLY LETS HER GUARD DOWN WITH HIM...
MY STOMACH'S TOO EMPTYYY... IT'S GONNA STICK TO MY BAAACK!
BUT...
ISN'T SHE LIKE THAT WITH US TOO?
I MEAN, OUT THERE, SHE HAS TO PUT ON HER "WORK" FACE.
SHE SHOULD BE ABLE TO RELAX AT HOME.
YOU'RE RIGHT.
DON'T BRING FLUFF-BALLS INTO THE KITCHEN!!
NOOO!
...BUT STILL, IS THAT REALLY "LETTING HER GUARD DOWN"?
FIRST OFF, GO CHANGE OUT OF YOUR UNIFORM.
THE LONGER YOU TAKE, THE LONGER TILL DINNER!
DA (DASH)
FINE.
I THINK SHE JUST WON'T BITE THE HAND THAT FEEDS HER.
WOOF!

PARTIALLY CAUGHT IN THE BLAST

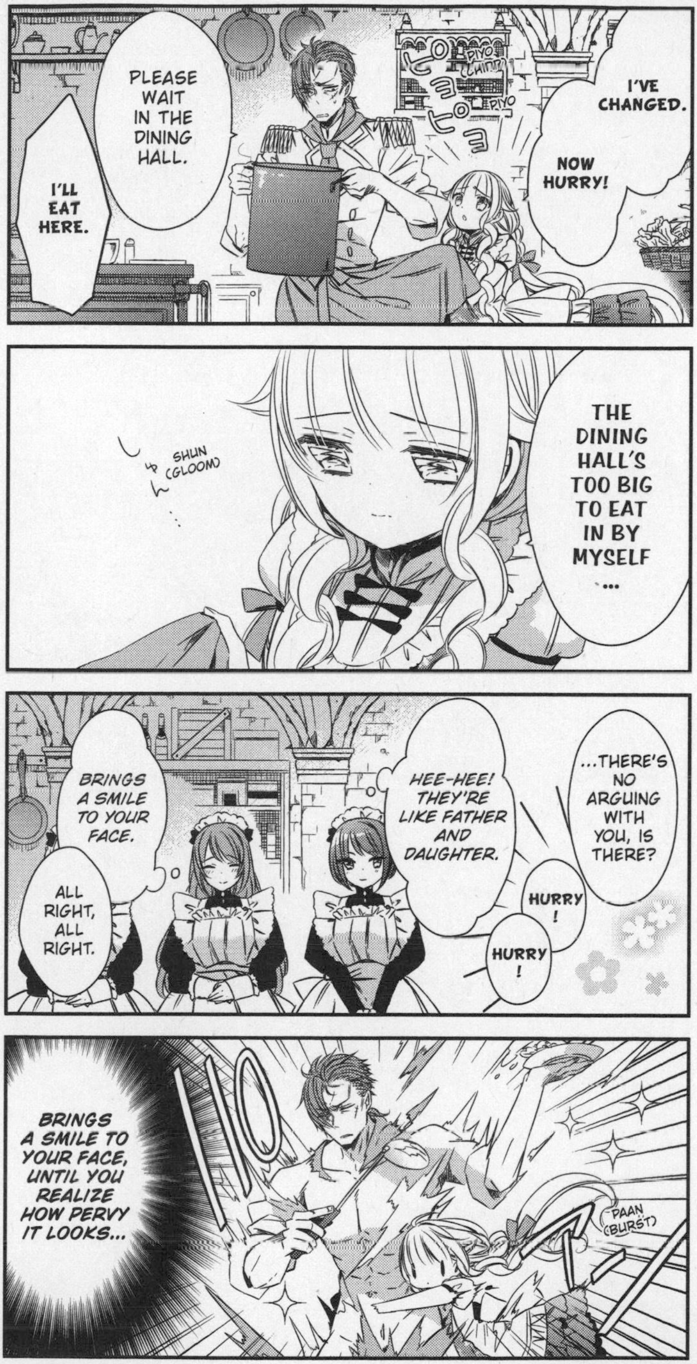
I'VE CHANGED.
NOW HURRY!
ピヨ ピヨ
PIYO (CHIRP) PIYO
PLEASE WAIT IN THE DINING HALL.
I'LL EAT HERE.
THE DINING HALL'S TOO BIG TO EAT IN BY MYSELF...
しゅん
SHUN (GLOOM)
...THERE'S NO ARGUING WITH YOU, IS THERE?
HURRY!
HURRY!
HEE-HEE! THEY'RE LIKE FATHER AND DAUGHTER.
BRINGS A SMILE TO YOUR FACE.
ALL RIGHT, ALL RIGHT.
PAAN (BURST)
BRINGS A SMILE TO YOUR FACE, UNTIL YOU REALIZE HOW PERVY IT LOOKS...

EDIBLE FLOWERS!

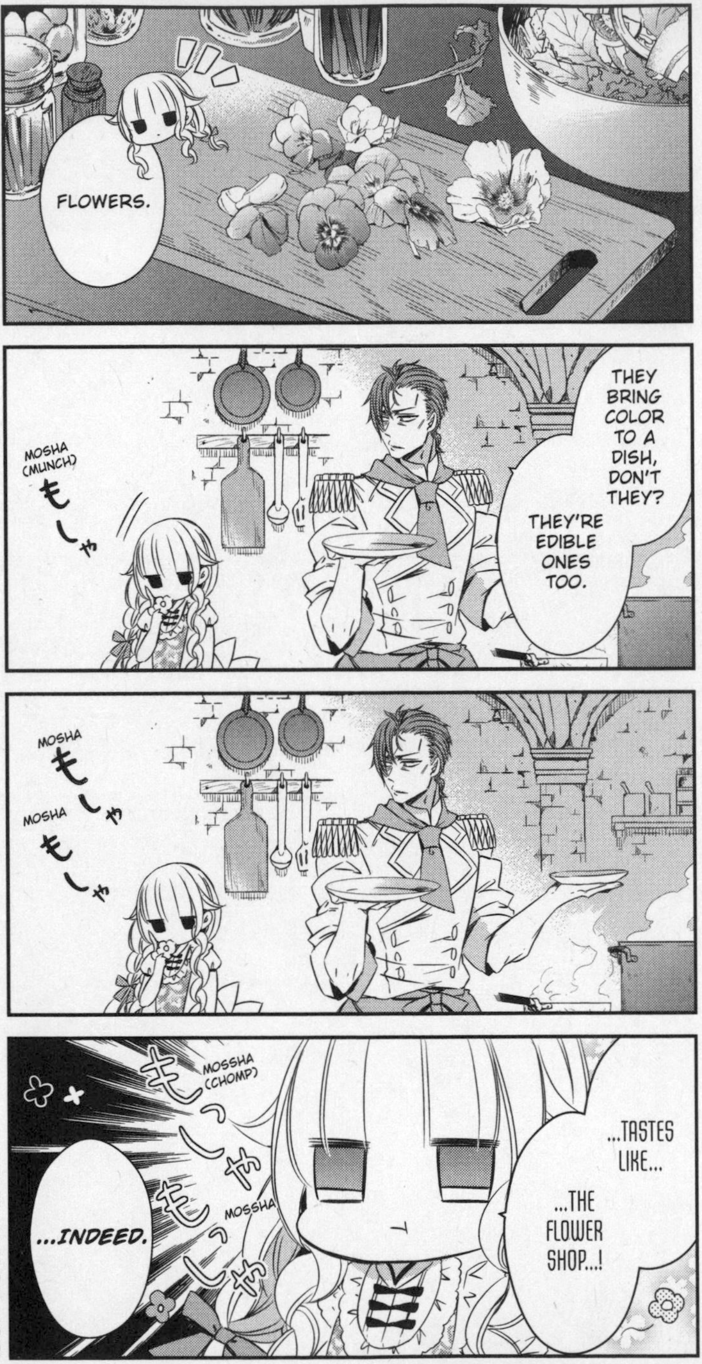
FLOWERS.
THEY BRING COLOR TO A DISH, DON'T THEY?
THEY'RE EDIBLE ONES TOO.
MOSHA (MUNCH)
もしゃ
MOSHA
もしゃ
MOSHA
もしゃ
...TASTES LIKE...
...THE FLOWER SHOP...!
MOSSHA (CHOMP)
もっしゃ
もっしゃ
MOSSHA
...INDEED.

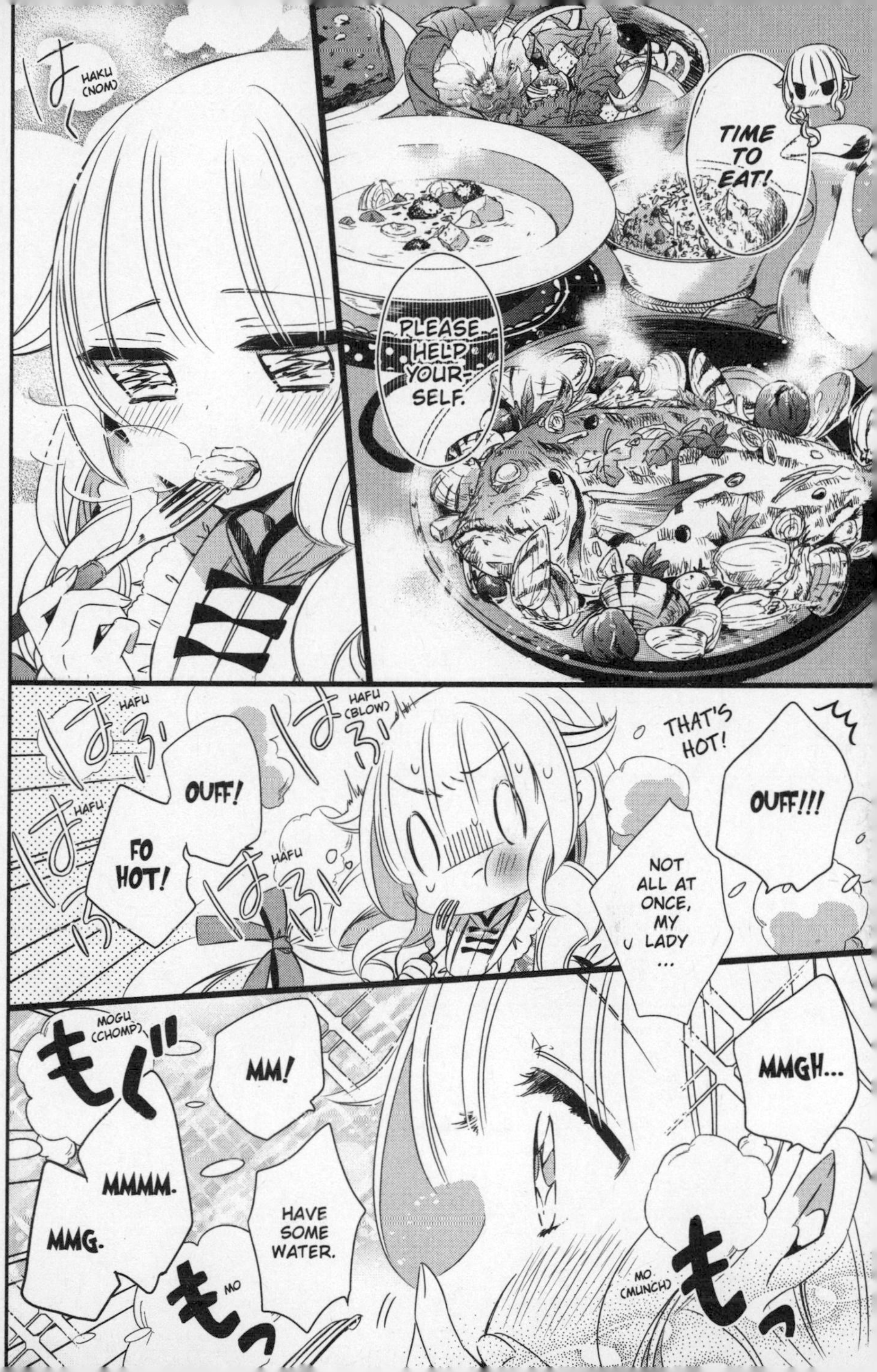
TIME TO EAT!
PLEASE HELP YOURSELF.
はく
HAKU (NOM)
OUFF!!!
THAT'S HOT!
NOT ALL AT ONCE, MY LADY ...
はふ
HAFU (BLOW)
OUFF!
はふ
HAFU
FO HOT!
HAFU
はふ
HAFU
MMGH...
もっ
MO (MUNCH)
HAVE SOME WATER.
もっ
MO
MM!
もぐ
MOGU (CHOMP)
MMMM.
MMG.

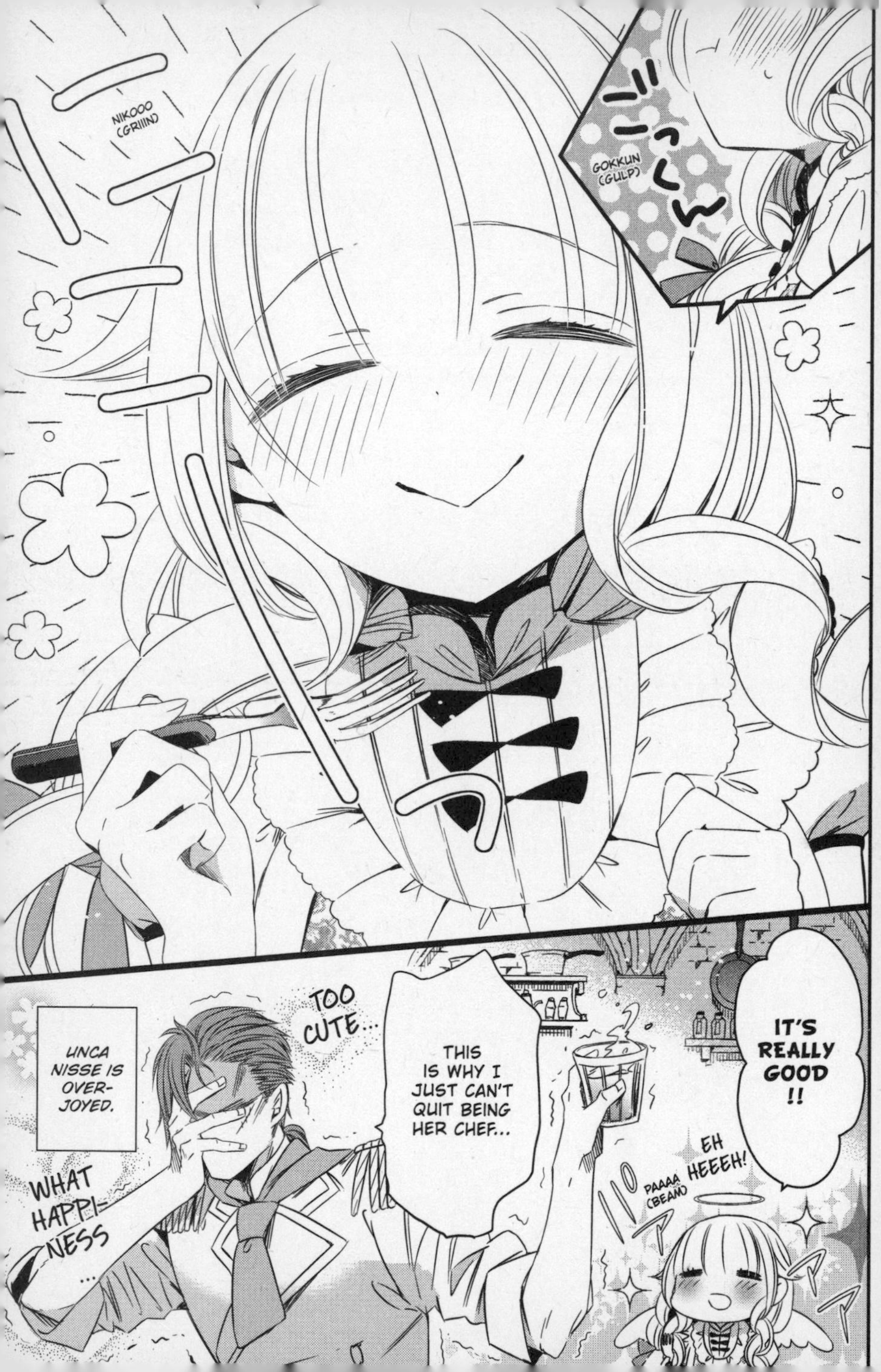
GOKKUN (GULP)
NIKOOO (GRIIIN)
IT'S REALLY GOOD!!
EH HEEEH!
PAAAA (BEAM)
THIS IS WHY I JUST CAN'T QUIT BEING HER CHEF...
TOO CUTE...
UNCA NISSE IS OVER-JOYED.
WHAT HAPPI-NESS...

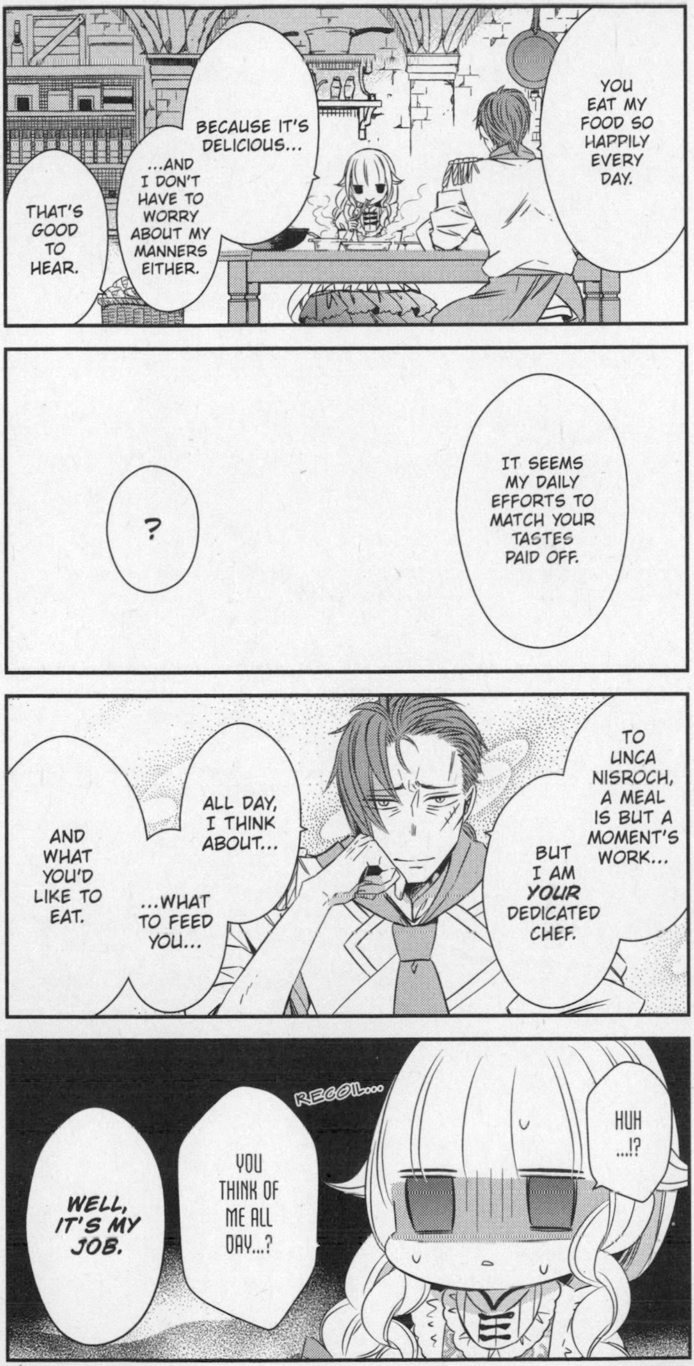
YOU EAT MY FOOD SO HAPPILY EVERY DAY.
BECAUSE IT'S DELICIOUS...
...AND I DON'T HAVE TO WORRY ABOUT MY MANNERS EITHER.
THAT'S GOOD TO HEAR.
IT SEEMS MY DAILY EFFORTS TO MATCH YOUR TASTES PAID OFF.
?
TO UNCA NISROCH, A MEAL IS BUT A MOMENT'S WORK...
BUT I AM *YOUR* DEDICATED CHEF.
ALL DAY, I THINK ABOUT...
...WHAT TO FEED YOU...
AND WHAT YOU'D LIKE TO EAT.
HUH ...!?
RECOIL...
YOU THINK OF ME ALL DAY...?
WELL, IT'S MY JOB.

THAT REACTION KIND OF HURTS UNCA NISROCH

THAT "COOKING IS LOVE" SPIEL

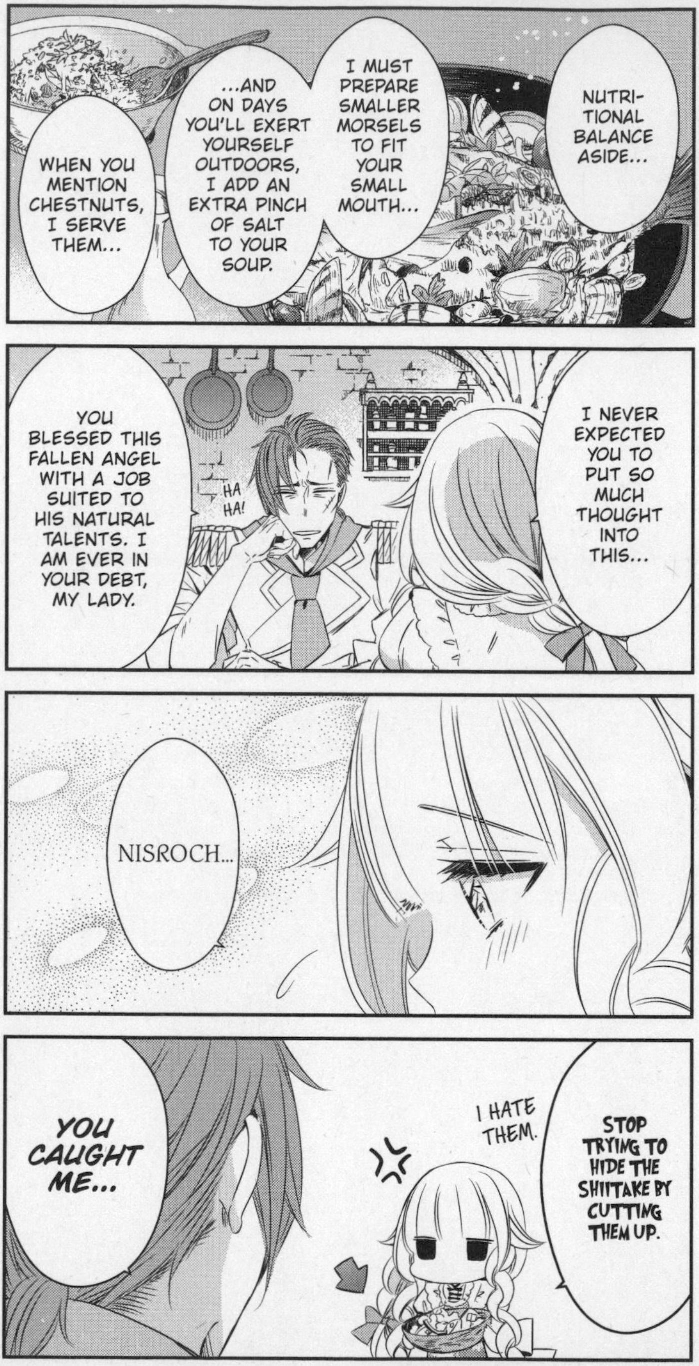
NUTRITIONAL BALANCE ASIDE...
I MUST PREPARE SMALLER MORSELS TO FIT YOUR SMALL MOUTH...
...AND ON DAYS YOU'LL EXERT YOURSELF OUTDOORS, I ADD AN EXTRA PINCH OF SALT TO YOUR SOUP.
WHEN YOU MENTION CHESTNUTS, I SERVE THEM...
I NEVER EXPECTED YOU TO PUT SO MUCH THOUGHT INTO THIS...
HA HA!
YOU BLESSED THIS FALLEN ANGEL WITH A JOB SUITED TO HIS NATURAL TALENTS. I AM EVER IN YOUR DEBT, MY LADY.
NISROCH...
STOP TRYING TO HIDE THE SHIITAKE BY CUTTING THEM UP.
I HATE THEM.
YOU CAUGHT ME...

EAT IN THE PROPER ORDER, MY LADY

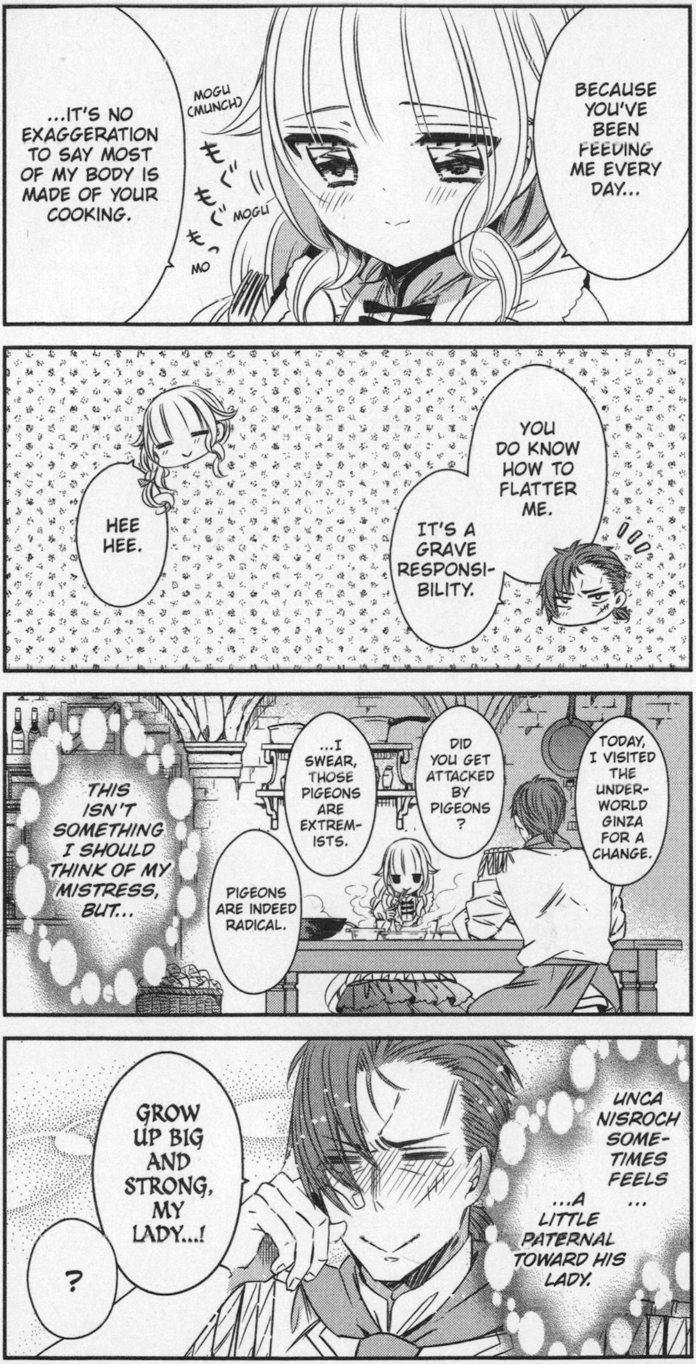
BECAUSE YOU'VE BEEN FEEDING ME EVERY DAY...
MOGU (MUNCH)
もぐ
MOGU
もぐ
MO
もっ
...IT'S NO EXAGGERATION TO SAY MOST OF MY BODY IS MADE OF YOUR COOKING.
YOU DO KNOW HOW TO FLATTER ME.
IT'S A GRAVE RESPONSIBILITY.
HEE HEE.
TODAY, I VISITED THE UNDERWORLD GINZA FOR A CHANGE.
DID YOU GET ATTACKED BY PIGEONS?
...I SWEAR, THOSE PIGEONS ARE EXTREMISTS.
PIGEONS ARE INDEED RADICAL.
THIS ISN'T SOMETHING I SHOULD THINK OF MY MISTRESS, BUT...
UNCA NISROCH SOMETIMES FEELS ...A LITTLE PATERNAL TOWARD HIS LADY.
GROW UP BIG AND STRONG, MY LADY...!
?

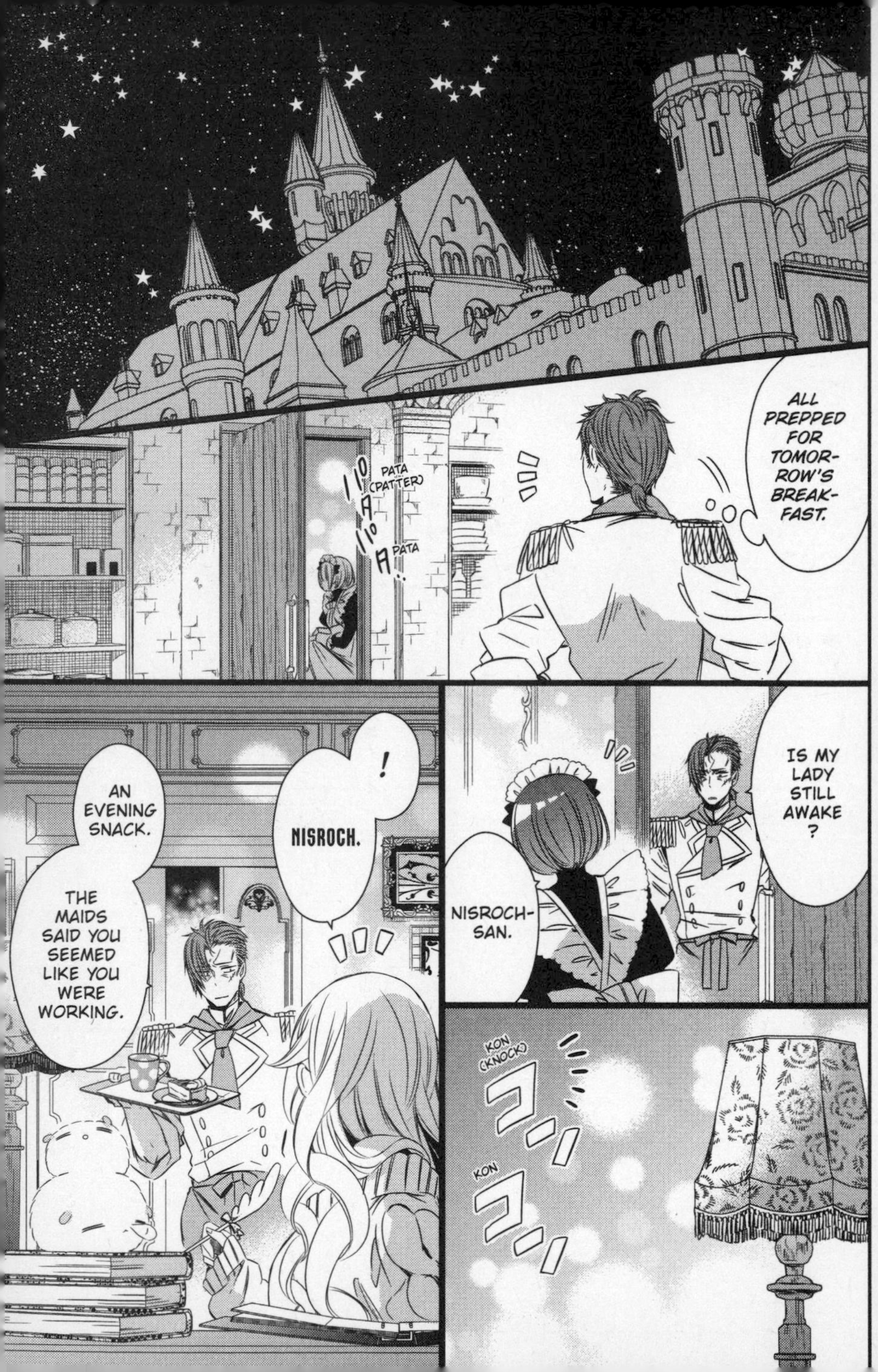
ALL PREPPED FOR TOMORROW'S BREAKFAST.
PATA (PATTER)
PATA
IS MY LADY STILL AWAKE?
NISROCH-SAN.
KON (KNOCK)
KON
!
NISROCH.
AN EVENING SNACK.
THE MAIDS SAID YOU SEEMED LIKE YOU WERE WORKING.

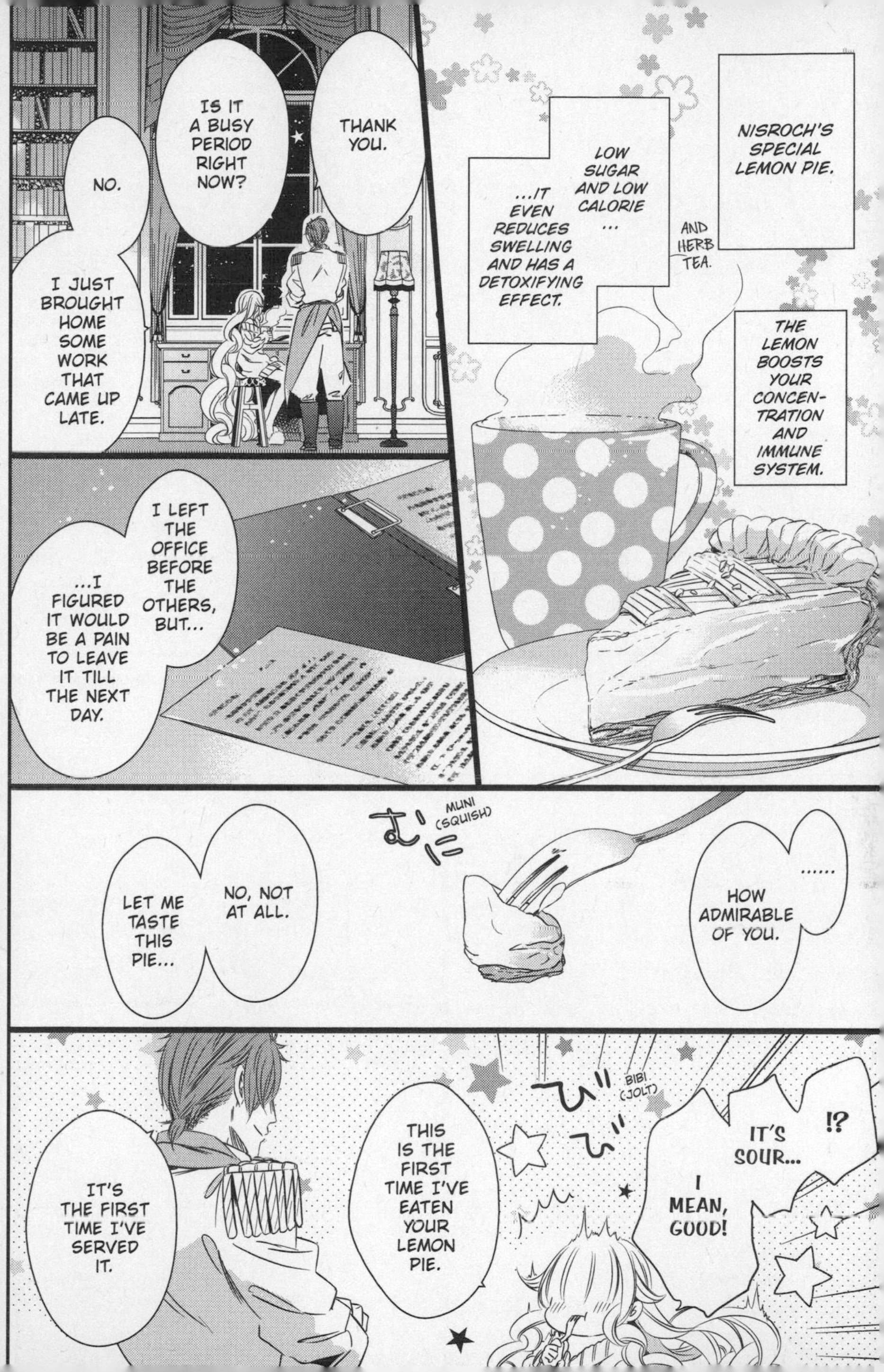
NISROCH'S SPECIAL LEMON PIE.
AND HERB TEA.
THE LEMON BOOSTS YOUR CONCENTRATION AND IMMUNE SYSTEM.
LOW SUGAR AND LOW CALORIE ...
...IT EVEN REDUCES SWELLING AND HAS A DETOXIFYING EFFECT.
THANK YOU.
IS IT A BUSY PERIOD RIGHT NOW?
NO.
I JUST BROUGHT HOME SOME WORK THAT CAME UP LATE.
I LEFT THE OFFICE BEFORE THE OTHERS, BUT...
...I FIGURED IT WOULD BE A PAIN TO LEAVE IT TILL THE NEXT DAY.
......
HOW ADMIRABLE OF YOU.
むに
MUNI (SQUISH)
NO, NOT AT ALL.
LET ME TASTE THIS PIE...
!?
IT'S SOUR...
I MEAN, GOOD!
BIBI (JOLT)
THIS IS THE FIRST TIME I'VE EATEN YOUR LEMON PIE.
IT'S THE FIRST TIME I'VE SERVED IT.

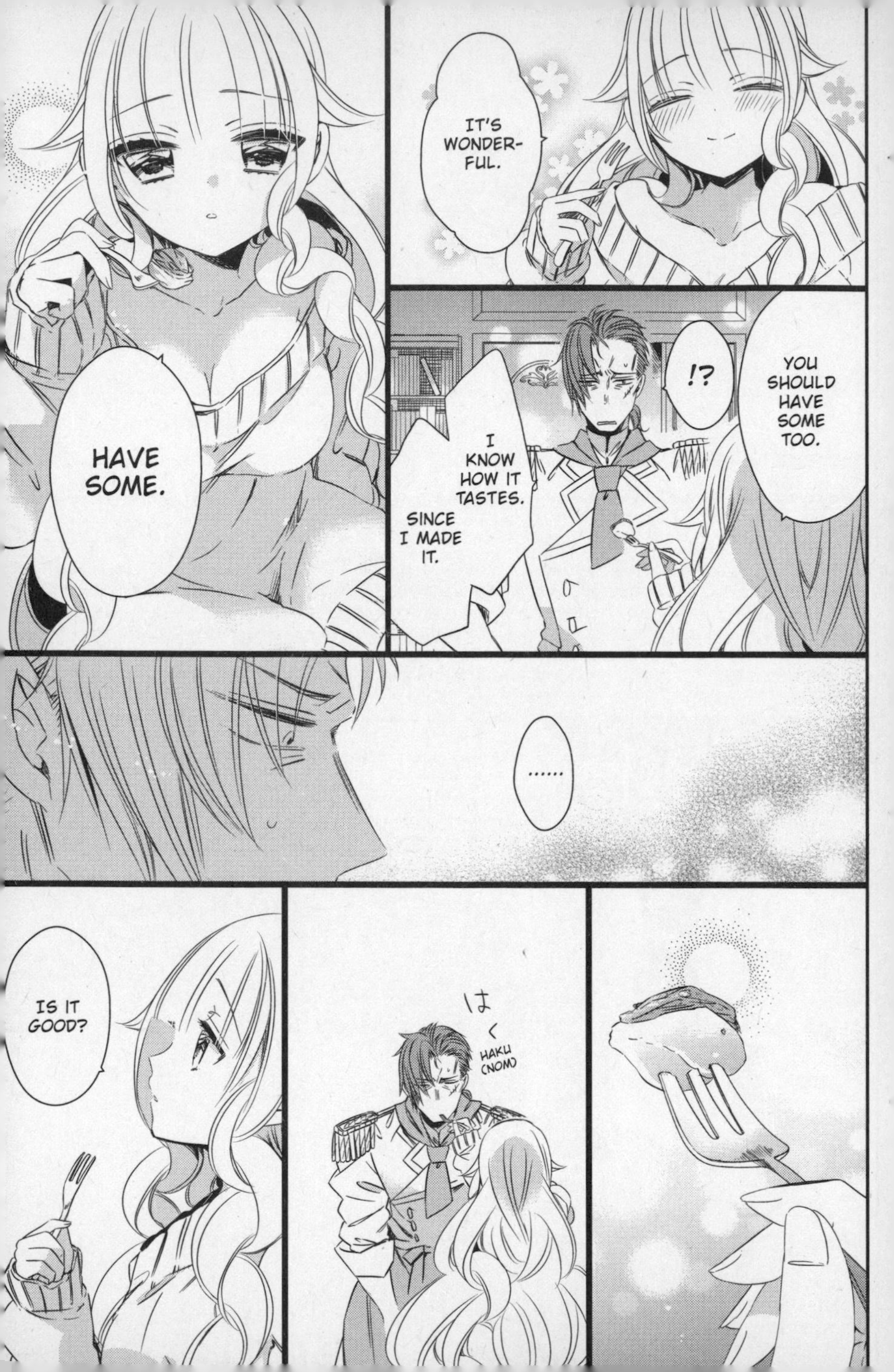
IT'S WONDERFUL.
YOU SHOULD HAVE SOME TOO.
!?
I KNOW HOW IT TASTES.
SINCE I MADE IT.
HAVE SOME.
......
はく
HAKU (NOM)
IS IT GOOD?

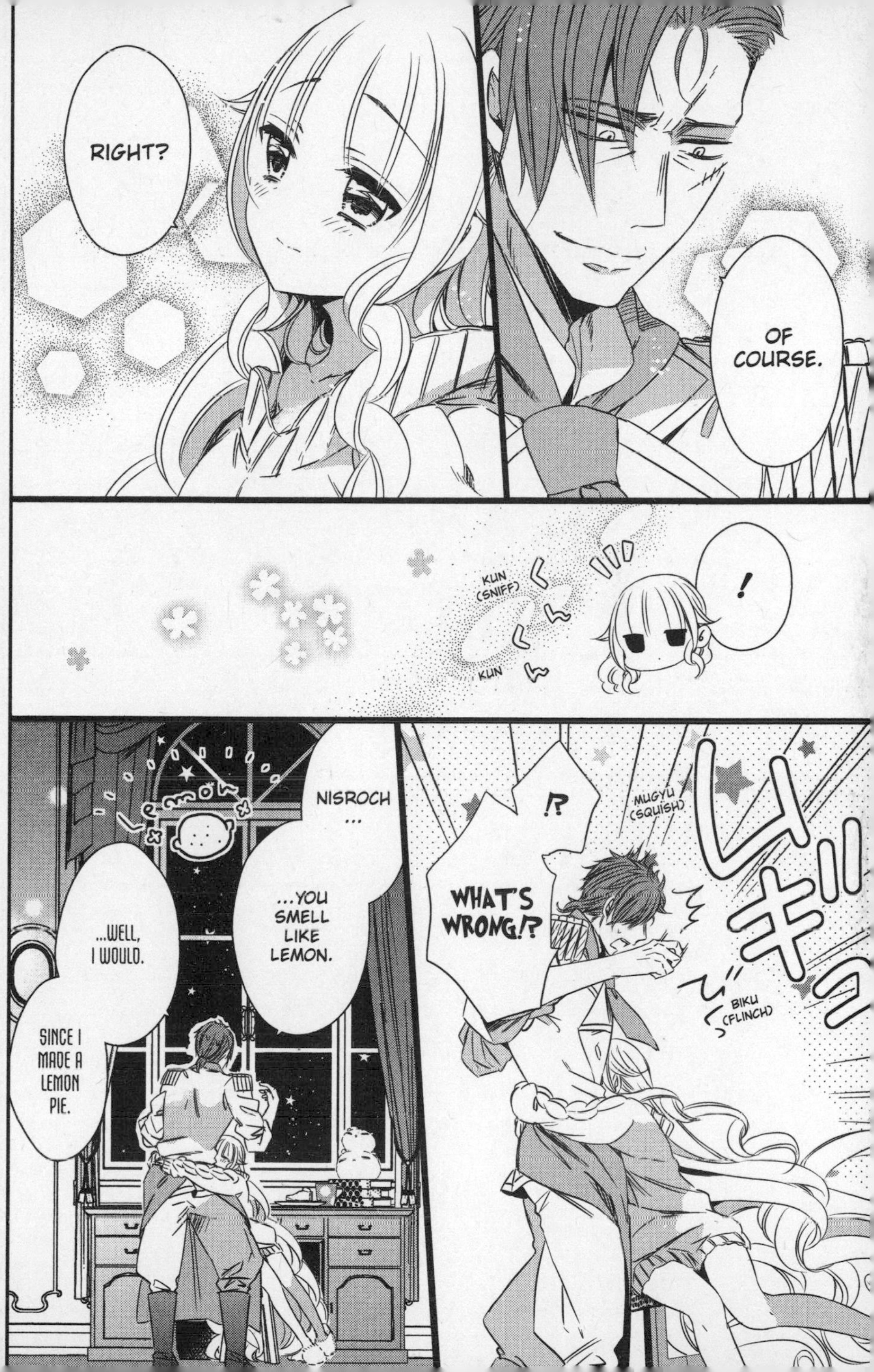
OF COURSE.
RIGHT?
!
KUN (SNIFF)
KUN
MUGYU (SQUISH)
!?
WHAT'S WRONG!?
BIKU (FLINCH)
NISROCH ...
...YOU SMELL LIKE LEMON.
Lemon
...WELL, I WOULD.
SINCE I MADE A LEMON PIE.

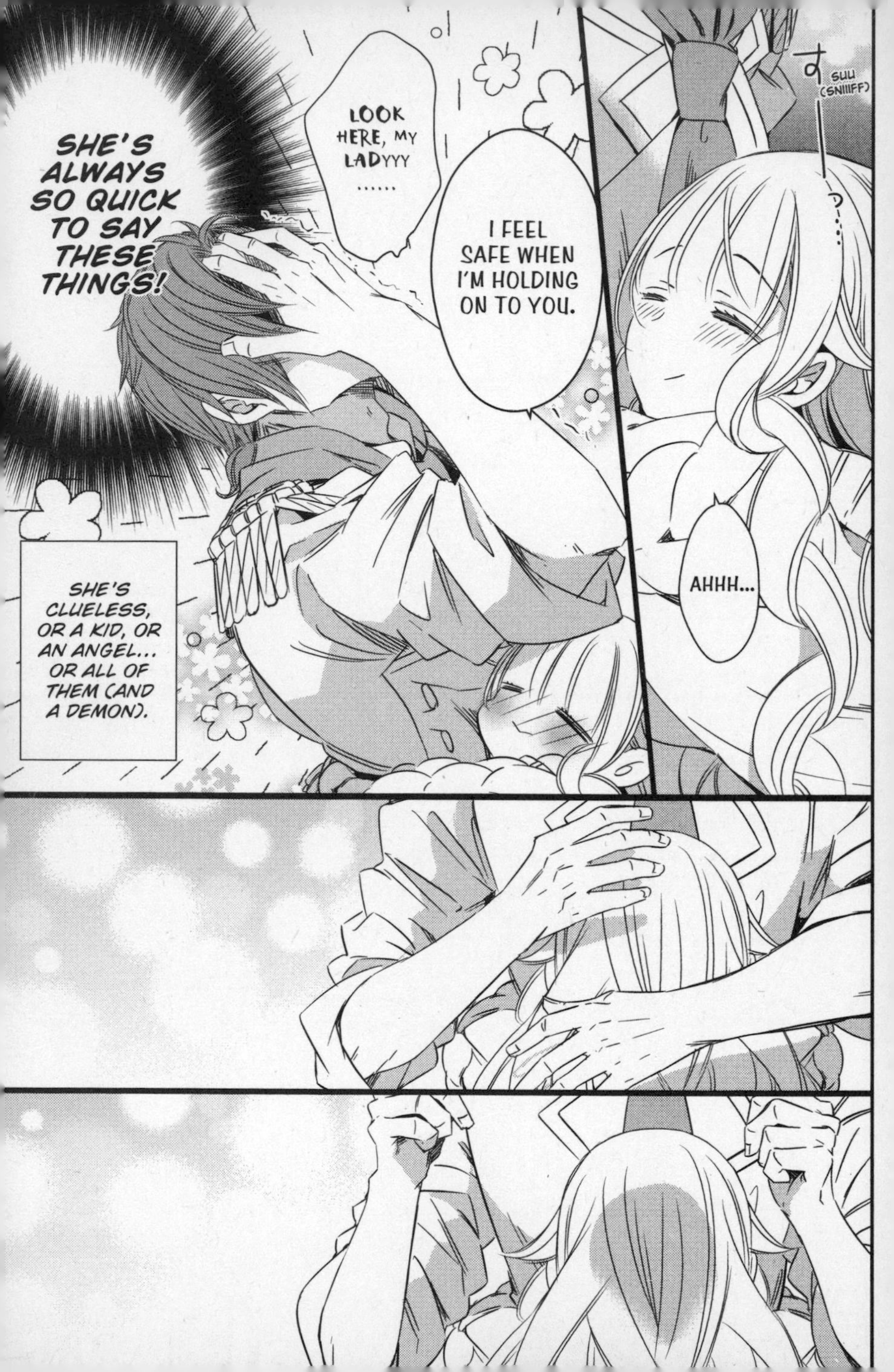
す
SUU (SNIIIFF)
AHHH...
I FEEL SAFE WHEN I'M HOLDING ON TO YOU.
LOOK HERE, MY LADYYY ......
SHE'S ALWAYS SO QUICK TO SAY THESE THINGS!
SHE'S CLUELESS, OR A KID, OR AN ANGEL... OR ALL OF THEM (AND A DEMON).

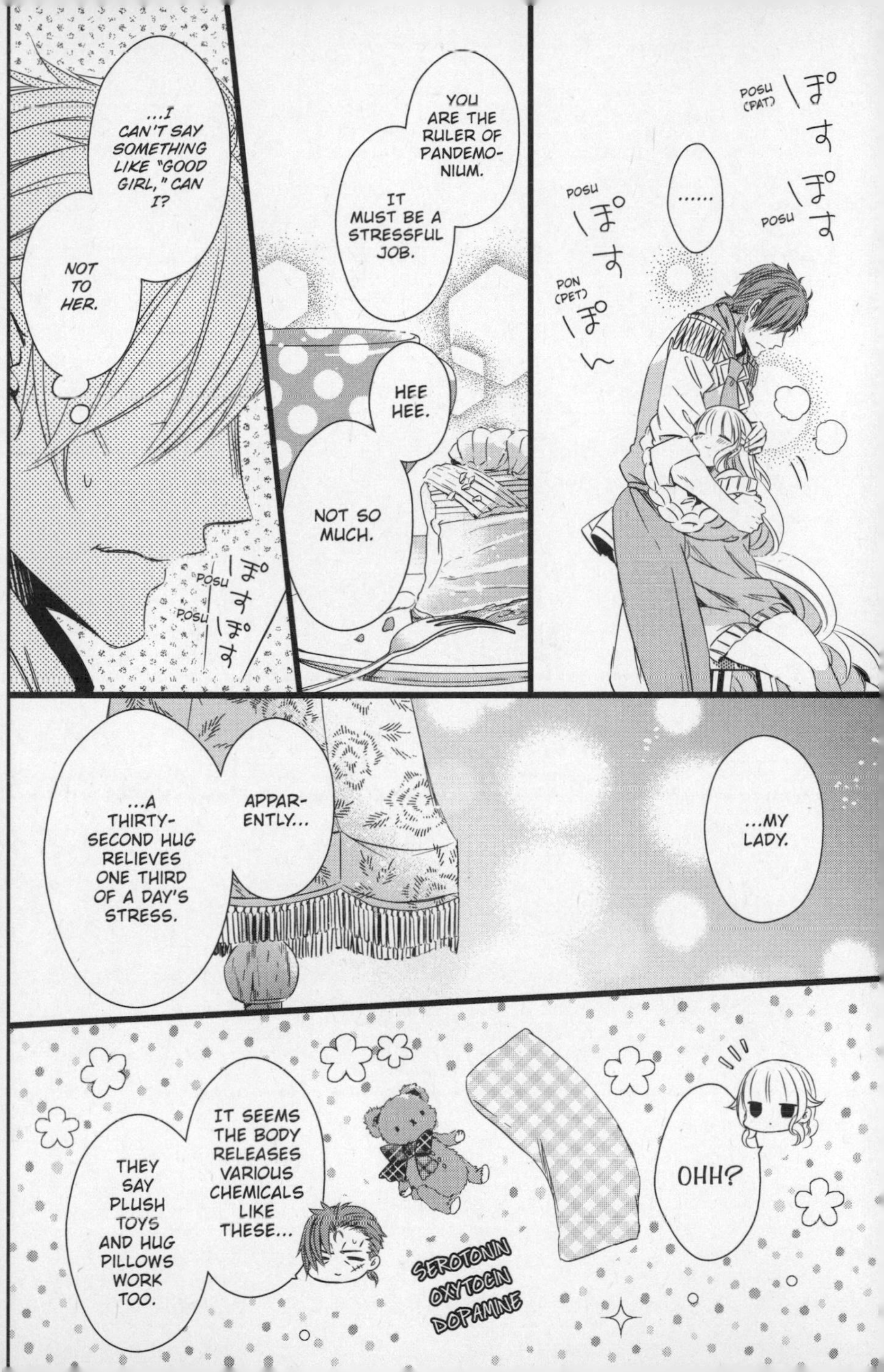
ぽす ぽす
POSU (PAT)
POSU
......
ぽす
POSU
ぽん
PON (PET)
YOU ARE THE RULER OF PANDEMONIUM.
IT MUST BE A STRESSFUL JOB.
HEE HEE.
NOT SO MUCH.
...I CAN'T SAY SOMETHING LIKE "GOOD GIRL," CAN I?
NOT TO HER.
ぽすぽす
POSU
POSU
...MY LADY.
APPARENTLY...
...A THIRTY-SECOND HUG RELIEVES ONE THIRD OF A DAY'S STRESS.
OHH?
IT SEEMS THE BODY RELEASES VARIOUS CHEMICALS LIKE THESE...
THEY SAY PLUSH TOYS AND HUG PILLOWS WORK TOO.
SEROTONIN
OXYTOCIN
DOPAMINE

UNDERSTANDING & ACCEPTANCE

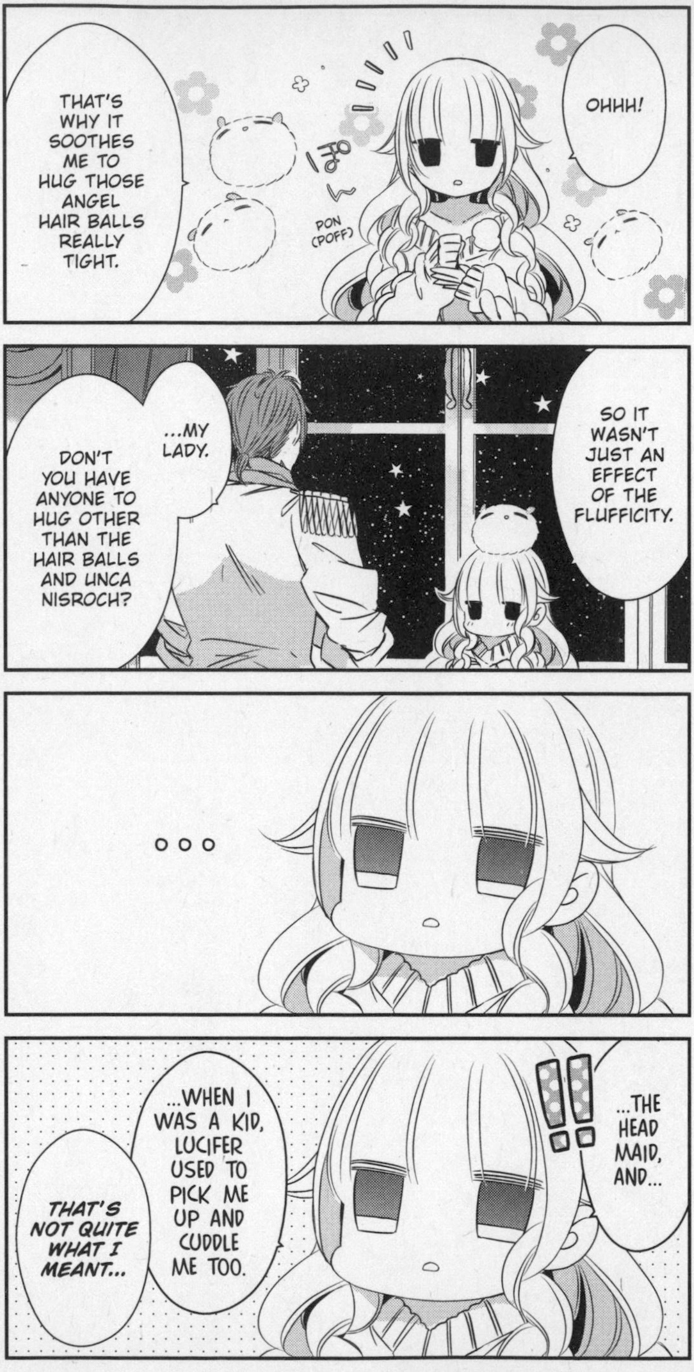
OHHH!
PON (POFF)
THAT'S WHY IT SOOTHES ME TO HUG THOSE ANGEL HAIR BALLS REALLY TIGHT.
SO IT WASN'T JUST AN EFFECT OF THE FLUFFICITY.
...MY LADY.
DON'T YOU HAVE ANYONE TO HUG OTHER THAN THE HAIR BALLS AND UNCA NISROCH?
ooo
!!
...THE HEAD MAID, AND...
...WHEN I WAS A KID, LUCIFER USED TO PICK ME UP AND CUDDLE ME TOO.
THAT'S NOT QUITE WHAT I MEANT...

WHEN YOUR JOKE HITS THE MARK, IT'S KIND OF A SHOCK

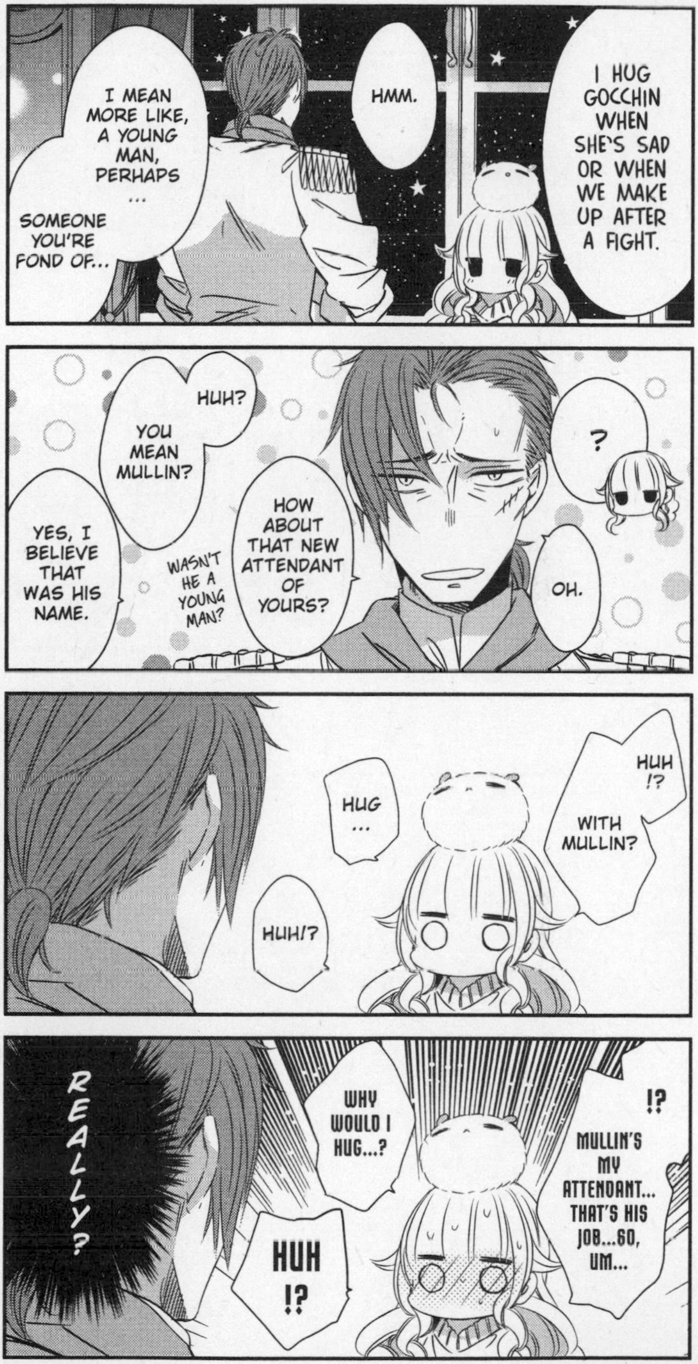
I HUG GOCCHIN WHEN SHE'S SAD OR WHEN WE MAKE UP AFTER A FIGHT.
HMM.
I MEAN MORE LIKE, A YOUNG MAN, PERHAPS...
SOMEONE YOU'RE FOND OF...
?
OH.
HOW ABOUT THAT NEW ATTENDANT OF YOURS?
WASN'T HE A YOUNG MAN?
HUH?
YOU MEAN MULLIN?
YES, I BELIEVE THAT WAS HIS NAME.
HUH !?
WITH MULLIN?
HUG ...
HUH!?
!?
MULLIN'S MY ATTENDANT... THAT'S HIS JOB...SO, UM...
WHY WOULD I HUG...?
HUH !?
REALLY?

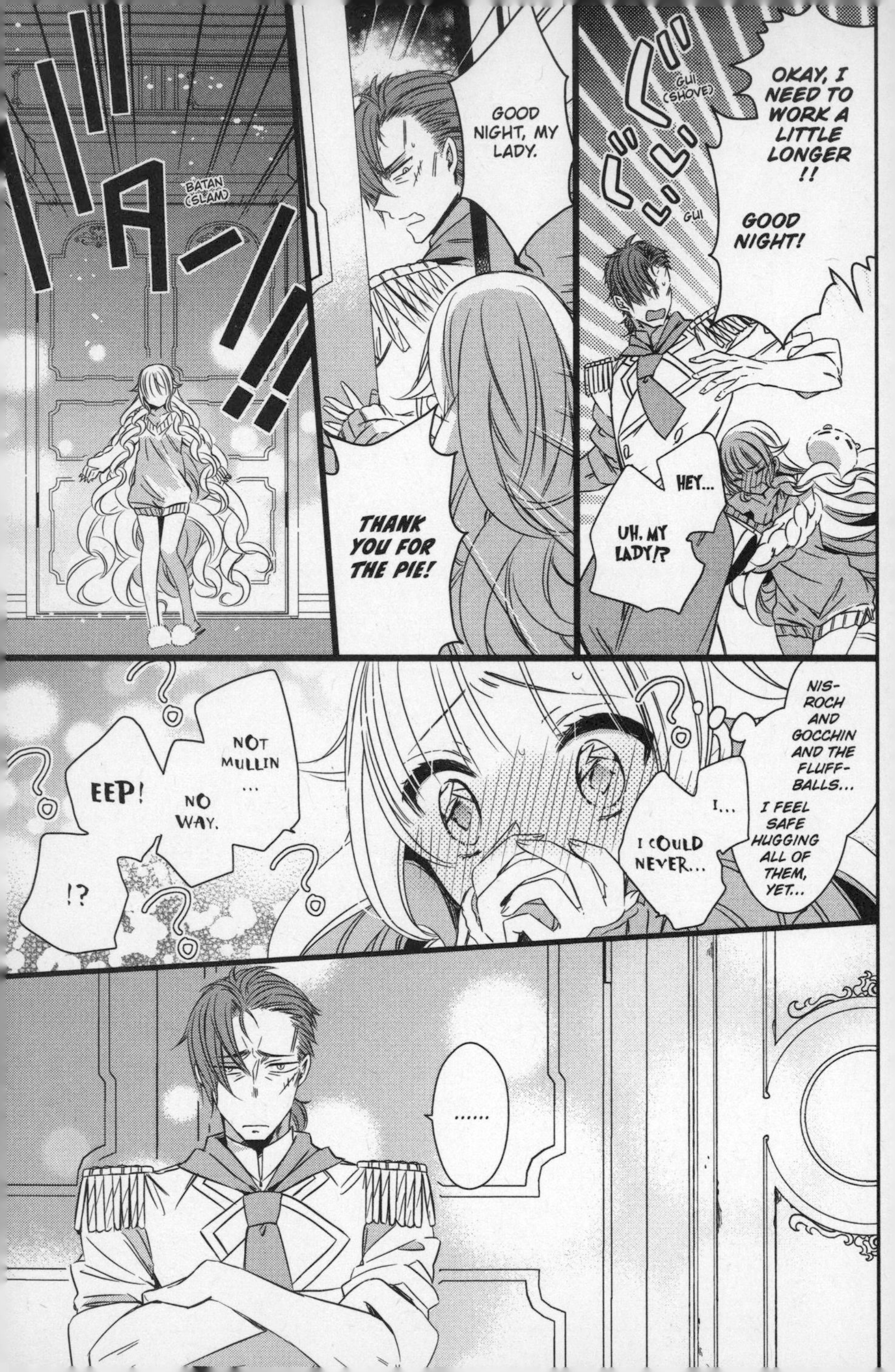
OKAY, I NEED TO WORK A LITTLE LONGER!!
GUI (SHOVE)
GOOD NIGHT!
GUI
HEY...
UH, MY LADY!?
GOOD NIGHT, MY LADY.
THANK YOU FOR THE PIE!
BATAN (SLAM)
NIS-ROCH AND GOCCHIN AND THE FLUFF-BALLS...
I FEEL SAFE HUGGING ALL OF THEM, YET...
I...
I COULD NEVER...
NOT MULLIN...
NO WAY.
EEP!
!?
......

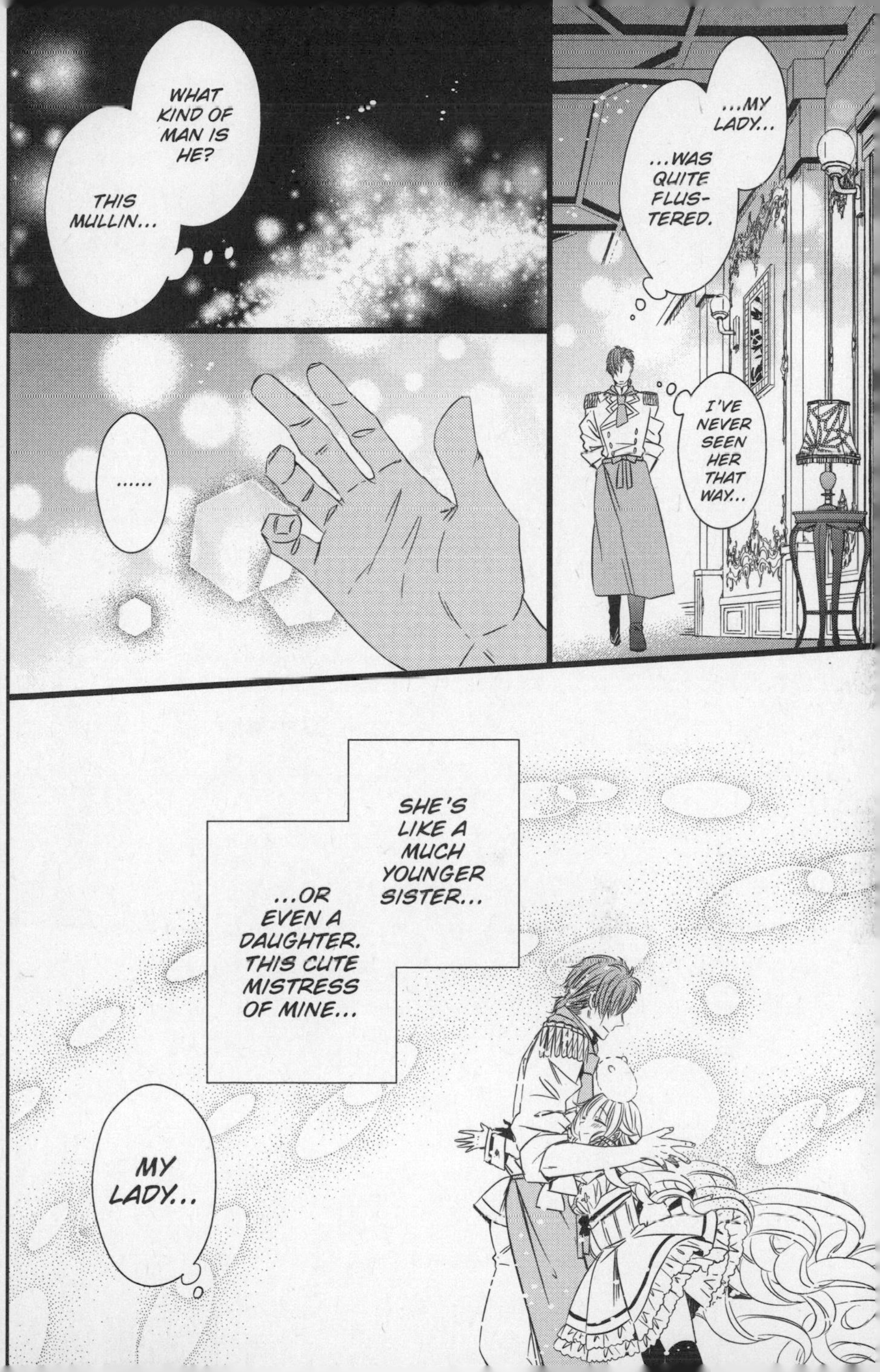
...MY LADY...
...WAS QUITE FLUS-TERED.
I'VE NEVER SEEN HER THAT WAY...
WHAT KIND OF MAN IS HE?
THIS MULLIN...
......
SHE'S LIKE A MUCH YOUNGER SISTER...
...OR EVEN A DAUGHTER. THIS CUTE MISTRESS OF MINE...
MY LADY...

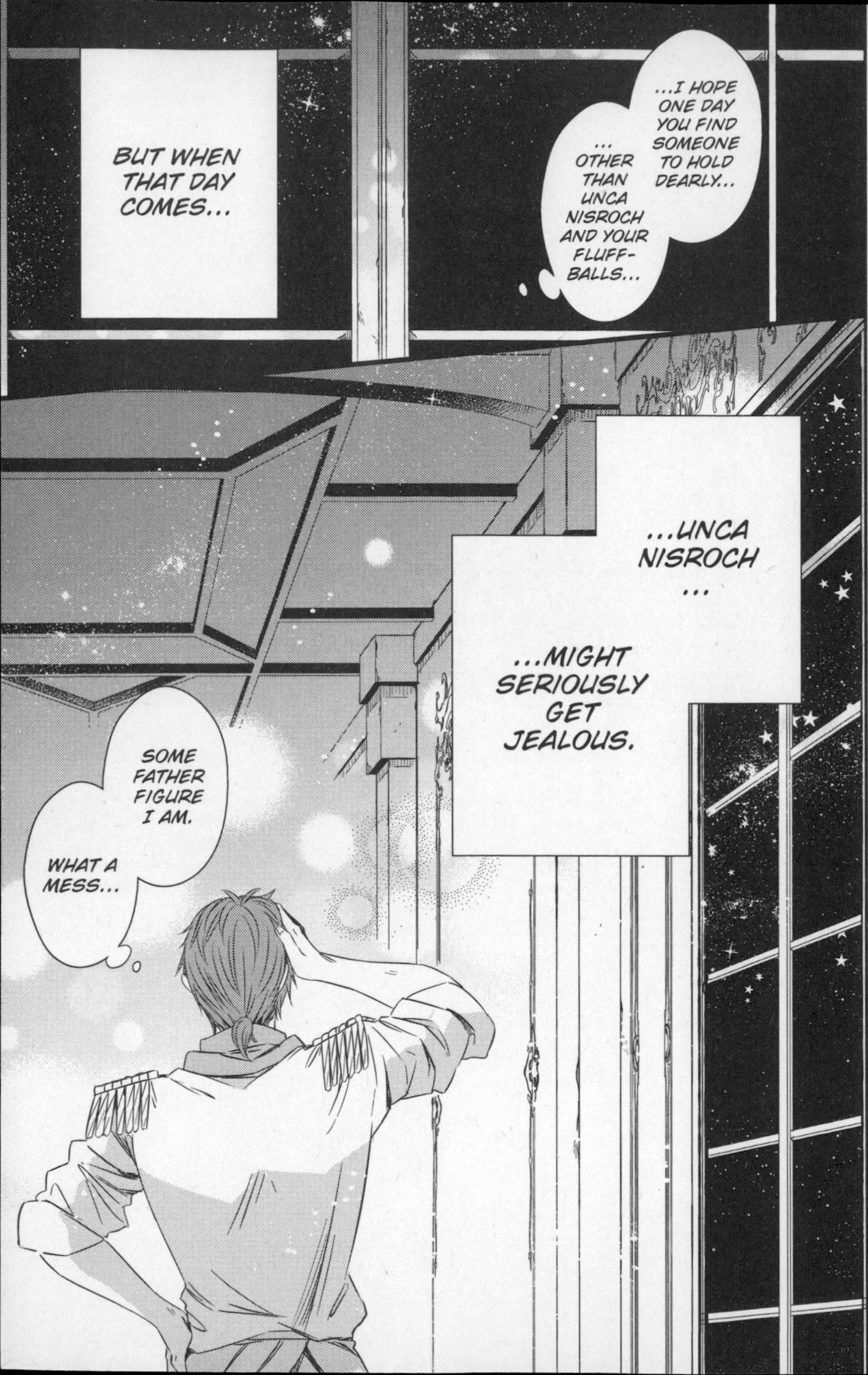
...I HOPE ONE DAY YOU FIND SOMEONE TO HOLD DEARLY...
...OTHER THAN UNCA NISROCH AND YOUR FLUFF-BALLS...
BUT WHEN THAT DAY COMES...
...UNCA NISROCH...
...MIGHT SERIOUSLY GET JEALOUS.
SOME FATHER FIGURE I AM.
WHAT A MESS...

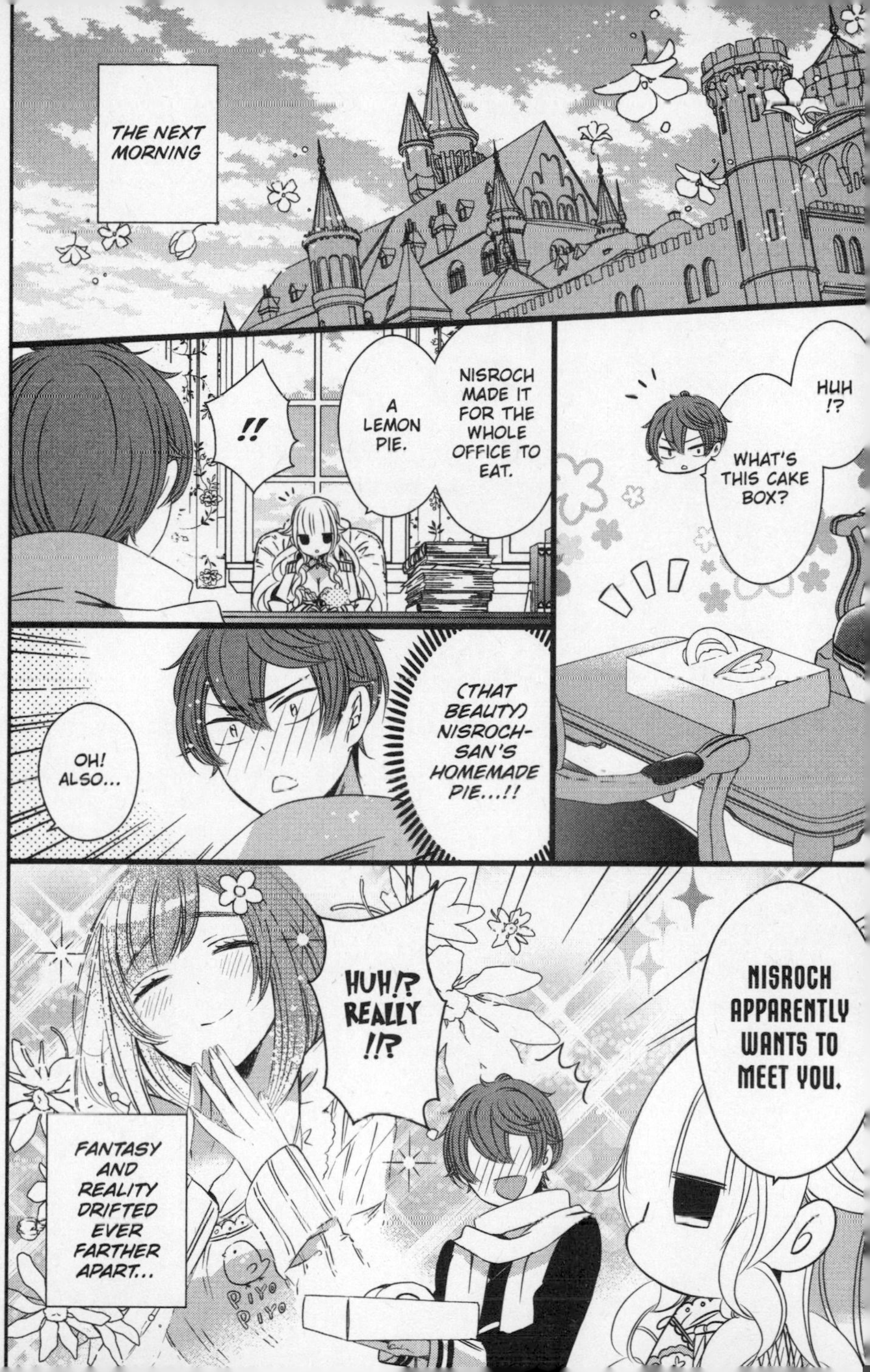
THE NEXT MORNING
HUH !?
WHAT'S THIS CAKE BOX?
NISROCH MADE IT FOR THE WHOLE OFFICE TO EAT.
A LEMON PIE.
!!
(THAT BEAUTY) NISROCH-SAN'S HOMEMADE PIE...!!
OH! ALSO...
NISROCH APPARENTLY WANTS TO MEET YOU.
HUH!? REALLY !!?
FANTASY AND REALITY DRIFTED EVER FARTHER APART...
PIYO PIYO

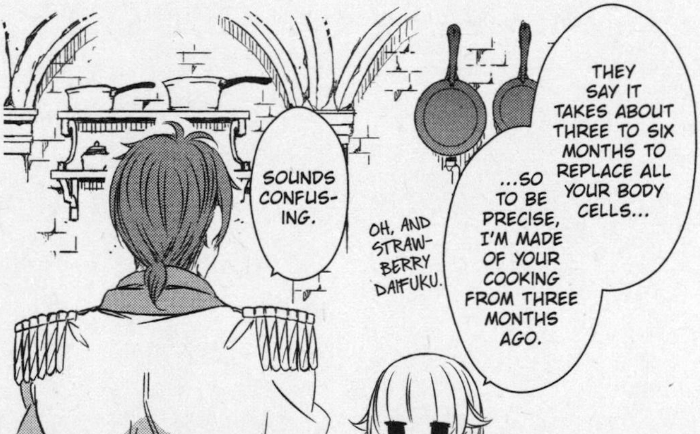
THEY SAY IT TAKES ABOUT THREE TO SIX MONTHS TO REPLACE ALL YOUR BODY CELLS...
...SO TO BE PRECISE, I'M MADE OF YOUR COOKING FROM THREE MONTHS AGO.
OH, AND STRAW-BERRY DAIFUKU.
SOUNDS CONFUS-ING.

As Miss Beelzebub Likes

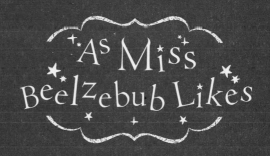

SO CUTE!

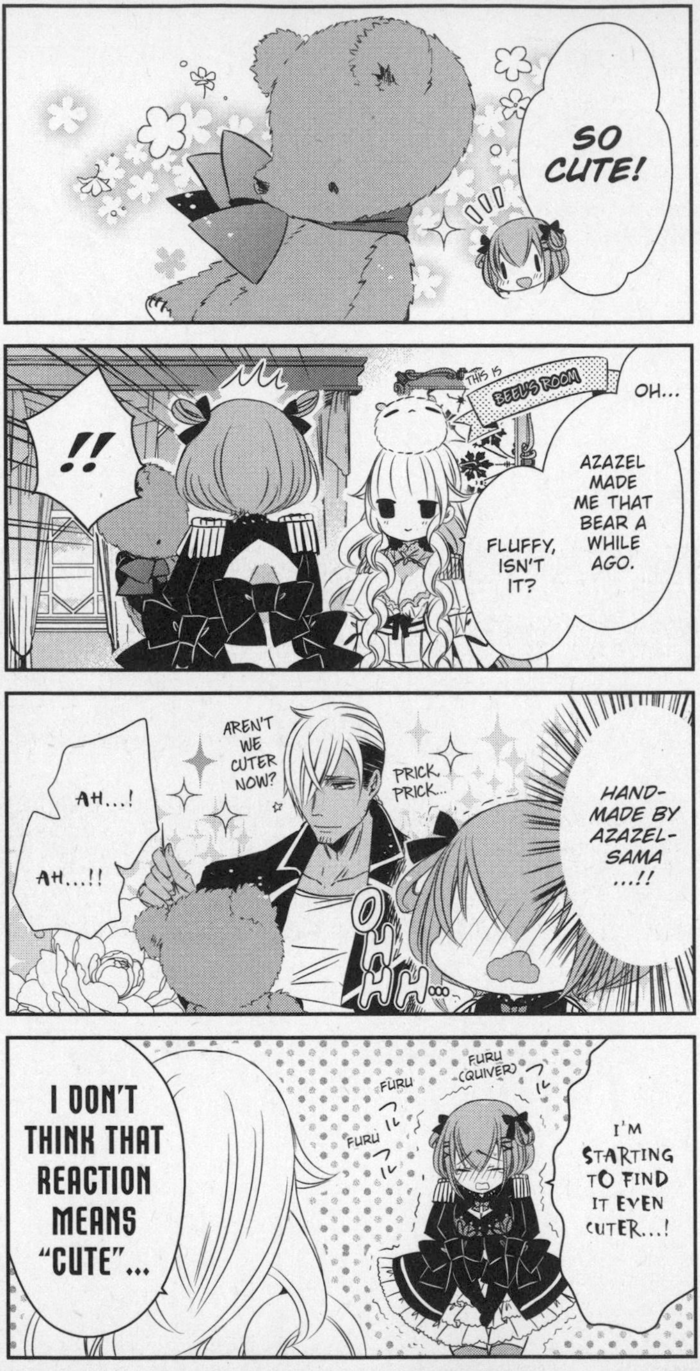

SO CUTE!
!!!
OH...
AZAZEL MADE ME THAT BEAR A WHILE AGO.
THIS IS BEEL'S ROOM
FLUFFY, ISN'T IT?
!!
HAND-MADE BY AZAZEL-SAMA ...!!
PRICK, PRICK...
AREN'T WE CUTER NOW?
AH...!
AH...!!
OHHHH...
I'M STARTING TO FIND IT EVEN CUTER...!
FURU (QUIVER) フル
FURU フル
FURU フル
I DON'T THINK THAT REACTION MEANS "CUTE"...

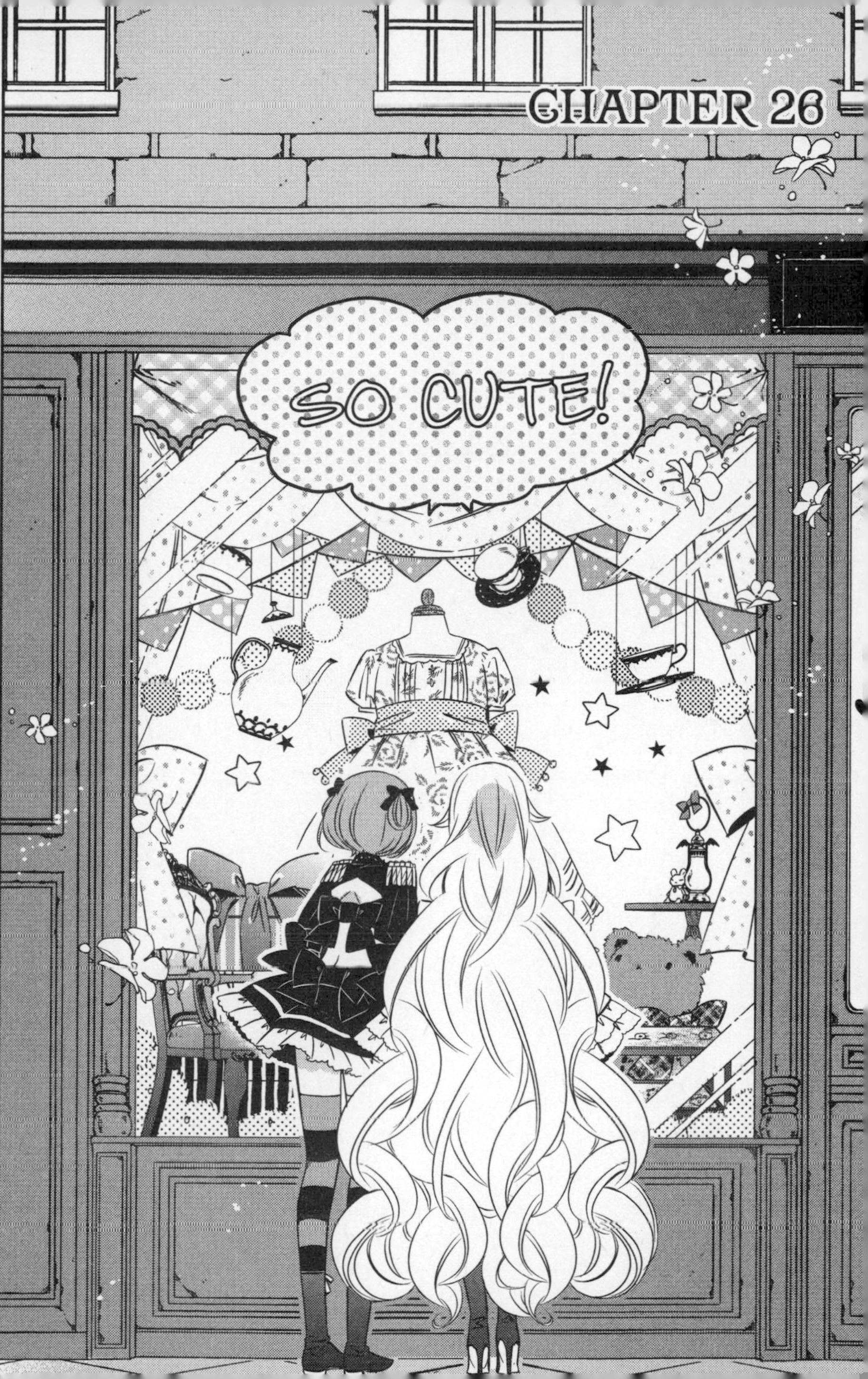
CHAPTER 26
SO CUTE!

SO CUTE (APPARENTLY, IT'S ALL ABOUT FLUFFINESS AND PROPORTIONS)

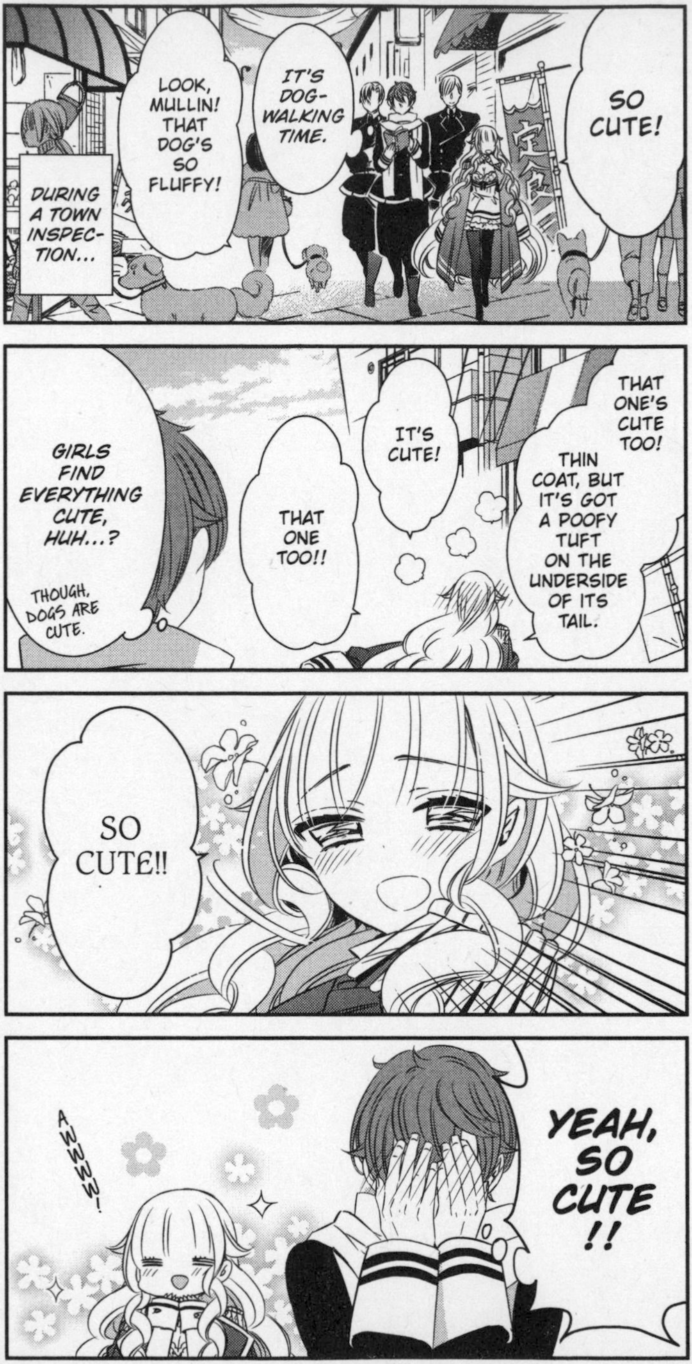
SO CUTE!
IT'S DOG-WALKING TIME.
LOOK, MULLIN! THAT DOG'S SO FLUFFY!
DURING A TOWN INSPECTION...
THAT ONE'S CUTE TOO!
THIN COAT, BUT IT'S GOT A POOFY TUFT ON THE UNDERSIDE OF ITS TAIL.
IT'S CUTE!
THAT ONE TOO!!
GIRLS FIND EVERYTHING CUTE, HUH...?
THOUGH, DOGS ARE CUTE.
SO CUTE!!
YEAH, SO CUTE!!
AWWWW!

AM I CUTE!? (NO)

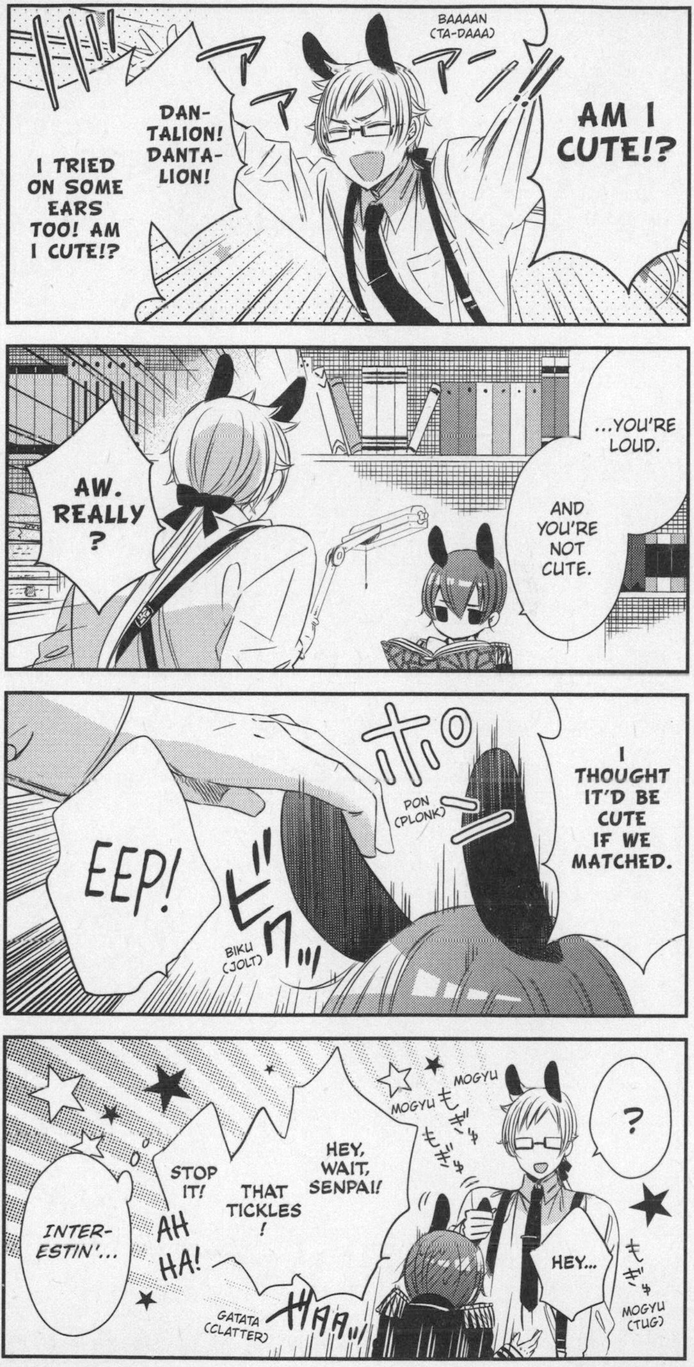
BAAAAN (TA-DAAA)
AM I CUTE!?
DAN-TALION! DANTA-LION!
I TRIED ON SOME EARS TOO! AM I CUTE!?
...YOU'RE LOUD.
AND YOU'RE NOT CUTE.
AW. REALLY?
I THOUGHT IT'D BE CUTE IF WE MATCHED.
PON (PLONK)
BIKU (JOLT)
EEP!
?
MOGYU MOGYU
MOGYU (TUG)
HEY...
HEY, WAIT, SENPAI!
THAT TICKLES!
STOP IT!
AH HA!
GATATA (CLATTER)
INTER-ESTIN'...

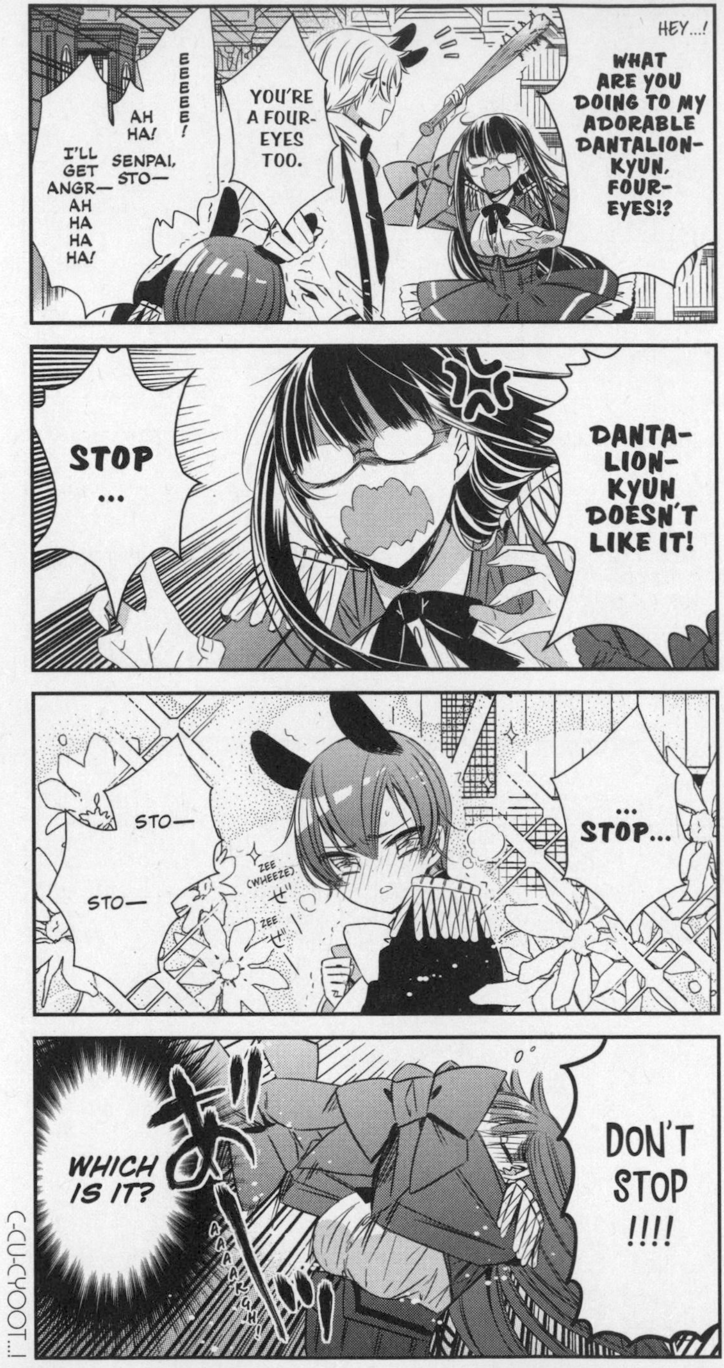
HEY...!
WHAT ARE YOU DOING TO MY ADORABLE DANTALION-KYUN, FOUR-EYES!?
YOU'RE A FOUR-EYES TOO.
EEEEEE!
AH HA! SENPAI, STO—
I'LL GET ANGR— AH HA HA HA HA!
DANTALION-KYUN DOESN'T LIKE IT!
STOP ...
... STOP...
ZEE (WHEEZE)
ZEE
STO—
STO—
DON'T STOP !!!!
WHICH IS IT?
AAAAARUH!
C-CU-CYOOT...!

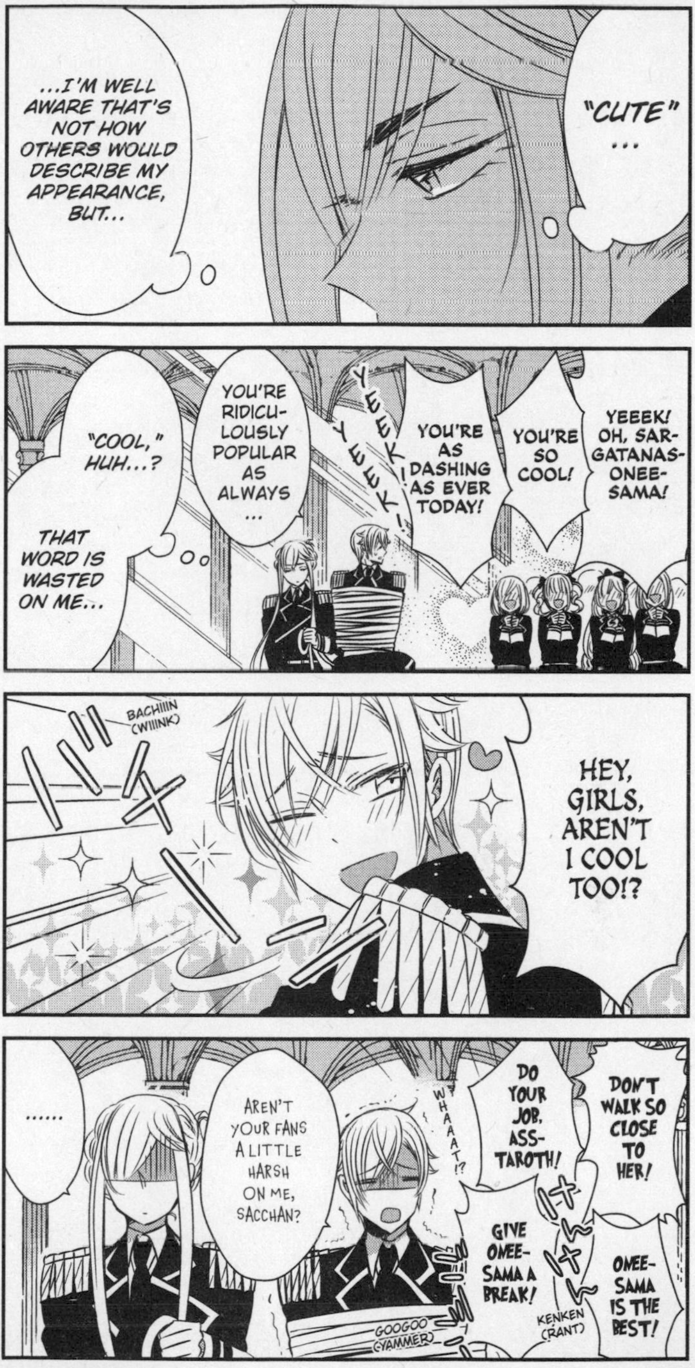
"CUTE"...
...I'M WELL AWARE THAT'S NOT HOW OTHERS WOULD DESCRIBE MY APPEARANCE, BUT...
YEEEK! OH, SARGATANAS-ONEE-SAMA!
YOU'RE SO COOL!
YOU'RE AS DASHING AS EVER TODAY!
YEEEK! YEEEK!
YOU'RE RIDICULOUSLY POPULAR AS ALWAYS...
"COOL," HUH...?
THAT WORD IS WASTED ON ME...
HEY, GIRLS, AREN'T I COOL TOO!?
BACHIIIN (WIIINK)
DON'T WALK SO CLOSE TO HER!
DO YOUR JOB, ASSTAROTH!
ONEE-SAMA IS THE BEST!
KENKEN (RANT)
GIVE ONEE-SAMA A BREAK!
WHAAAAT!?
GOOGOO (YAMMER)
AREN'T YOUR FANS A LITTLE HARSH ON ME, SACCHAN?
......

CUTE =/= COOL

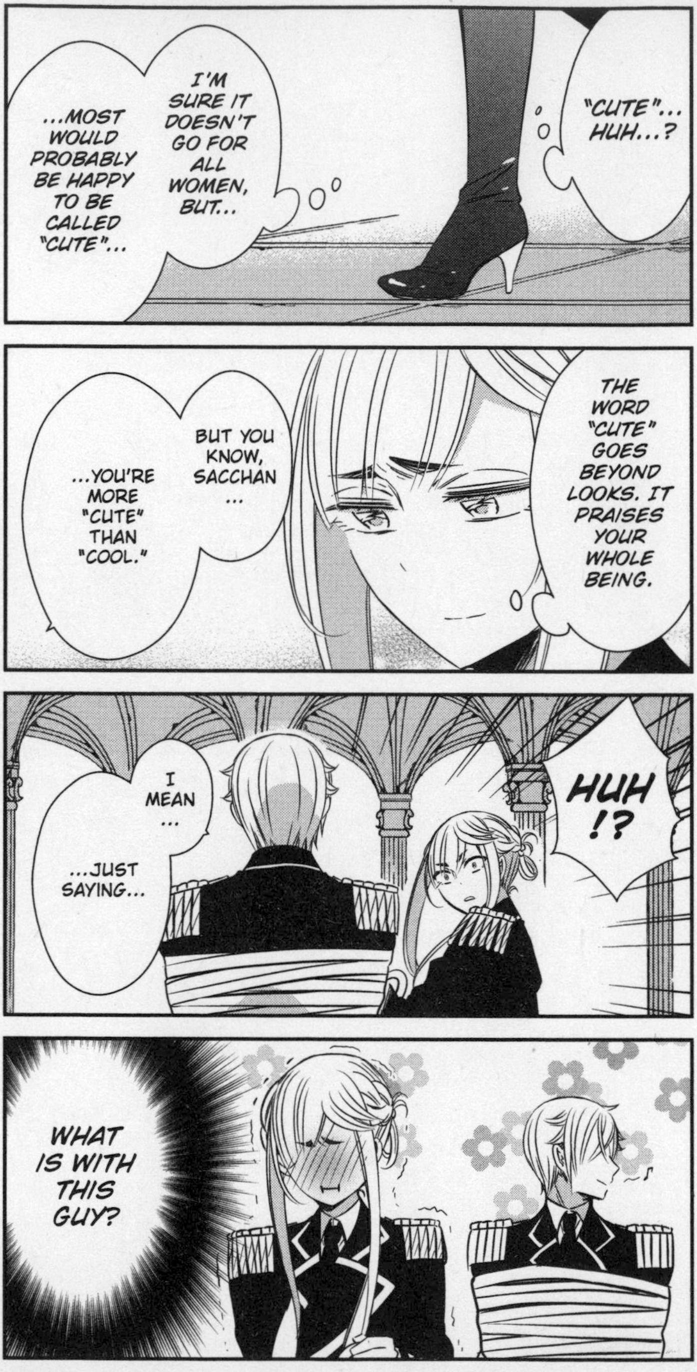
"CUTE"... HUH...?
I'M SURE IT DOESN'T GO FOR ALL WOMEN, BUT...
...MOST WOULD PROBABLY BE HAPPY TO BE CALLED "CUTE"...
THE WORD "CUTE" GOES BEYOND LOOKS. IT PRAISES YOUR WHOLE BEING.
BUT YOU KNOW, SACCHAN...
...YOU'RE MORE "CUTE" THAN "COOL."
HUH!?
I MEAN...
...JUST SAYING...
WHAT IS WITH THIS GUY?

SO...CUTE...

CUTE (I WANT TO BE CALLED THAT TOO)

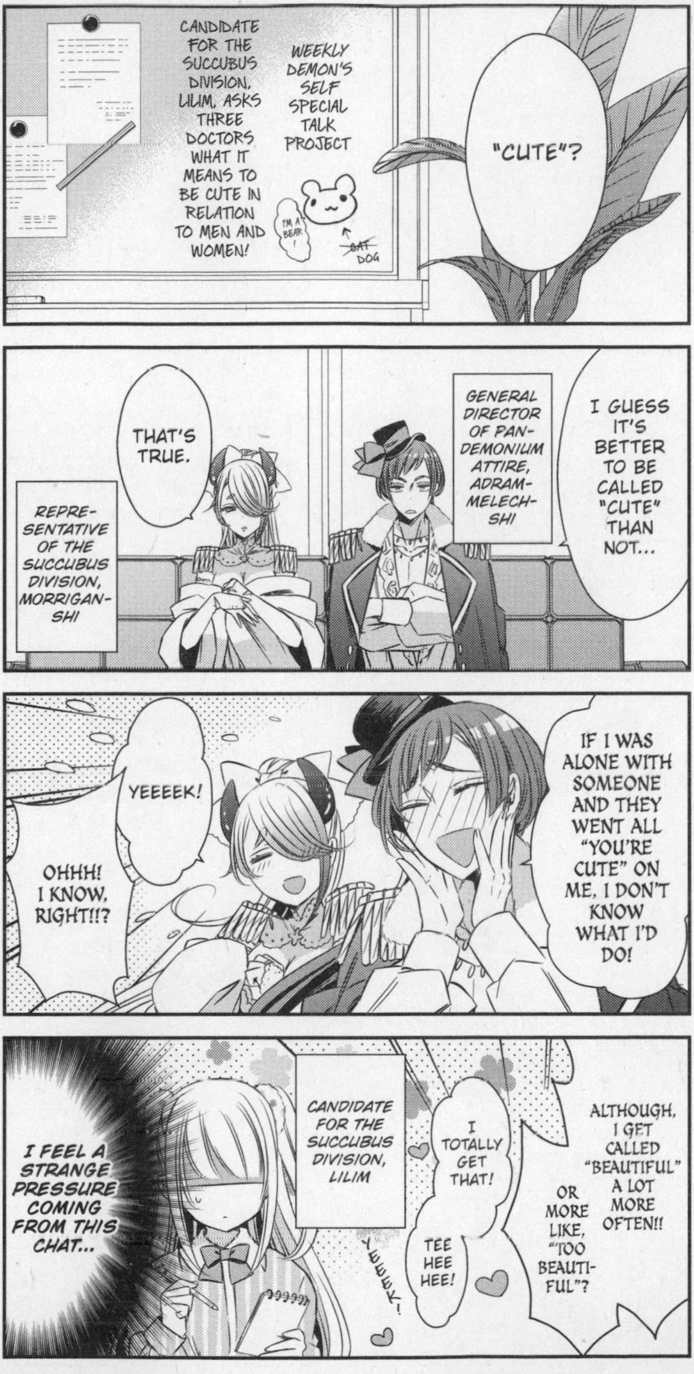
"CUTE"?
WEEKLY DEMON'S SELF SPECIAL TALK PROJECT
CANDIDATE FOR THE SUCCUBUS DIVISION, LILIM, ASKS THREE DOCTORS WHAT IT MEANS TO BE CUTE IN RELATION TO MEN AND WOMEN!
CAT DOG
I'M A BEAR!
I GUESS IT'S BETTER TO BE CALLED "CUTE" THAN NOT...
GENERAL DIRECTOR OF PAN-DEMONIUM ATTIRE, ADRAM-MELECH-SHI
THAT'S TRUE.
REPRE-SENTATIVE OF THE SUCCUBUS DIVISION, MORRIGAN-SHI
IF I WAS ALONE WITH SOMEONE AND THEY WENT ALL "YOU'RE CUTE" ON ME, I DON'T KNOW WHAT I'D DO!
YEEEEK!
OHHH! I KNOW, RIGHT!!?
ALTHOUGH, I GET CALLED "BEAUTIFUL" A LOT MORE OFTEN!!
OR MORE LIKE, "TOO BEAUTI-FUL"?
I TOTALLY GET THAT!
TEE HEE HEE!
YEEEEK!
CANDIDATE FOR THE SUCCUBUS DIVISION, LILIM
I FEEL A STRANGE PRESSURE COMING FROM THIS CHAT...

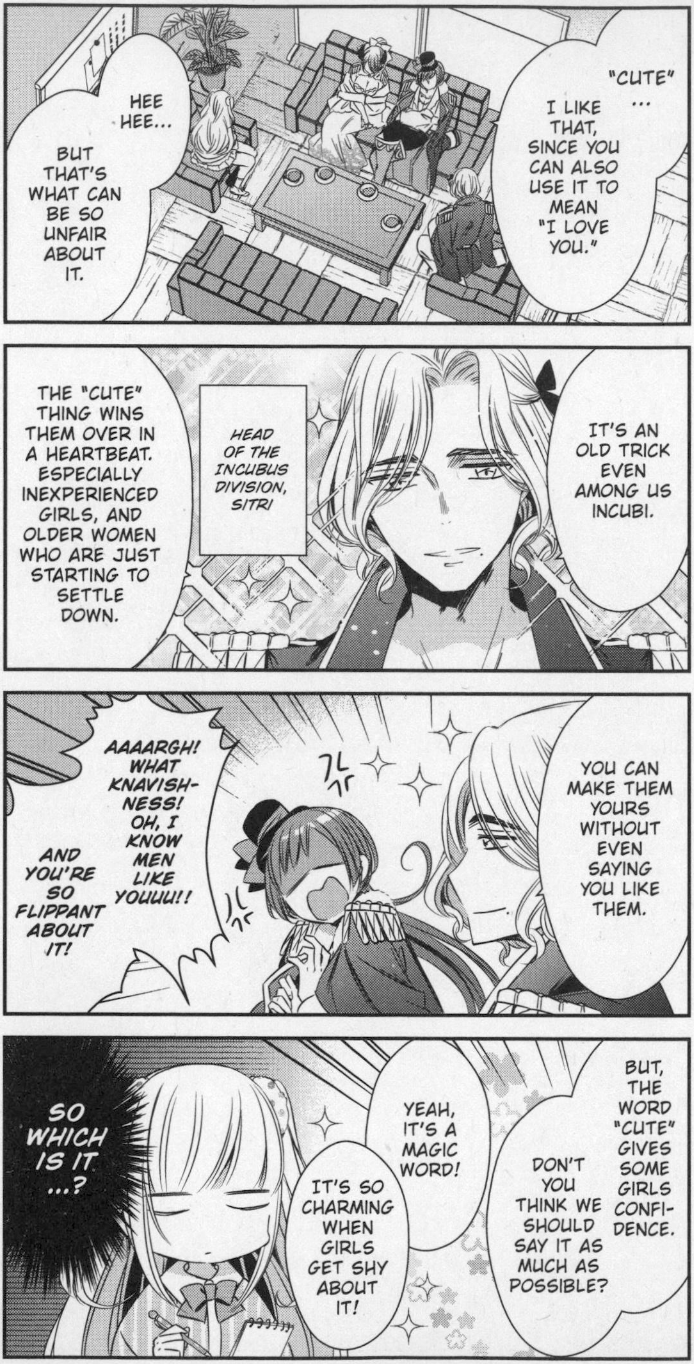
"CUTE"...
I LIKE THAT, SINCE YOU CAN ALSO USE IT TO MEAN "I LOVE YOU."
HEE HEE...
BUT THAT'S WHAT CAN BE SO UNFAIR ABOUT IT.
IT'S AN OLD TRICK EVEN AMONG US INCUBI.
HEAD OF THE INCUBUS DIVISION, SITRI
THE "CUTE" THING WINS THEM OVER IN A HEARTBEAT. ESPECIALLY INEXPERIENCED GIRLS, AND OLDER WOMEN WHO ARE JUST STARTING TO SETTLE DOWN.
YOU CAN MAKE THEM YOURS WITHOUT EVEN SAYING YOU LIKE THEM.
AAAARGH! WHAT KNAVISHNESS! OH, I KNOW MEN LIKE YOUUU!!
AND YOU'RE SO FLIPPANT ABOUT IT!
BUT, THE WORD "CUTE" GIVES SOME GIRLS CONFIDENCE.
DON'T YOU THINK WE SHOULD SAY IT AS MUCH AS POSSIBLE?
YEAH, IT'S A MAGIC WORD!
IT'S SO CHARMING WHEN GIRLS GET SHY ABOUT IT!
SO WHICH IS IT ...?

CUTE (THE MAGIC WORD)

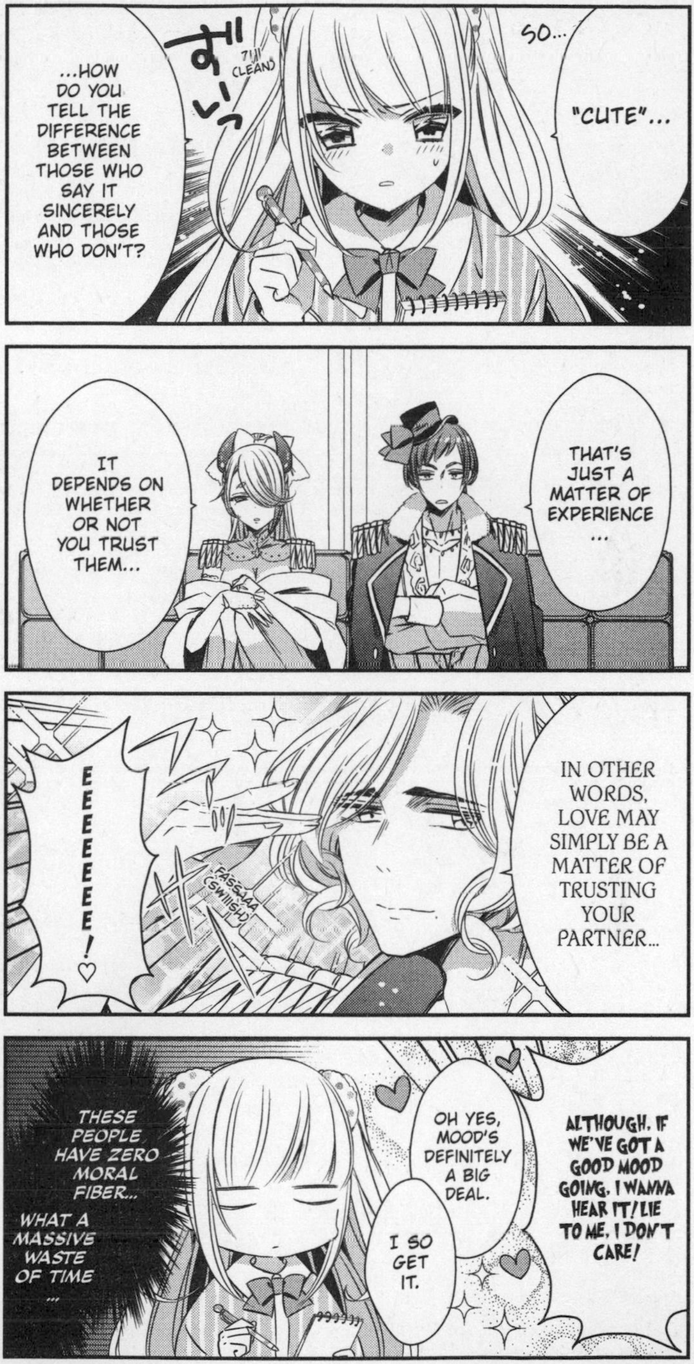
SO... "CUTE"...
...HOW DO YOU TELL THE DIFFERENCE BETWEEN THOSE WHO SAY IT SINCERELY AND THOSE WHO DON'T?
ずいっ
ZUII (LEAN)
THAT'S JUST A MATTER OF EXPERIENCE ...
IT DEPENDS ON WHETHER OR NOT YOU TRUST THEM...
IN OTHER WORDS, LOVE MAY SIMPLY BE A MATTER OF TRUSTING YOUR PARTNER...
FASSAA (SWIIISH)
EEEEEEEE!♡
ALTHOUGH, IF WE'VE GOT A GOOD MOOD GOING, I WANNA HEAR IT! LIE TO ME, I DON'T CARE!
OH YES, MOOD'S DEFINITELY A BIG DEAL.
I SO GET IT.
THESE PEOPLE HAVE ZERO MORAL FIBER...
WHAT A MASSIVE WASTE OF TIME ...

CUTE (IT'S ABOUT SENSING THE MOOD) (WHATEVER)

BLACK-MARKET (NOT) DEALINGS IN CUTE STUFF

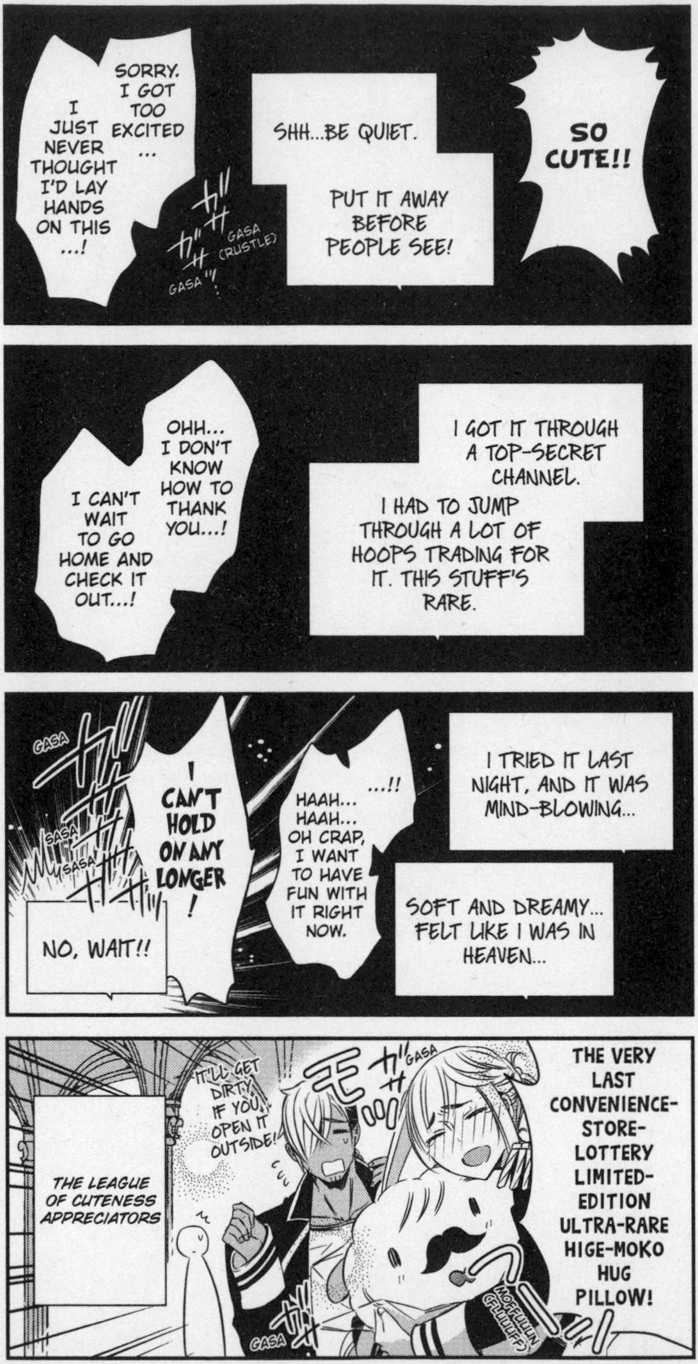
SO CUTE!!
SHH...BE QUIET.
PUT IT AWAY BEFORE PEOPLE SEE!
SORRY. I GOT TOO EXCITED...
I JUST NEVER THOUGHT I'D LAY HANDS ON THIS...!
GASA (RUSTLE)
GASA
I GOT IT THROUGH A TOP-SECRET CHANNEL.
I HAD TO JUMP THROUGH A LOT OF HOOPS TRADING FOR IT. THIS STUFF'S RARE.
OHH... I DON'T KNOW HOW TO THANK YOU...!
I CAN'T WAIT TO GO HOME AND CHECK IT OUT...!
I TRIED IT LAST NIGHT, AND IT WAS MIND-BLOWING...
SOFT AND DREAMY... FELT LIKE I WAS IN HEAVEN...
...!!
HAAH... HAAH... OH CRAP, I WANT TO HAVE FUN WITH IT RIGHT NOW.
I CAN'T HOLD ON ANY LONGER!
GASA
SASA
SASA
NO, WAIT!!
THE VERY LAST CONVENIENCE-STORE-LOTTERY LIMITED-EDITION ULTRA-RARE HIGE-MOKO HUG PILLOW!
GASA
IT'LL GET DIRTY IF YOU OPEN IT OUTSIDE!
MOFFULUN (FLUUUFF)
GASA
THE LEAGUE OF CUTENESS APPRECIATORS

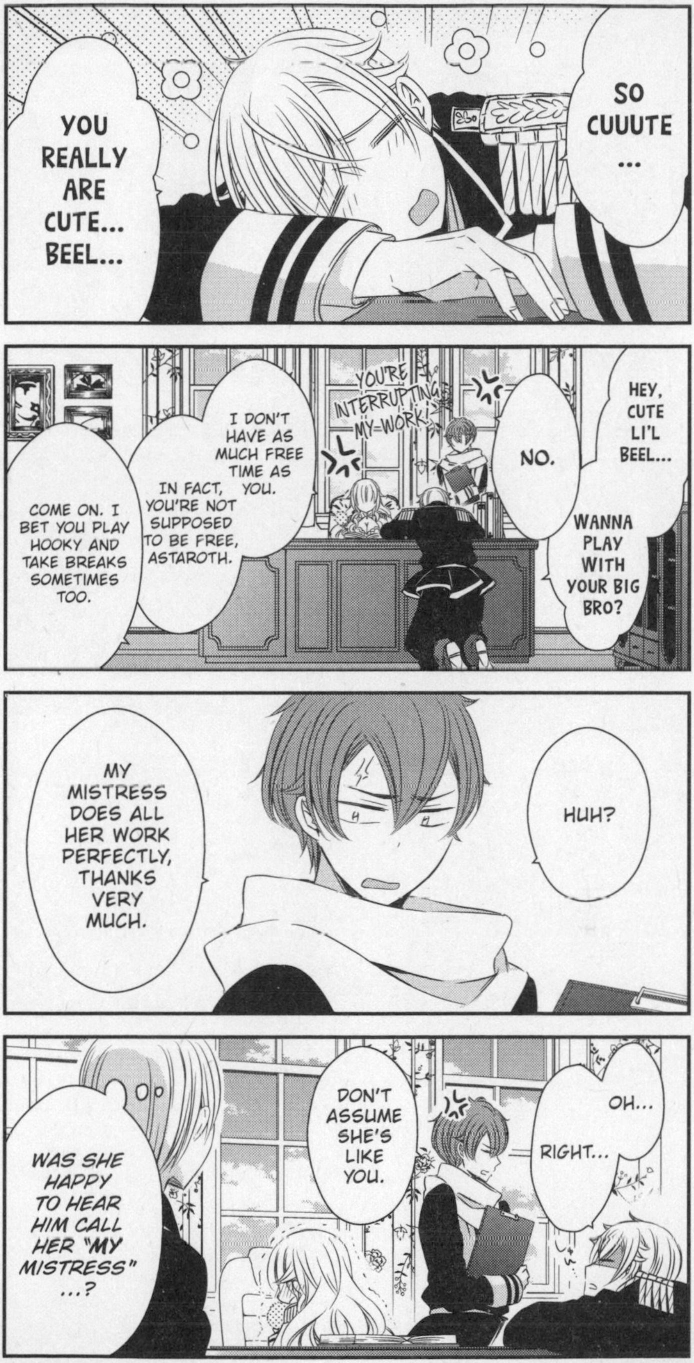
SO CUUUTE ...
YOU REALLY ARE CUTE... BEEL...
HEY, CUTE LI'L BEEL...
WANNA PLAY WITH YOUR BIG BRO?
NO.
YOU'RE INTERRUPTING MY WORK!
I DON'T HAVE AS MUCH FREE TIME AS YOU.
IN FACT, YOU'RE NOT SUPPOSED TO BE FREE, ASTAROTH.
COME ON. I BET YOU PLAY HOOKY AND TAKE BREAKS SOMETIMES TOO.
HUH?
MY MISTRESS DOES ALL HER WORK PERFECTLY, THANKS VERY MUCH.
OH...
RIGHT...
DON'T ASSUME SHE'S LIKE YOU.
WAS SHE HAPPY TO HEAR HIM CALL HER "MY MISTRESS" ...?

CUTE, CUTE BEEL

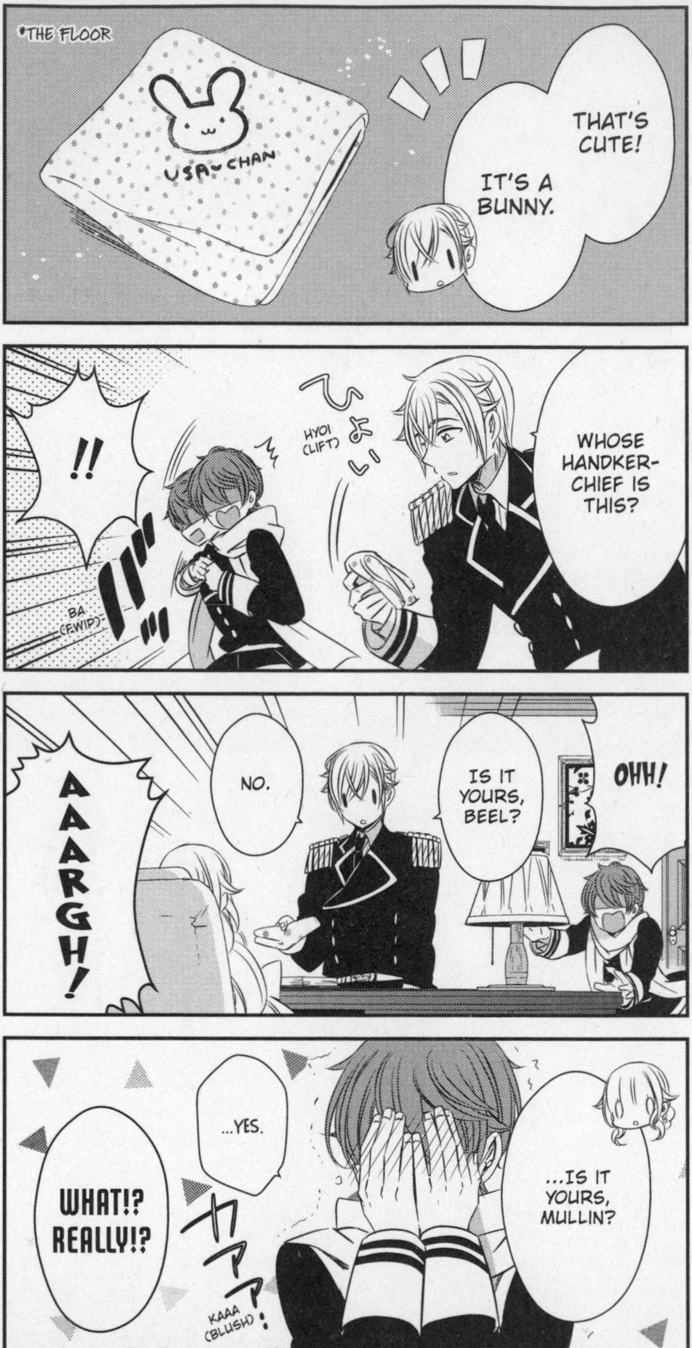
*THE FLOOR
THAT'S CUTE! IT'S A BUNNY.
USA~CHAN
WHOSE HANDKER-CHIEF IS THIS?
ひょい
HYOI (LIFT)
!!
BA (F-WIP)
OHH!
IS IT YOURS, BEEL?
NO.
AAAARGH!
...IS IT YOURS, MULLIN?
...YES.
カァァ
KAAA (BLUSH)
WHAT!? REALLY!?

CUTE LITTLE BUNNY-SAN

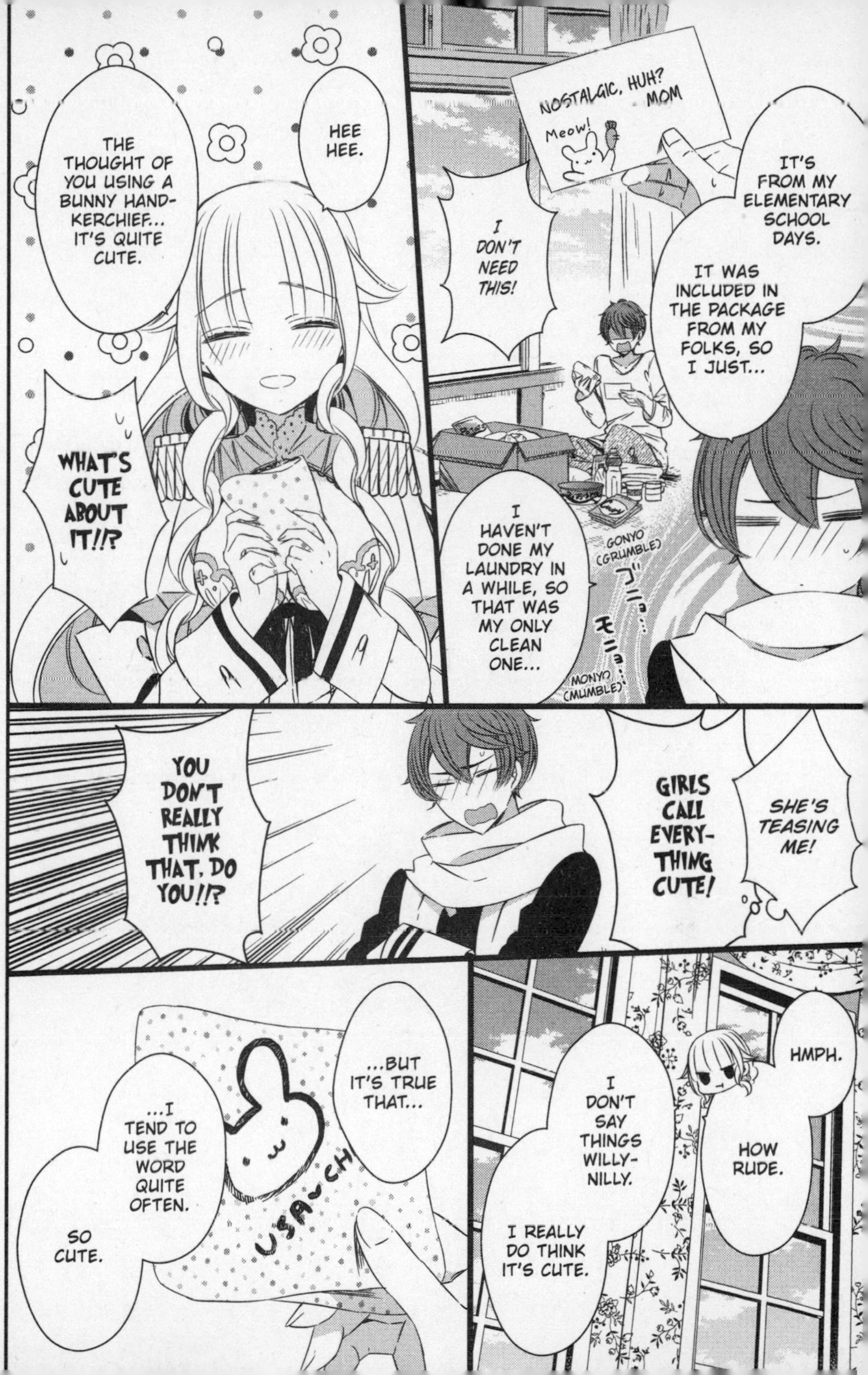
NOSTALGIC, HUH? MOM
Meow!
IT'S FROM MY ELEMENTARY SCHOOL DAYS.
IT WAS INCLUDED IN THE PACKAGE FROM MY FOLKS, SO I JUST...
I DON'T NEED THIS!
I HAVEN'T DONE MY LAUNDRY IN A WHILE, SO THAT WAS MY ONLY CLEAN ONE...
GONYO (GRUMBLE)
ゴニョ...
モニョ...
MONYO (MUMBLE)
HEE HEE.
THE THOUGHT OF YOU USING A BUNNY HAND-KERCHIEF... IT'S QUITE CUTE.
WHAT'S CUTE ABOUT IT!!?
SHE'S TEASING ME!
GIRLS CALL EVERY-THING CUTE!
YOU DON'T REALLY THINK THAT, DO YOU!!?
HMPH.
HOW RUDE.
I DON'T SAY THINGS WILLY-NILLY.
I REALLY DO THINK IT'S CUTE.
...BUT IT'S TRUE THAT...
...I TEND TO USE THE WORD QUITE OFTEN.
USA♥CH
SO CUTE.

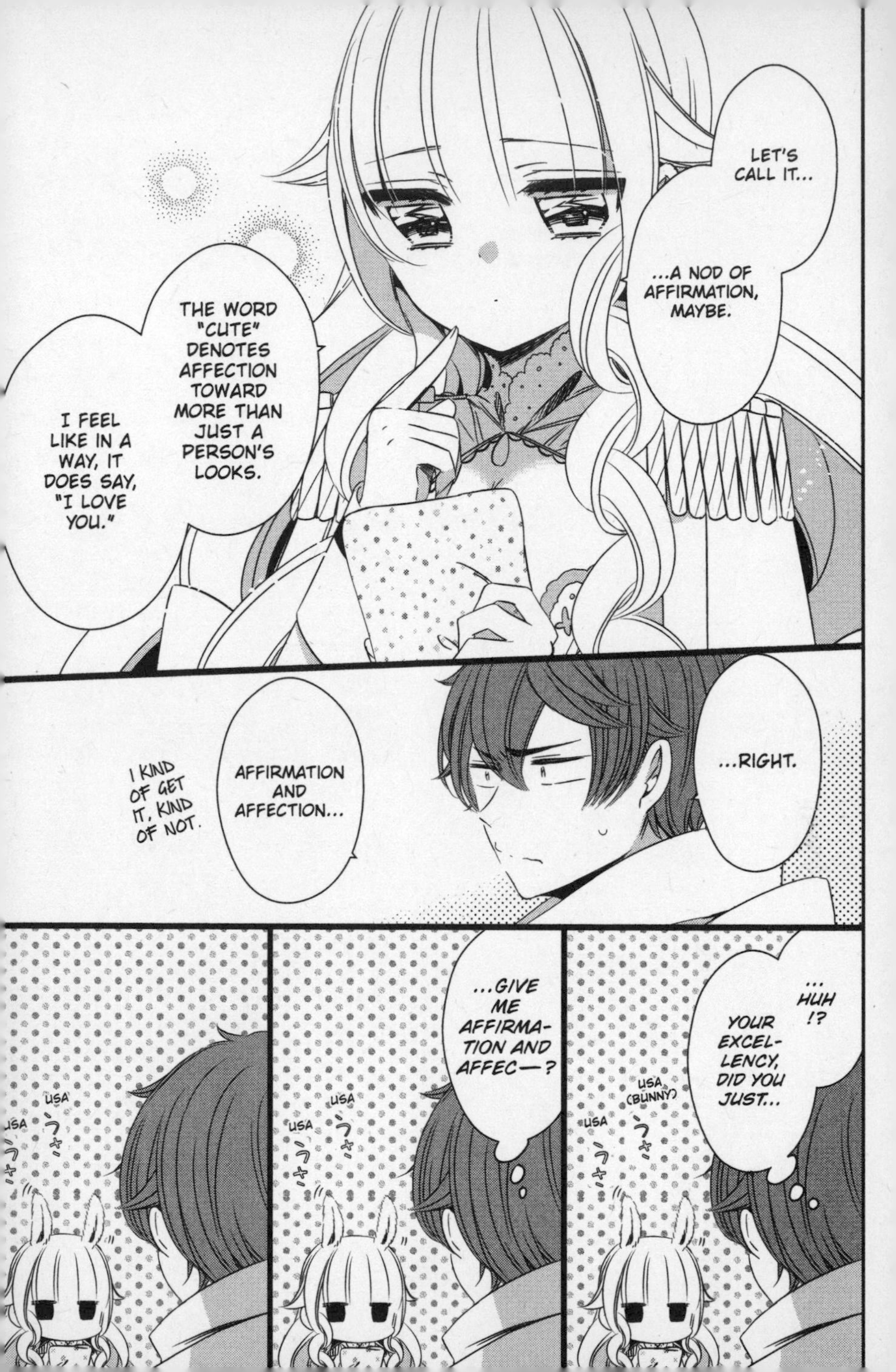
LET'S CALL IT...
...A NOD OF AFFIRMATION, MAYBE.
THE WORD "CUTE" DENOTES AFFECTION TOWARD MORE THAN JUST A PERSON'S LOOKS.
I FEEL LIKE IN A WAY, IT DOES SAY, "I LOVE YOU."
...RIGHT.
AFFIRMATION AND AFFECTION...
I KIND OF GET IT, KIND OF NOT.
...HUH!?
YOUR EXCELLENCY, DID YOU JUST...
USA (BUNNY)
USA
...GIVE ME AFFIRMATION AND AFFEC—?
USA
USA
USA
USA

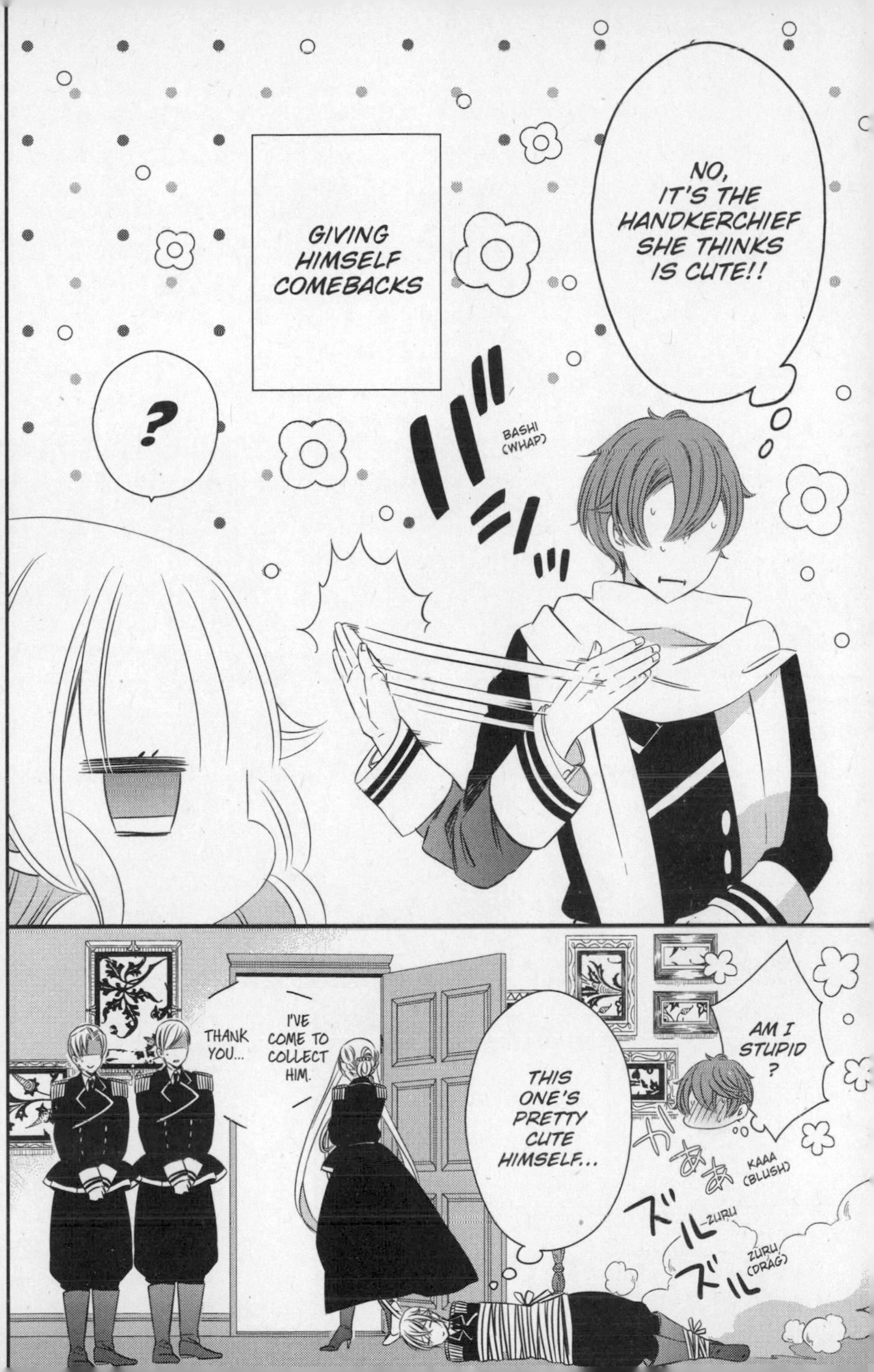
NO, IT'S THE HANDKERCHIEF SHE THINKS IS CUTE!!
GIVING HIMSELF COMEBACKS
BASHI (WHAP)
?
AM I STUPID?
KAAA (BLUSH)
ZURU
ZURU (DRAG)
THIS ONE'S PRETTY CUTE HIMSELF...
I'VE COME TO COLLECT HIM.
THANK YOU...

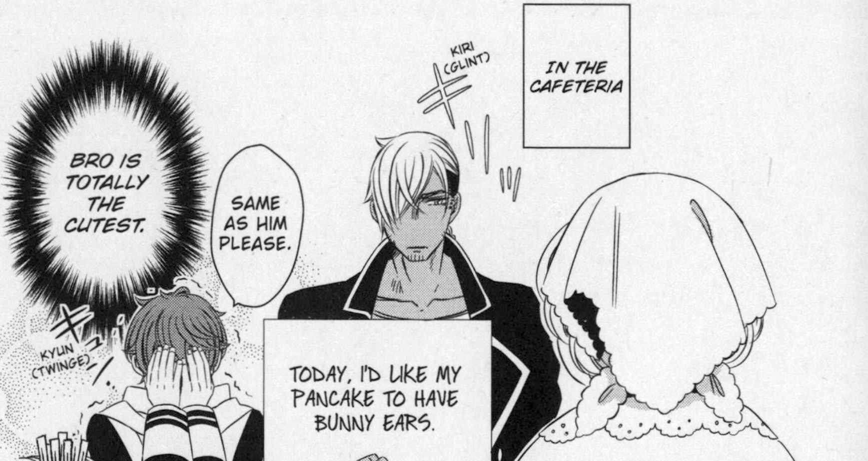
IN THE CAFETERIA
KIRI (GLINT)
TODAY, I'D LIKE MY PANCAKE TO HAVE BUNNY EARS.
SAME AS HIM PLEASE.
BRO IS TOTALLY THE CUTEST.
KYUN (TWINGE)

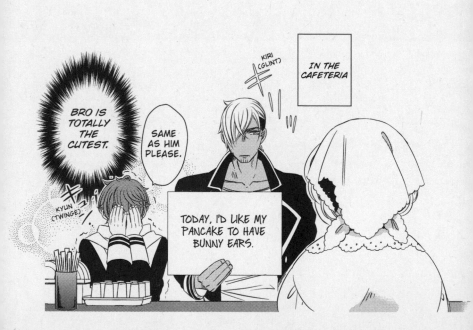

As Miss Beelzebub Likes

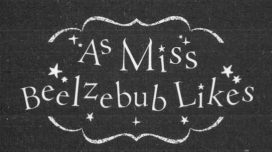

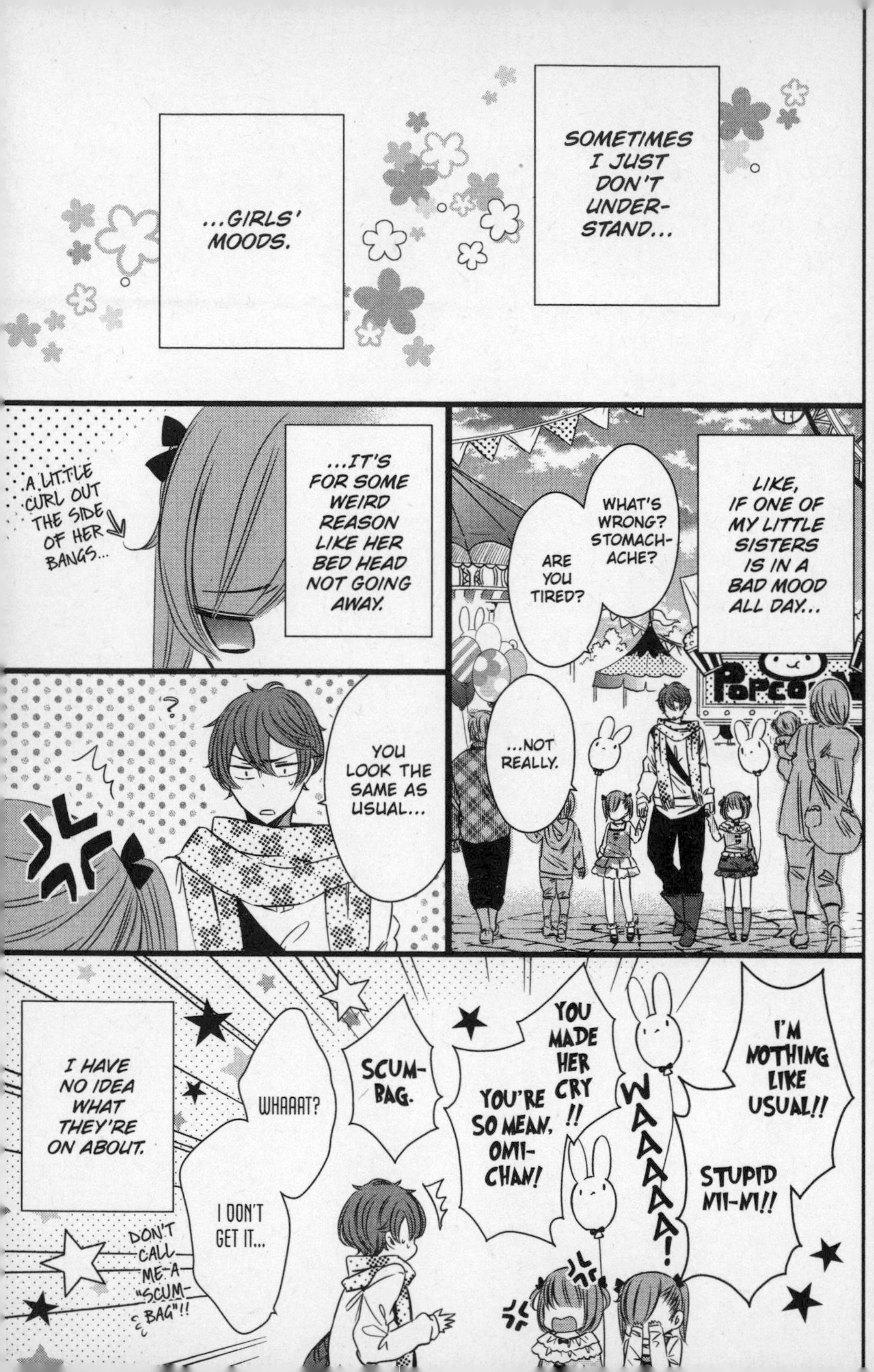
SOMETIMES I JUST DON'T UNDERSTAND...
...GIRLS' MOODS.
LIKE, IF ONE OF MY LITTLE SISTERS IS IN A BAD MOOD ALL DAY...
WHAT'S WRONG? STOMACHACHE?
ARE YOU TIRED?
...NOT REALLY.
...IT'S FOR SOME WEIRD REASON LIKE HER BED HEAD NOT GOING AWAY.
A LITTLE CURL OUT THE SIDE OF HER BANGS...
YOU LOOK THE SAME AS USUAL...
I'M NOTHING LIKE USUAL!!
STUPID NII-NII!!
WAAAAA!
YOU MADE HER CRY!!
YOU'RE SO MEAN, OMI-CHAN!
SCUMBAG.
WHAAAT?
I DON'T GET IT...
DON'T CALL ME A "SCUMBAG"!!
I HAVE NO IDEA WHAT THEY'RE ON ABOUT.

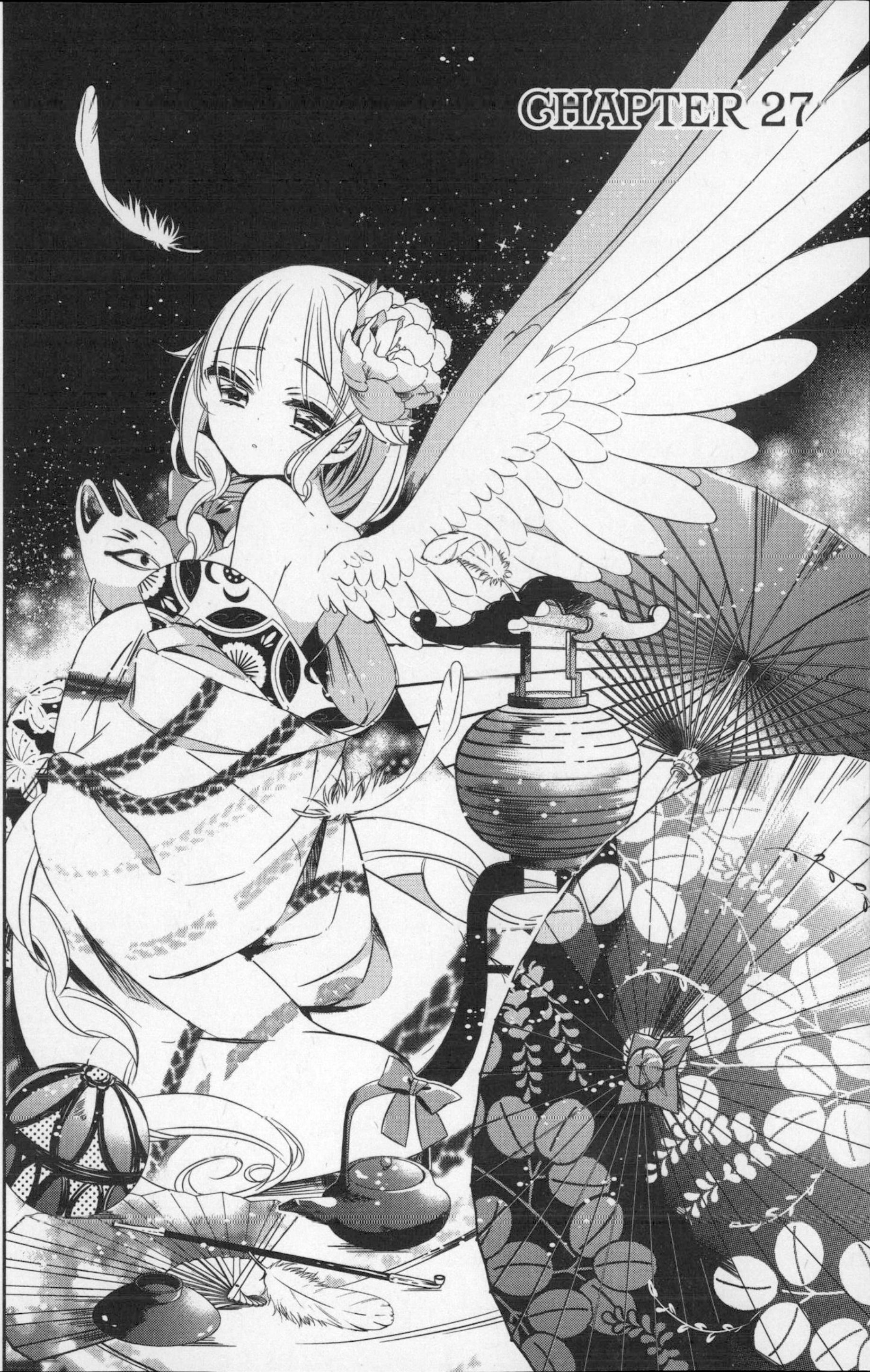
CHAPTER 27

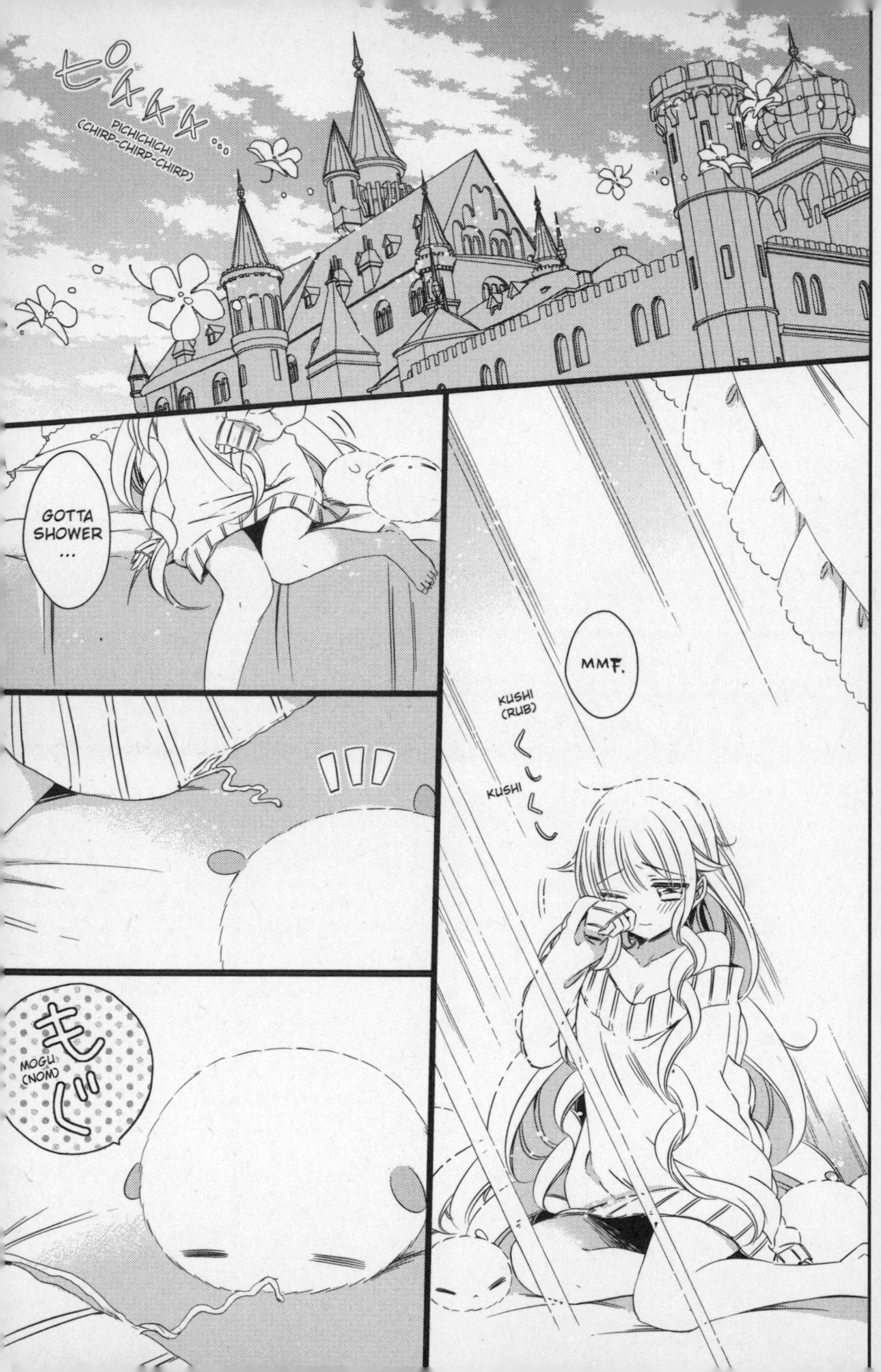
ピチチチ…
PICHICHICHI (CHIRP-CHIRP-CHIRP)
MMF.
KUSHI (RUB)
くしくし
KUSHI
GOTTA SHOWER …
もぐ
MOGU (NOM)

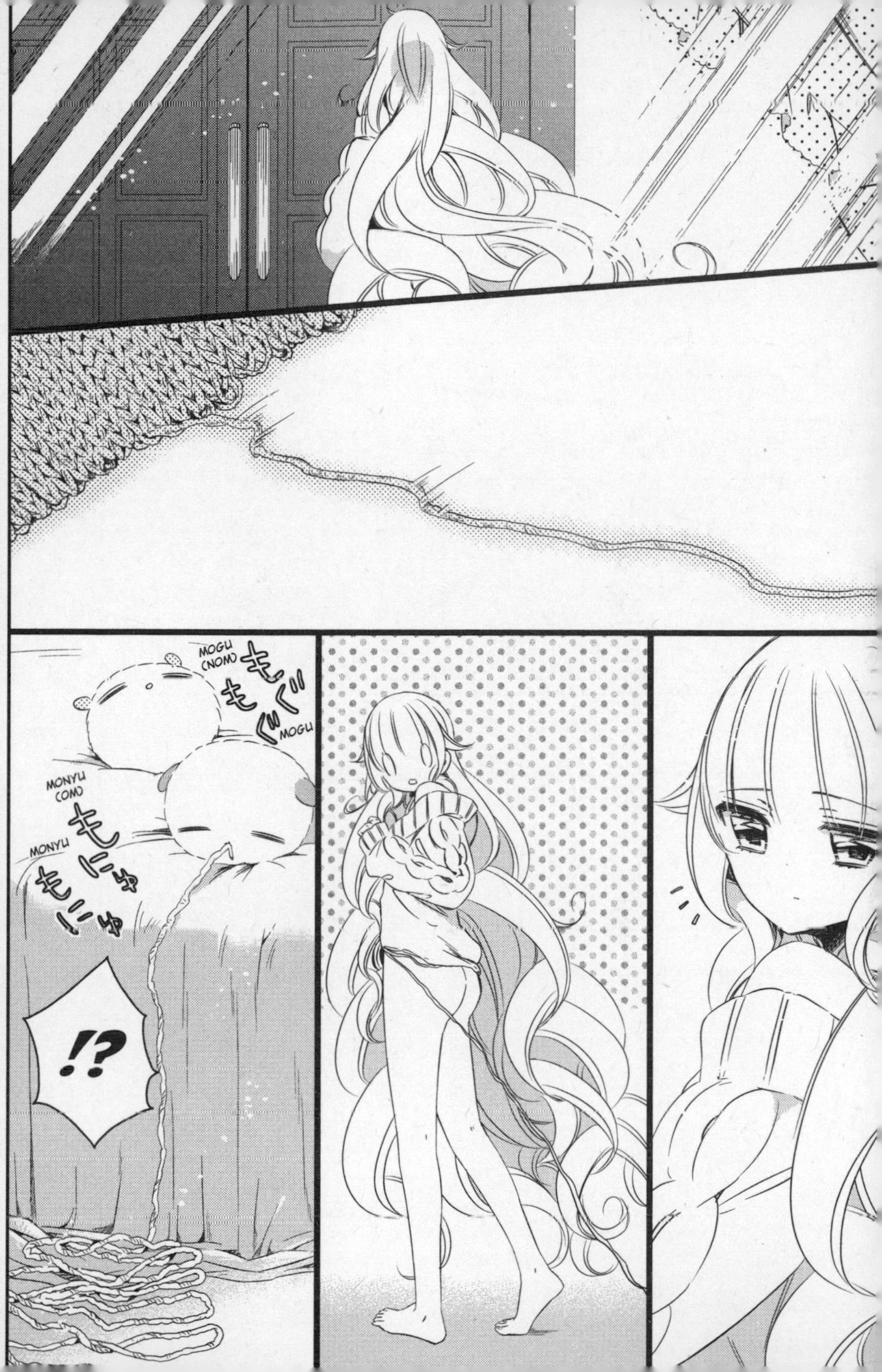
...
MOGU (NOM)
もぐもぐ
MOGU
MONYU (OM)
もにゅ
MONYU
もにゅ
!?

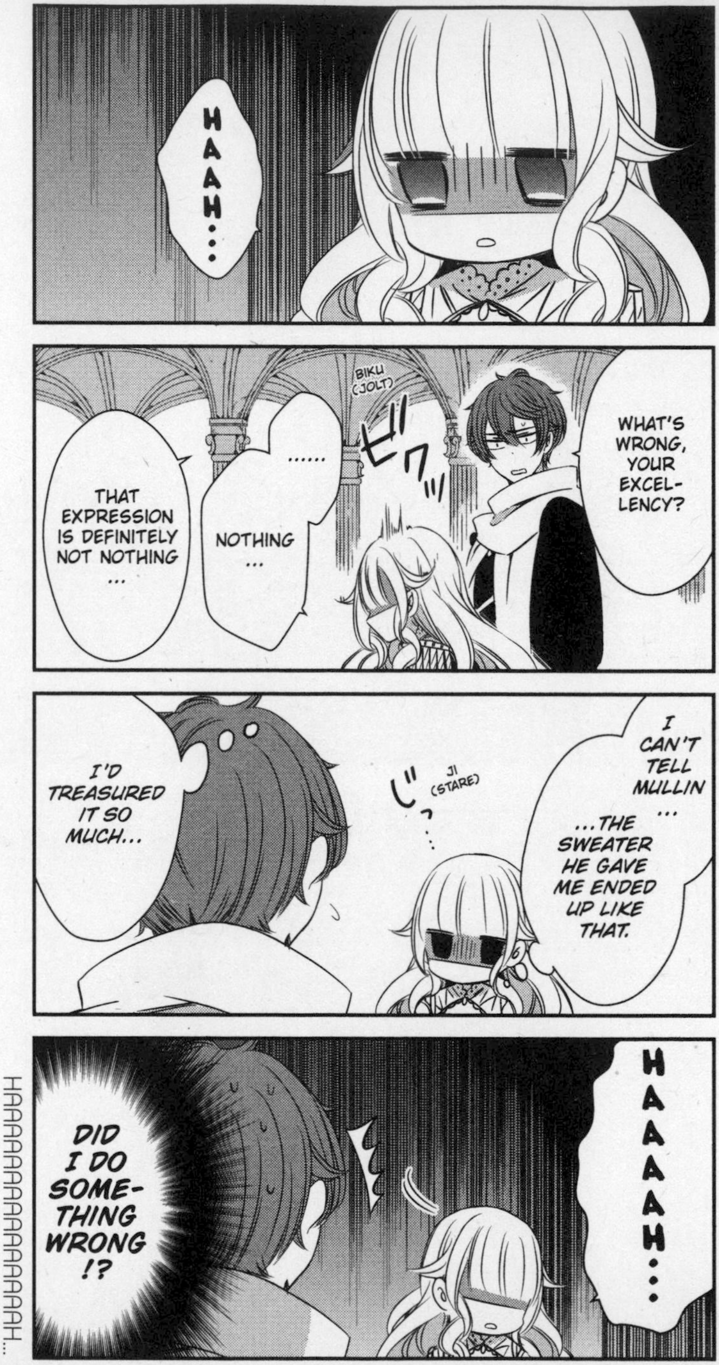
HAAH...
WHAT'S WRONG, YOUR EXCELLENCY?
BIKU (JOLT)
......
NOTHING ...
THAT EXPRESSION IS DEFINITELY NOT NOTHING ...
I CAN'T TELL MULLIN ...
...THE SWEATER HE GAVE ME ENDED UP LIKE THAT.
JI (STARE)
I'D TREASURED IT SO MUCH...
HAAAAH...
DID I DO SOMETHING WRONG!?
HAAAAAAAAAAAAAAAAAAAH...

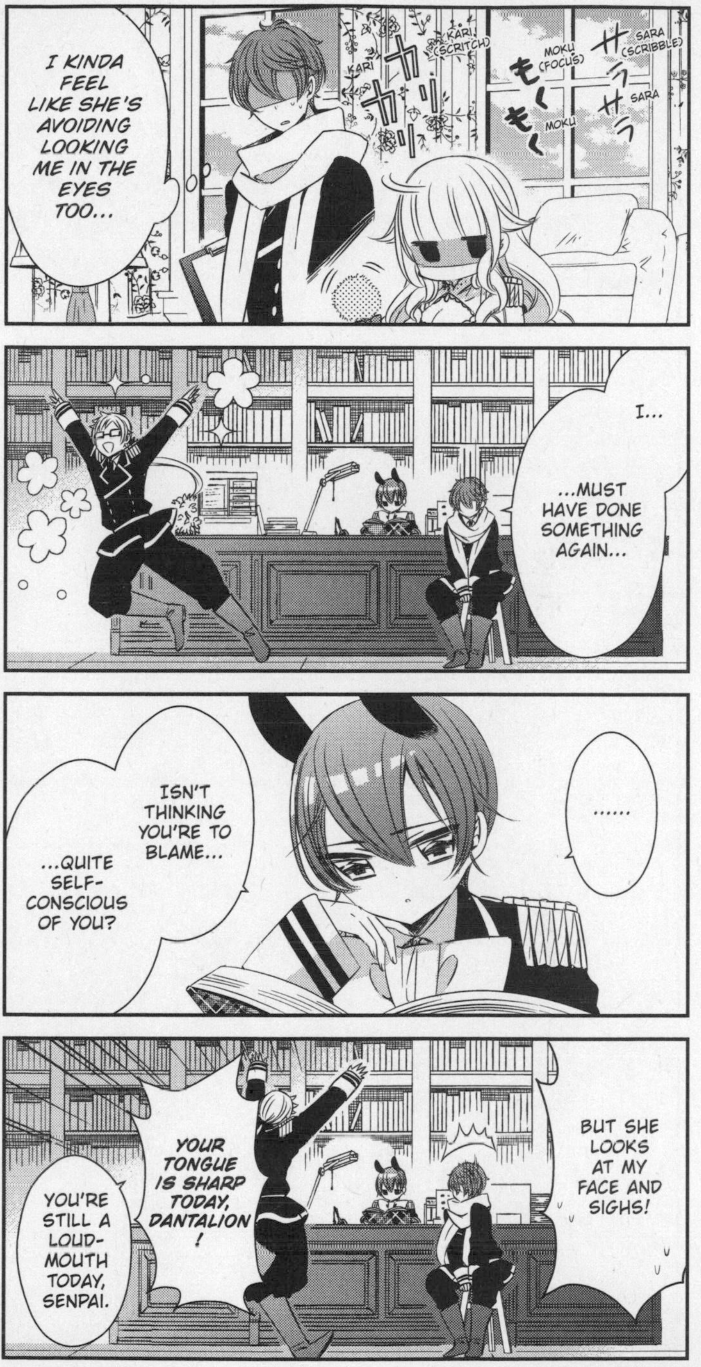
SARA (SCRIBBLE)
SARA
MOKU (FOCUS)
MOKU
KARI (SCRITCH)
KARI
I KINDA FEEL LIKE SHE'S AVOIDING LOOKING ME IN THE EYES TOO...
I...
...MUST HAVE DONE SOMETHING AGAIN...
......
ISN'T THINKING YOU'RE TO BLAME...
...QUITE SELF-CONSCIOUS OF YOU?
BUT SHE LOOKS AT MY FACE AND SIGHS!
YOUR TONGUE IS SHARP TODAY, DANTALION!
YOU'RE STILL A LOUDMOUTH TODAY, SENPAI.

SLIGHTLY PISSED THE LATEST EDITION DIDN'T ARRIVE ON ITS RELEASE DATE

IT'S JUST YARN

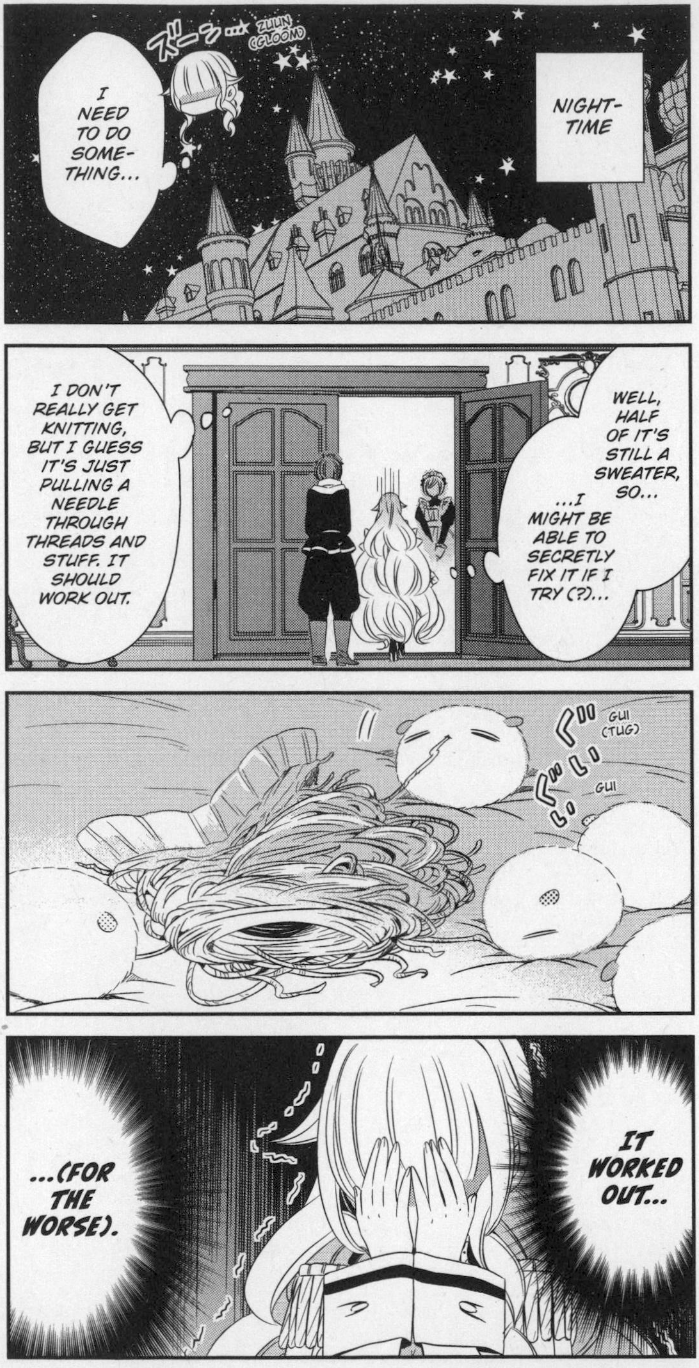
NIGHT-TIME
ズーン… ZUUN (GLOOM)
I NEED TO DO SOME-THING…
WELL, HALF OF IT'S STILL A SWEATER, SO…
…I MIGHT BE ABLE TO SECRETLY FIX IT IF I TRY (?)…
I DON'T REALLY GET KNITTING, BUT I GUESS IT'S JUST PULLING A NEEDLE THROUGH THREADS AND STUFF. IT SHOULD WORK OUT.
GUI (TUG)
GUI
IT WORKED OUT…
…(FOR THE WORSE).

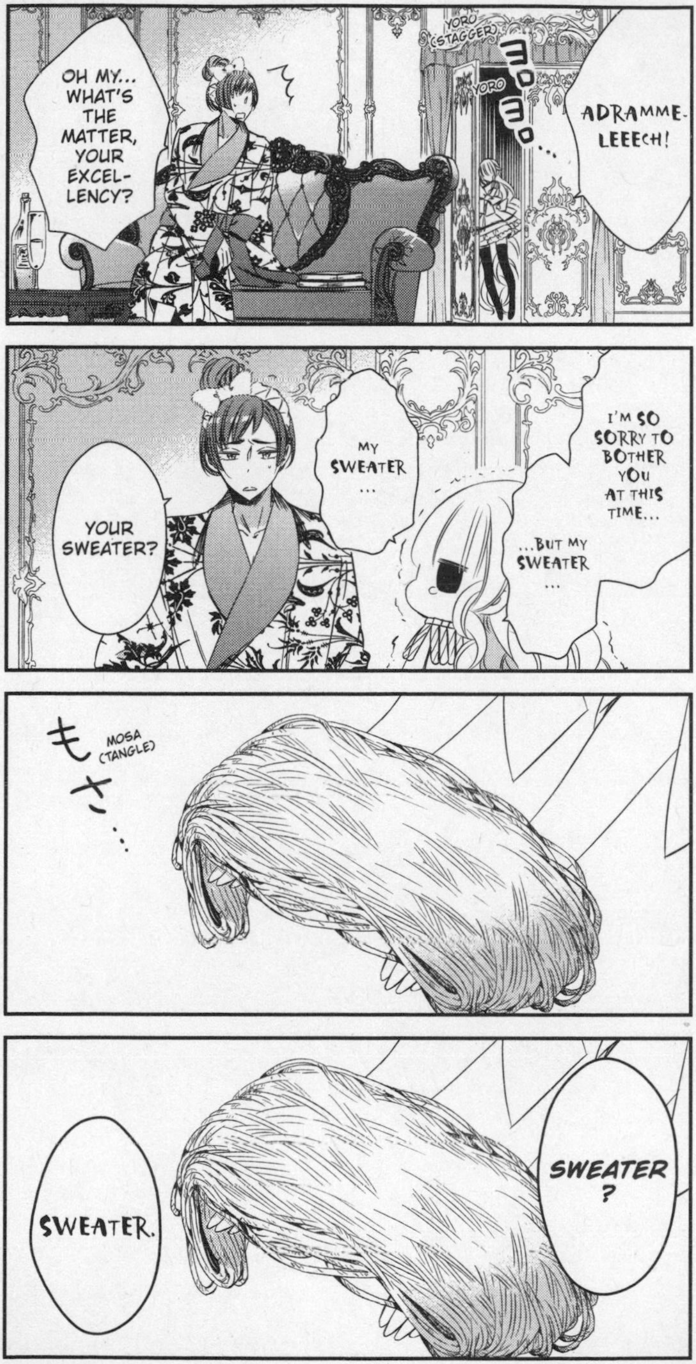
ADRAMME-LEEECH!
YORO (STAGGER)
YORO
OH MY... WHAT'S THE MATTER, YOUR EXCELLENCY?
I'M SO SORRY TO BOTHER YOU AT THIS TIME...
...BUT MY SWEATER...
MY SWEATER...
YOUR SWEATER?
MOSA (TANGLE)
SWEATER?
SWEATER.

FORMERLY

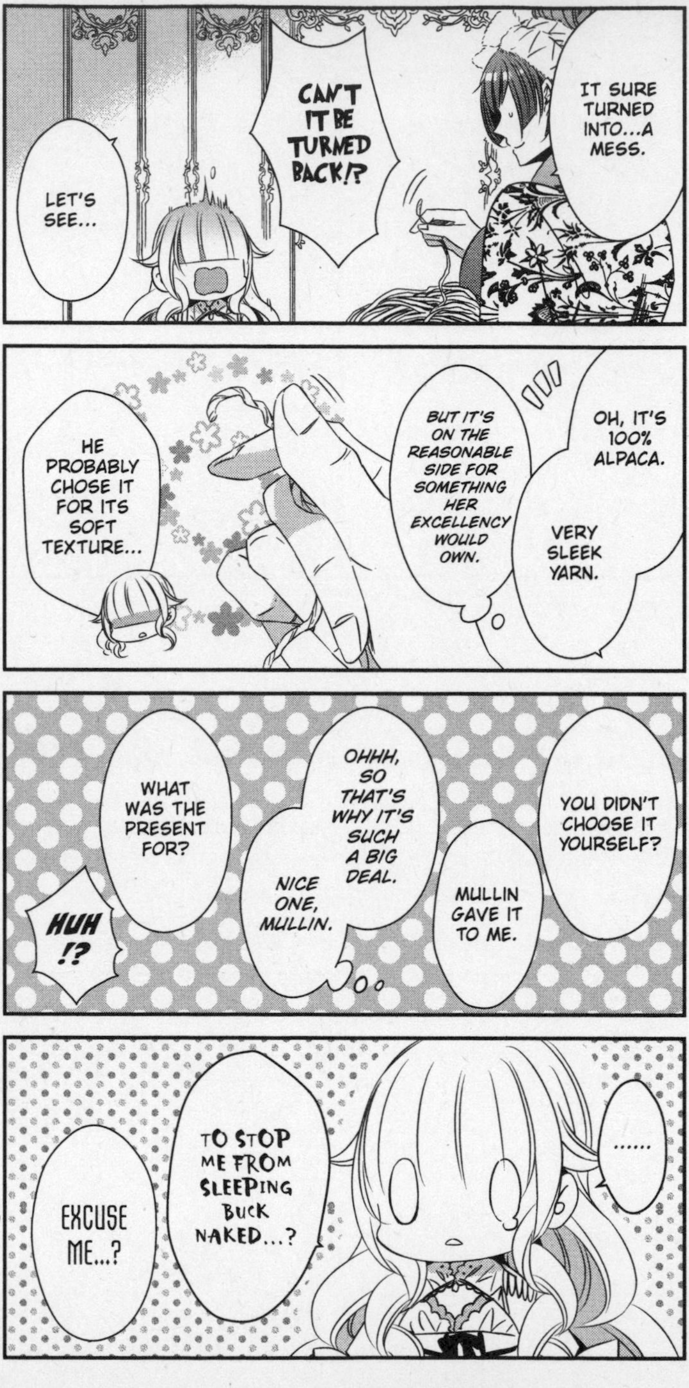
IT SURE TURNED INTO...A MESS.
CAN'T IT BE TURNED BACK!?
LET'S SEE...
OH, IT'S 100% ALPACA.
VERY SLEEK YARN.
BUT IT'S ON THE REASONABLE SIDE FOR SOMETHING HER EXCELLENCY WOULD OWN.
HE PROBABLY CHOSE IT FOR ITS SOFT TEXTURE...
YOU DIDN'T CHOOSE IT YOURSELF?
MULLIN GAVE IT TO ME.
OHHH, SO THAT'S WHY IT'S SUCH A BIG DEAL.
NICE ONE, MULLIN.
WHAT WAS THE PRESENT FOR?
HUH!?
......
TO STOP ME FROM SLEEPING BUCK NAKED...?
EXCUSE ME...?

BUCK

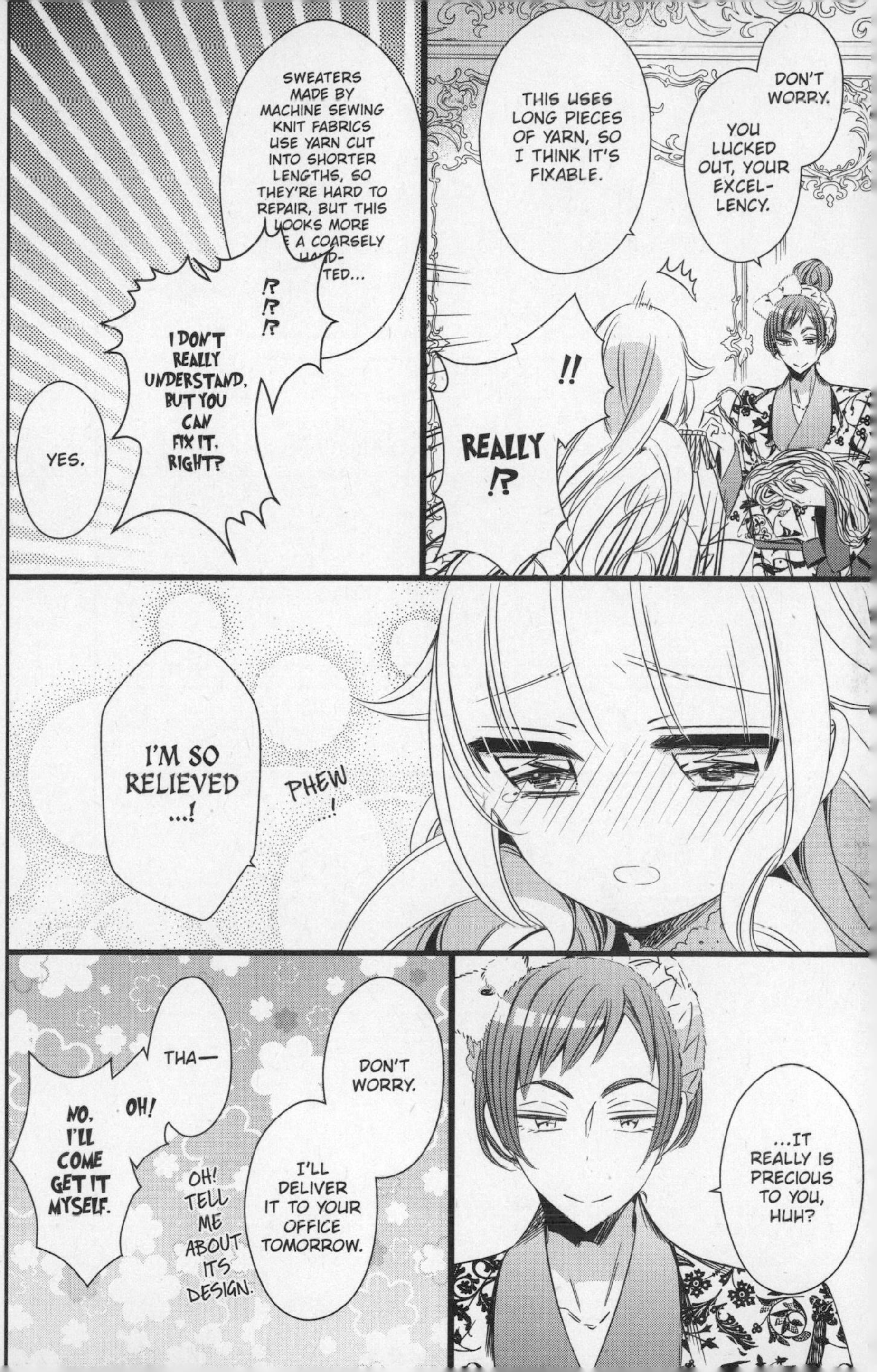
DON'T WORRY.
YOU LUCKED OUT, YOUR EXCEL-LENCY.
THIS USES LONG PIECES OF YARN, SO I THINK IT'S FIXABLE.
!!
REALLY!?
SWEATERS MADE BY MACHINE SEWING KNIT FABRICS USE YARN CUT INTO SHORTER LENGTHS, SO THEY'RE HARD TO REPAIR, BUT THIS LOOKS MORE A COARSELY HAND- TED...
!?!?!?
I DON'T REALLY UNDERSTAND, BUT YOU CAN FIX IT, RIGHT?
YES.
I'M SO RELIEVED ...!
PHEW ...!
...IT REALLY IS PRECIOUS TO YOU, HUH?
DON'T WORRY.
I'LL DELIVER IT TO YOUR OFFICE TOMORROW.
THA—
OH!
NO. I'LL COME GET IT MYSELF.
OH! TELL ME ABOUT ITS DESIGN.

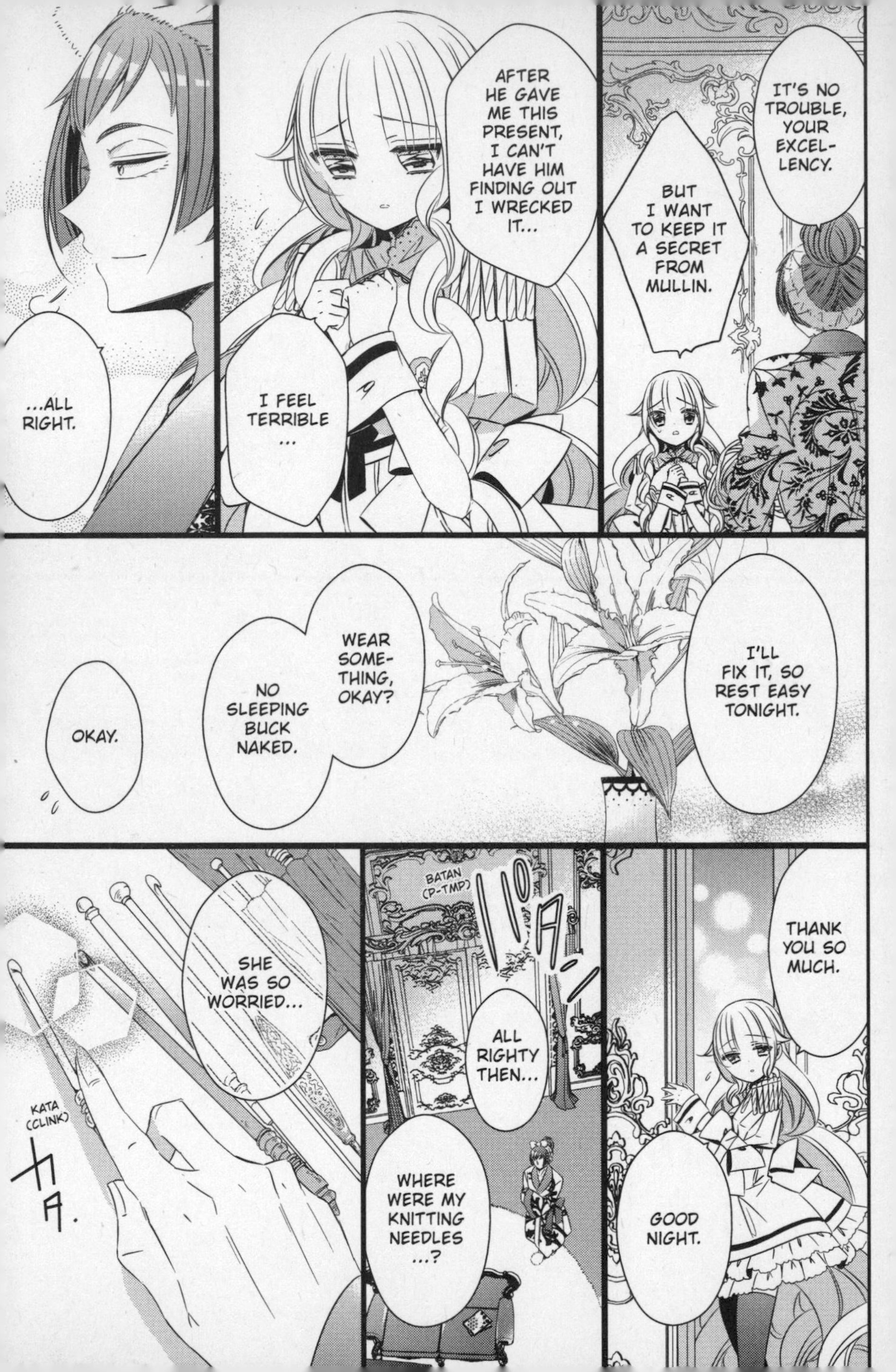
IT'S NO TROUBLE, YOUR EXCEL-LENCY.
BUT I WANT TO KEEP IT A SECRET FROM MULLIN.
AFTER HE GAVE ME THIS PRESENT, I CAN'T HAVE HIM FINDING OUT I WRECKED IT...
I FEEL TERRIBLE ...
...ALL RIGHT.
I'LL FIX IT, SO REST EASY TONIGHT.
WEAR SOME-THING, OKAY?
NO SLEEPING BUCK NAKED.
OKAY.
THANK YOU SO MUCH.
GOOD NIGHT.
BATAN (P-TMP)
ALL RIGHTY THEN...
WHERE WERE MY KNITTING NEEDLES ...?
SHE WAS SO WORRIED...
KATA (CLINK)

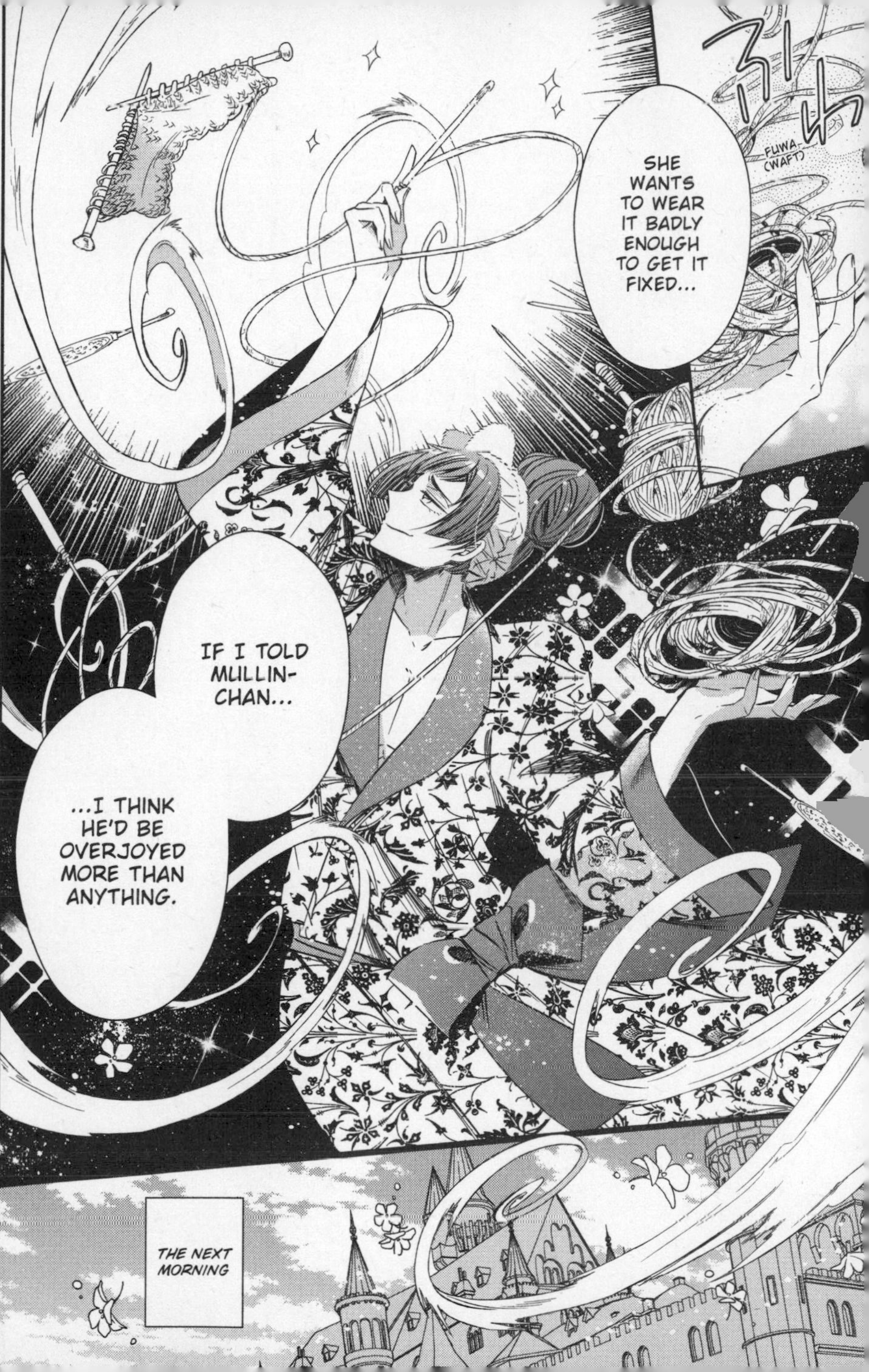
FUWA-
(WAFT)
SHE WANTS TO WEAR IT BADLY ENOUGH TO GET IT FIXED...
IF I TOLD MULLIN-CHAN...
...I THINK HE'D BE OVERJOYED MORE THAN ANYTHING.
THE NEXT MORNING

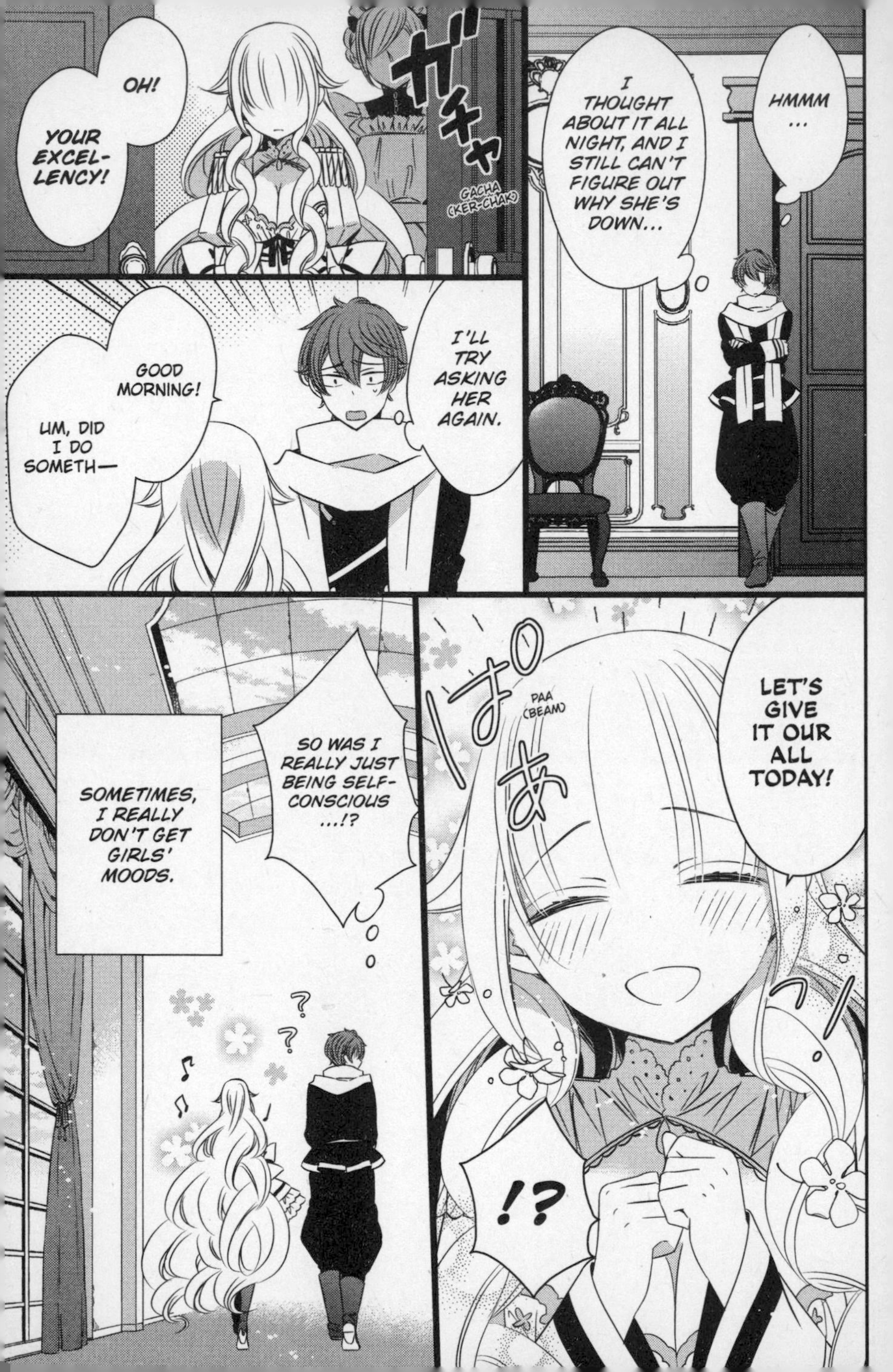
HMMM...
I THOUGHT ABOUT IT ALL NIGHT, AND I STILL CAN'T FIGURE OUT WHY SHE'S DOWN...
ガチャ
GACHA (KER-CHAK)
OH!
YOUR EXCELLENCY!
I'LL TRY ASKING HER AGAIN.
GOOD MORNING!
UM, DID I DO SOMETH—
LET'S GIVE IT OUR ALL TODAY!
ぱぁ
PAA (BEAM)
!?
SO WAS I REALLY JUST BEING SELF-CONSCIOUS...!?
SOMETIMES, I REALLY DON'T GET GIRLS' MOODS.

As Miss Beelzebub Likes

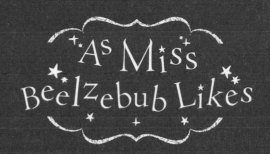

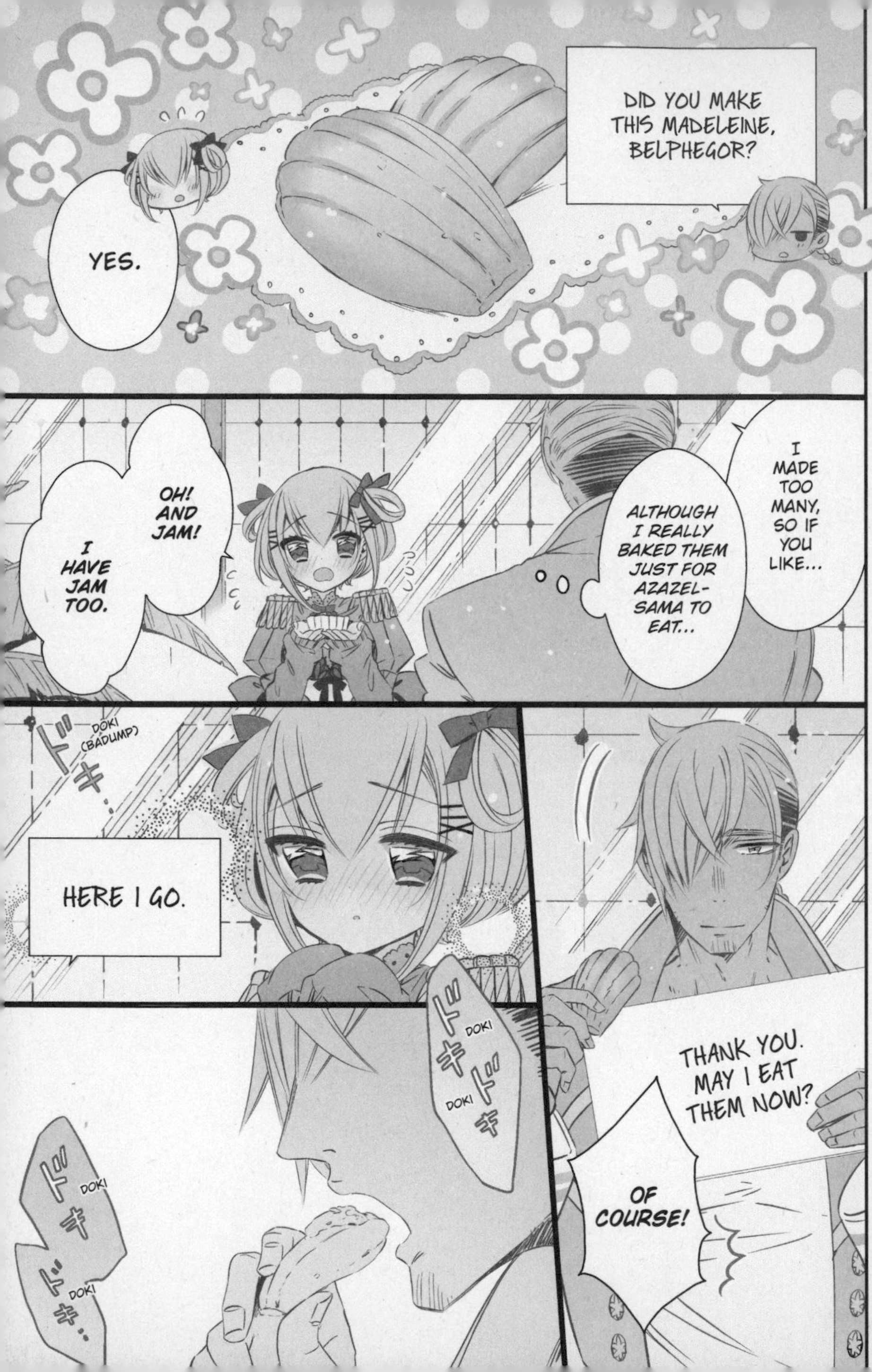
DID YOU MAKE THIS MADELEINE, BELPHEGOR?
YES.
I MADE TOO MANY, SO IF YOU LIKE...
ALTHOUGH I REALLY BAKED THEM JUST FOR AZAZEL-SAMA TO EAT...
OH! AND JAM!
I HAVE JAM TOO.
ドキ... DOKI (BADUMP)
HERE I GO.
THANK YOU. MAY I EAT THEM NOW?
OF COURSE!
ドキ DOKI
ドキ DOKI
ドキ DOKI
ドキ... DOKI

CHAPTER 28

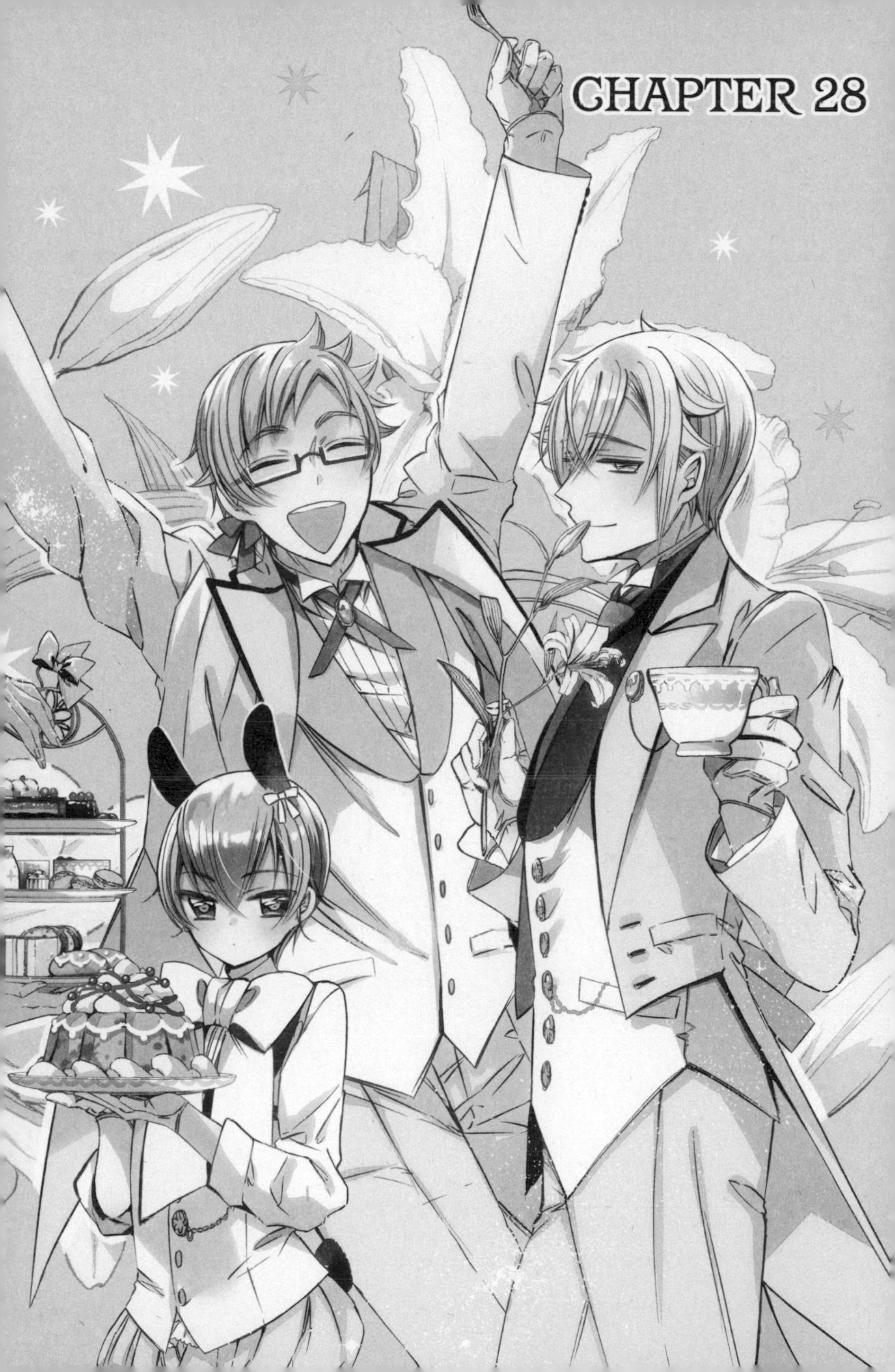

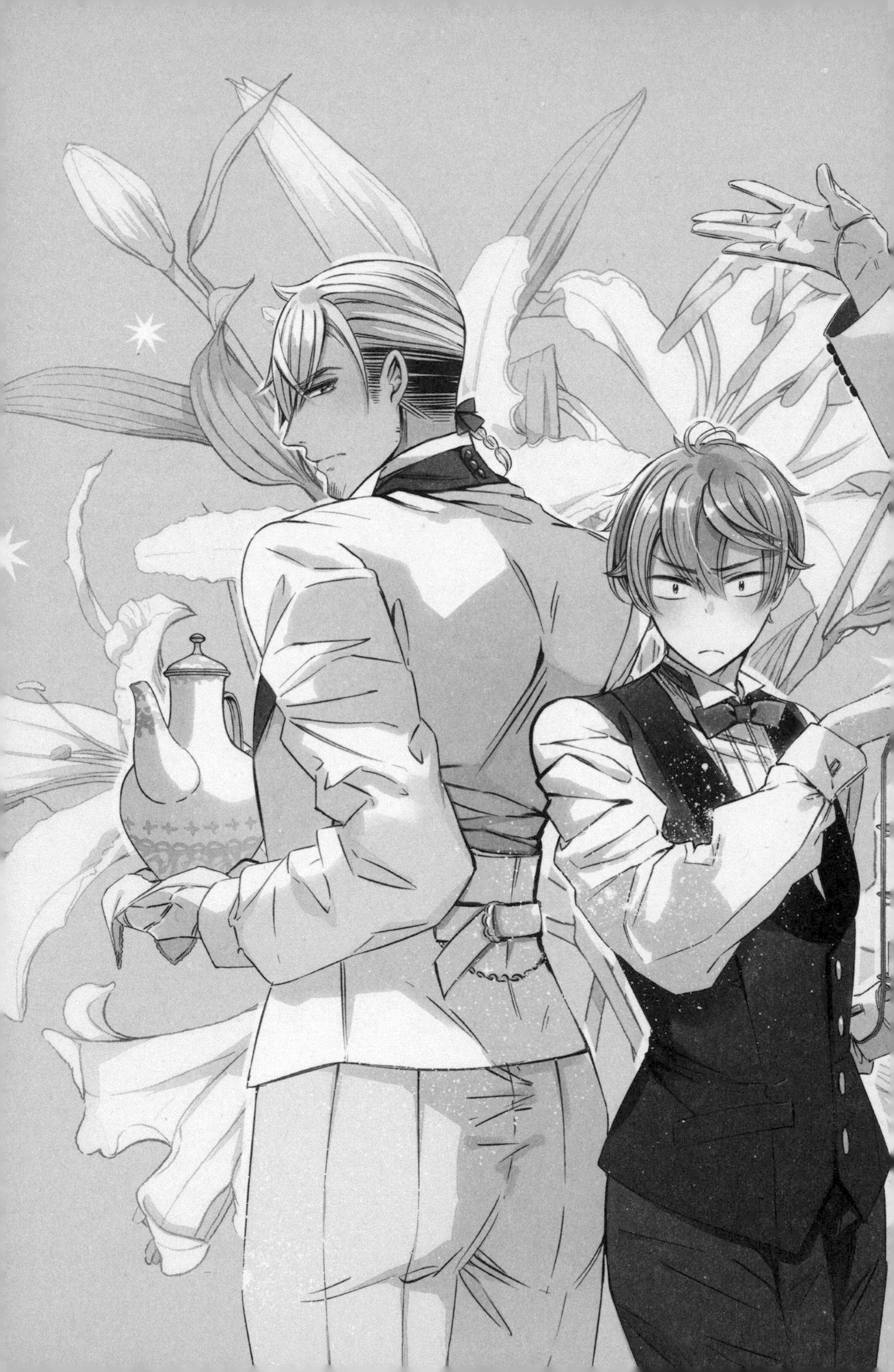

As Miss Beelzebub Likes

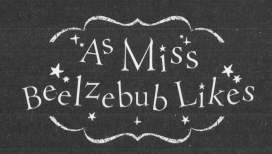

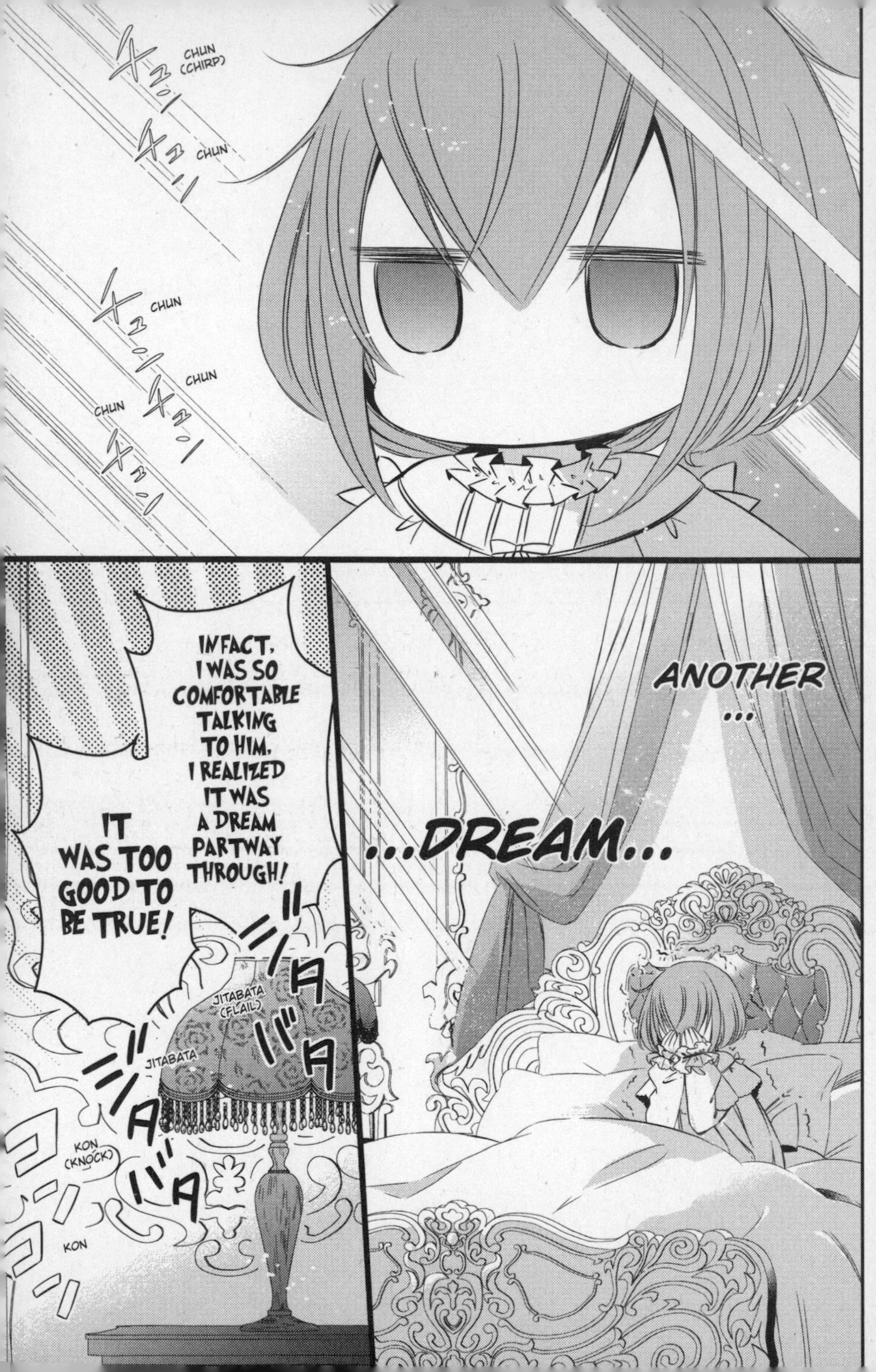
CHUN (CHIRP)
CHUN
CHUN
CHUN
CHUN
ANOTHER ...
...DREAM...
INFACT, I WAS SO COMFORTABLE TALKING TO HIM, I REALIZED IT WAS A DREAM PARTWAY THROUGH!
IT WAS TOO GOOD TO BE TRUE!
JITABATA (FLAIL)
JITABATA
KON (KNOCK)
KON

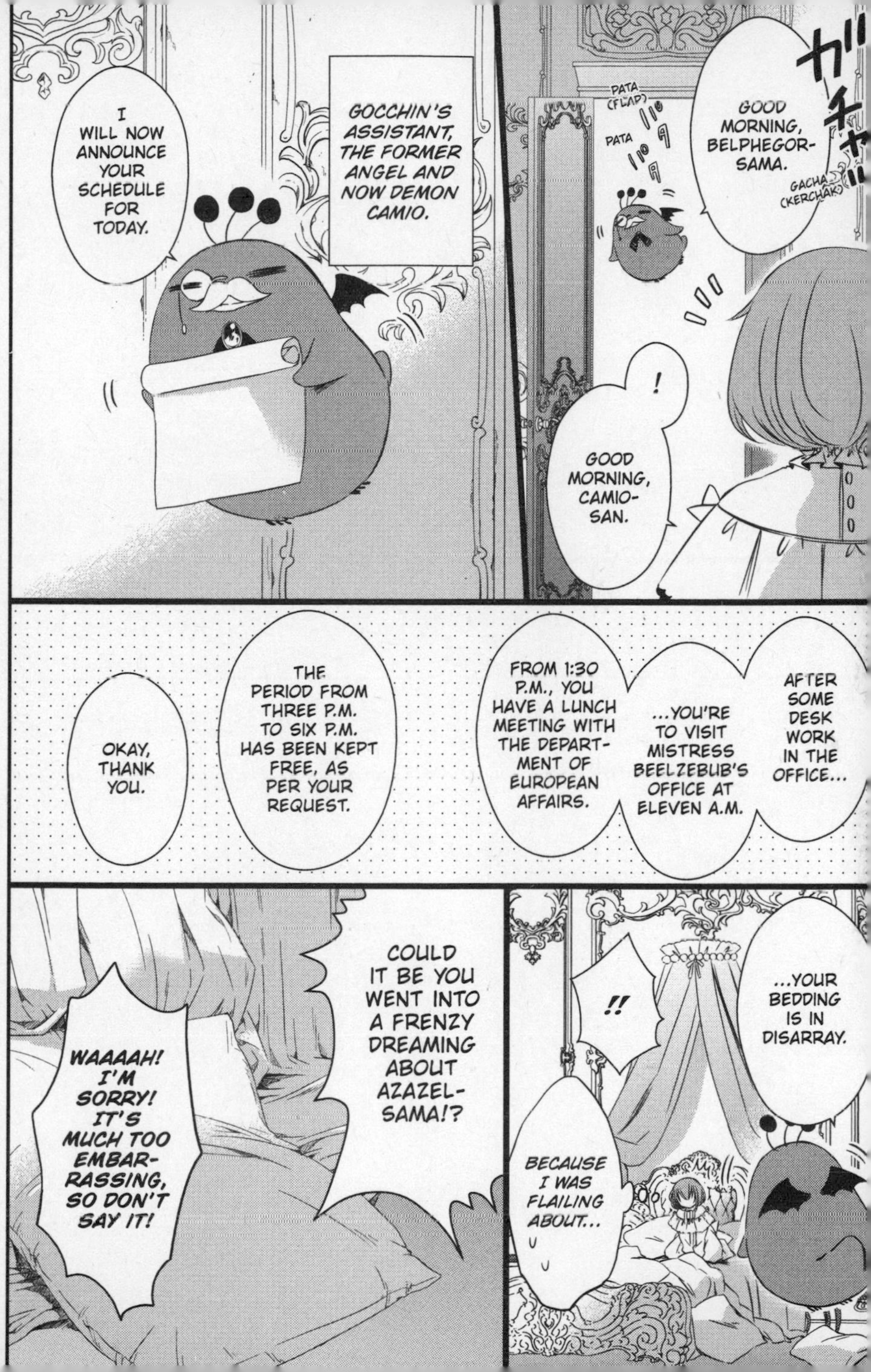
ガチャ
GACHA (KERCHAK)
GOOD MORNING, BELPHEGOR-SAMA.
PATA (FLAP)
PATA
!
GOOD MORNING, CAMIO-SAN.
GOCCHIN'S ASSISTANT, THE FORMER ANGEL AND NOW DEMON CAMIO.
I WILL NOW ANNOUNCE YOUR SCHEDULE FOR TODAY.
AFTER SOME DESK WORK IN THE OFFICE...
...YOU'RE TO VISIT MISTRESS BEELZEBUB'S OFFICE AT ELEVEN A.M.
FROM 1:30 P.M., YOU HAVE A LUNCH MEETING WITH THE DEPART-MENT OF EUROPEAN AFFAIRS.
THE PERIOD FROM THREE P.M. TO SIX P.M. HAS BEEN KEPT FREE, AS PER YOUR REQUEST.
OKAY, THANK YOU.
...YOUR BEDDING IS IN DISARRAY.
!!
BECAUSE I WAS FLAILING ABOUT...
COULD IT BE YOU WENT INTO A FRENZY DREAMING ABOUT AZAZEL-SAMA!?
WAAAAH! I'M SORRY! IT'S MUCH TOO EMBAR-RASSING, SO DON'T SAY IT!

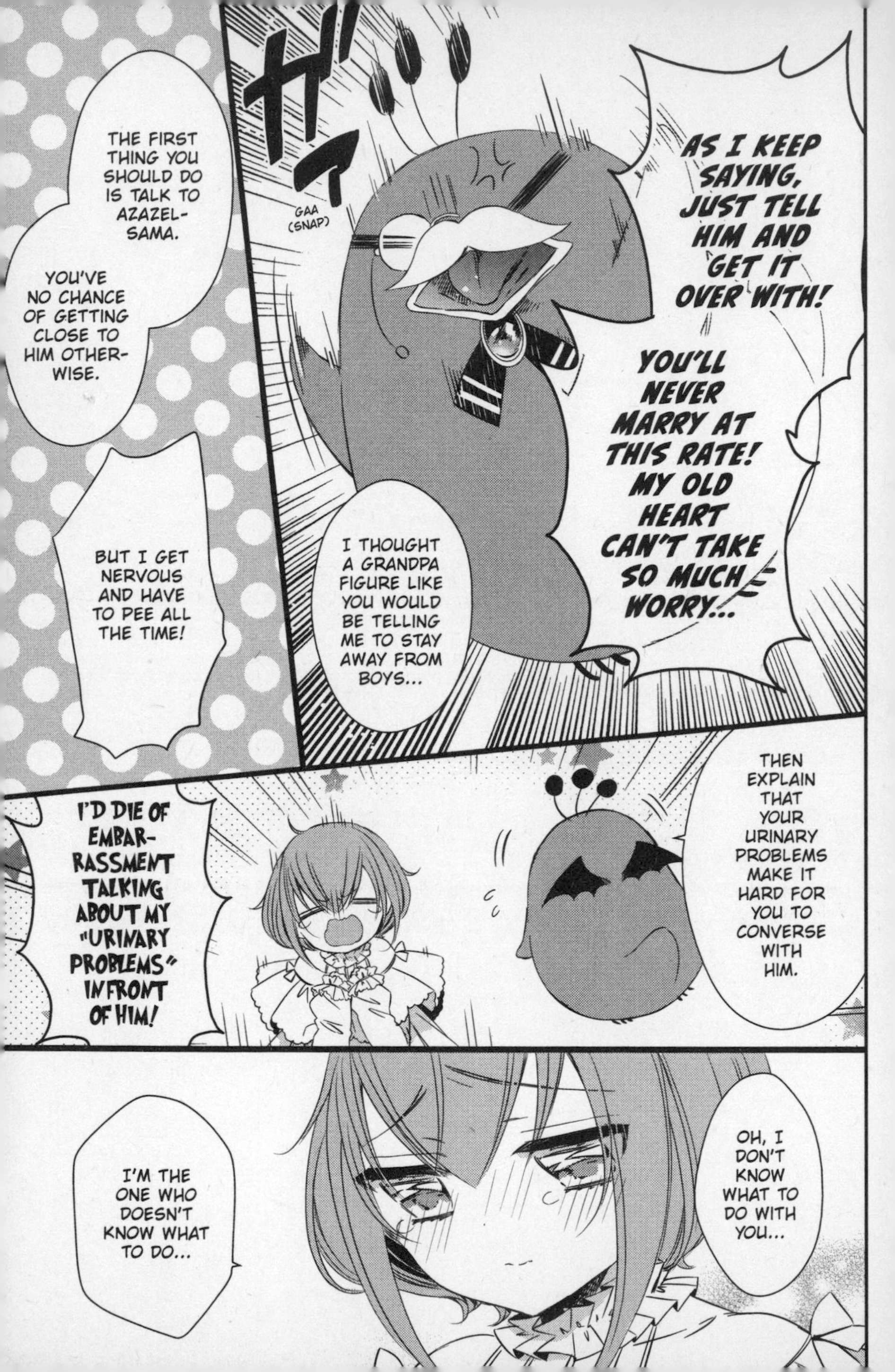

GAA (SNAP)
AS I KEEP SAYING, JUST TELL HIM AND GET IT OVER WITH!
YOU'LL NEVER MARRY AT THIS RATE! MY OLD HEART CAN'T TAKE SO MUCH WORRY...
I THOUGHT A GRANDPA FIGURE LIKE YOU WOULD BE TELLING ME TO STAY AWAY FROM BOYS...
THE FIRST THING YOU SHOULD DO IS TALK TO AZAZEL-SAMA.
YOU'VE NO CHANCE OF GETTING CLOSE TO HIM OTHERWISE.
BUT I GET NERVOUS AND HAVE TO PEE ALL THE TIME!
THEN EXPLAIN THAT YOUR URINARY PROBLEMS MAKE IT HARD FOR YOU TO CONVERSE WITH HIM.
I'D DIE OF EMBARRASSMENT TALKING ABOUT MY "URINARY PROBLEMS" IN FRONT OF HIM!
OH, I DON'T KNOW WHAT TO DO WITH YOU...
I'M THE ONE WHO DOESN'T KNOW WHAT TO DO...

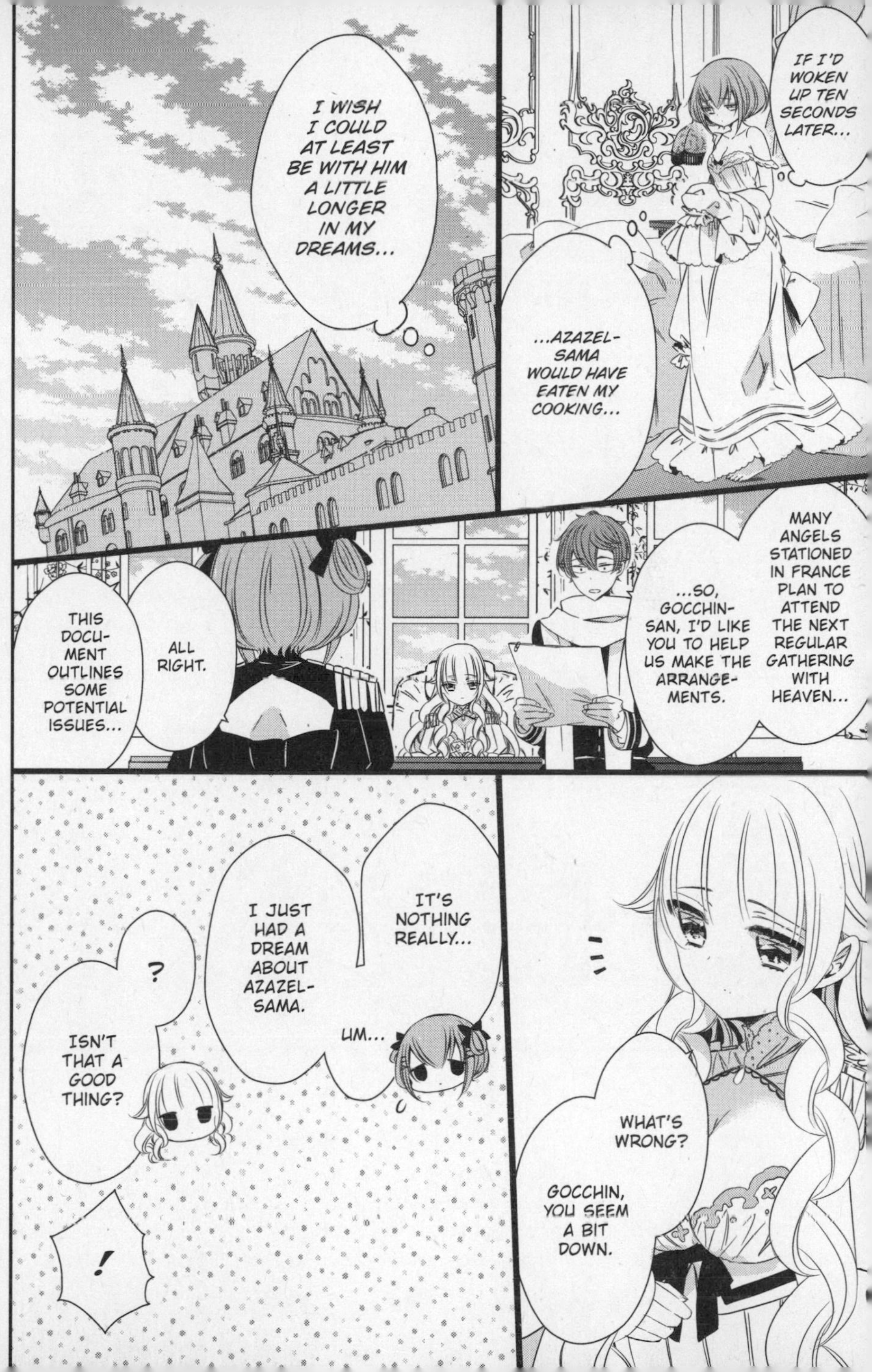
IF I'D WOKEN UP TEN SECONDS LATER...
...AZAZEL-SAMA WOULD HAVE EATEN MY COOKING...
I WISH I COULD AT LEAST BE WITH HIM A LITTLE LONGER IN MY DREAMS...
MANY ANGELS STATIONED IN FRANCE PLAN TO ATTEND THE NEXT REGULAR GATHERING WITH HEAVEN...
...SO, GOCCHIN-SAN, I'D LIKE YOU TO HELP US MAKE THE ARRANGE-MENTS.
ALL RIGHT.
THIS DOCU-MENT OUTLINES SOME POTENTIAL ISSUES...
WHAT'S WRONG?
GOCCHIN, YOU SEEM A BIT DOWN.
IT'S NOTHING REALLY...
I JUST HAD A DREAM ABOUT AZAZEL-SAMA.
UM...
?
ISN'T THAT A GOOD THING?
!

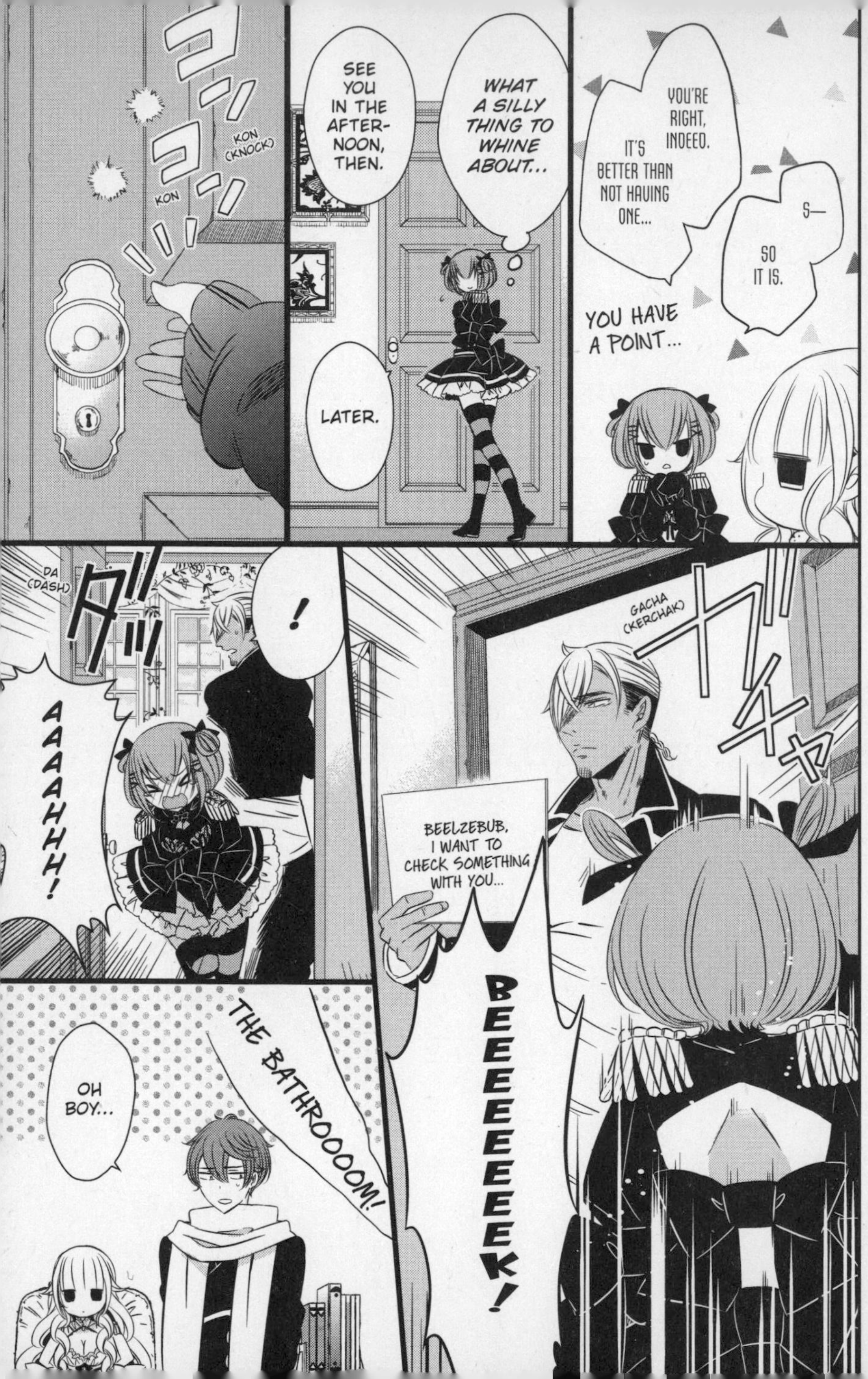

YOU'RE RIGHT, INDEED.
IT'S BETTER THAN NOT HAVING ONE...
S— SO IT IS.
YOU HAVE A POINT...
WHAT A SILLY THING TO WHINE ABOUT...
SEE YOU IN THE AFTERNOON, THEN.
LATER.
KON (KNOCK)
KON
GACHA (KERCHAK)
BEELZEBUB, I WANT TO CHECK SOMETHING WITH YOU...
BEEEEEEEEEEK!
!
DA (DASH)
AAAAAHHH!
THE BATHROOOOOM!
OH BOY...

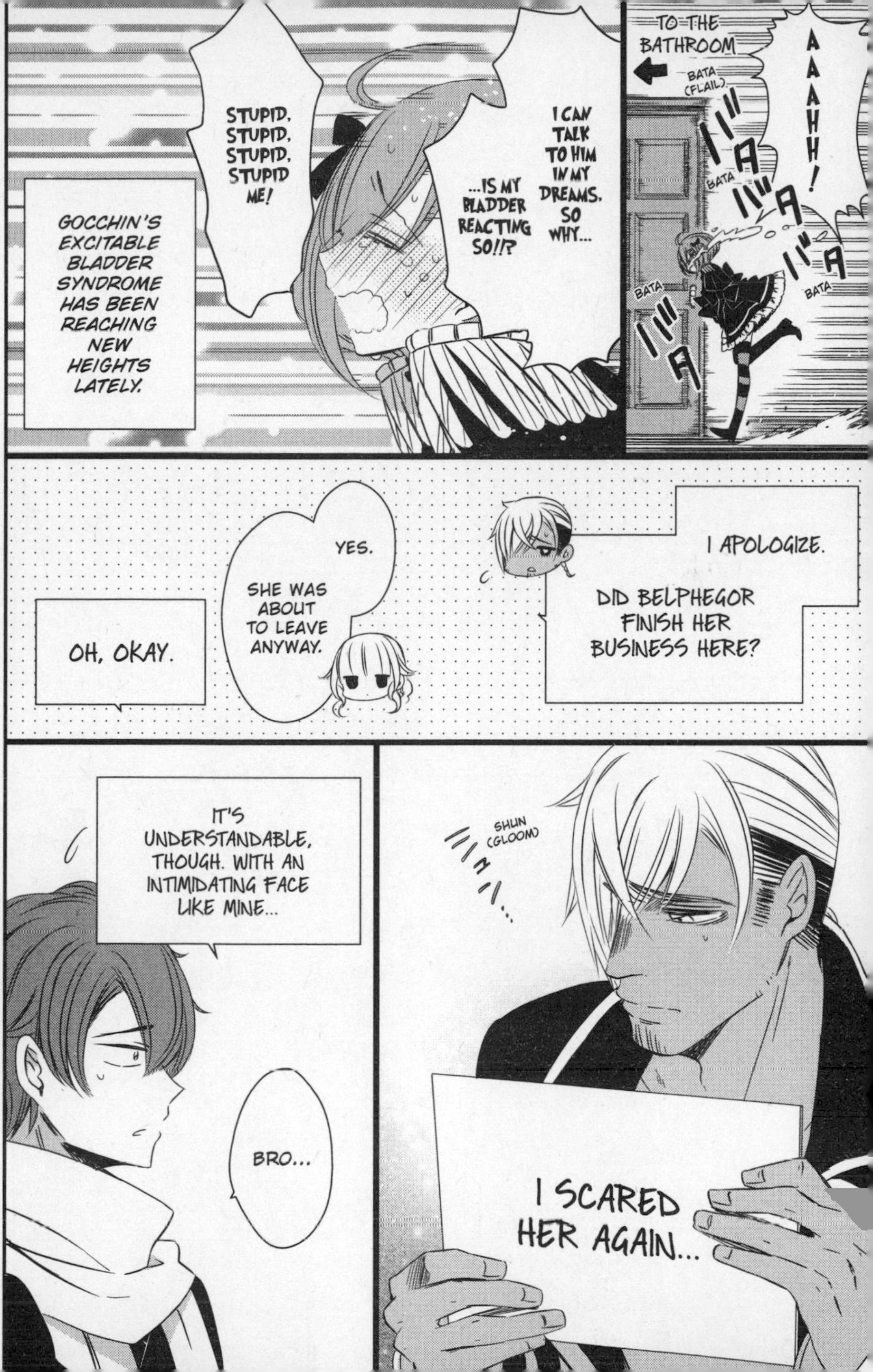

TO THE BATHROOM
AAAAHH!
BATA (FLAIL)
BATA
BATA
BATA
I CAN TALK TO HIM IN MY DREAMS. SO WHY...
...IS MY BLADDER REACTING SO!!?
STUPID, STUPID, STUPID, STUPID ME!
GOCCHIN'S EXCITABLE BLADDER SYNDROME HAS BEEN REACHING NEW HEIGHTS LATELY.
I APOLOGIZE.
DID BELPHEGOR FINISH HER BUSINESS HERE?
YES.
SHE WAS ABOUT TO LEAVE ANYWAY.
OH, OKAY.
SHUN (GLOOM)
I SCARED HER AGAIN...
IT'S UNDERSTANDABLE, THOUGH. WITH AN INTIMIDATING FACE LIKE MINE...
BRO...

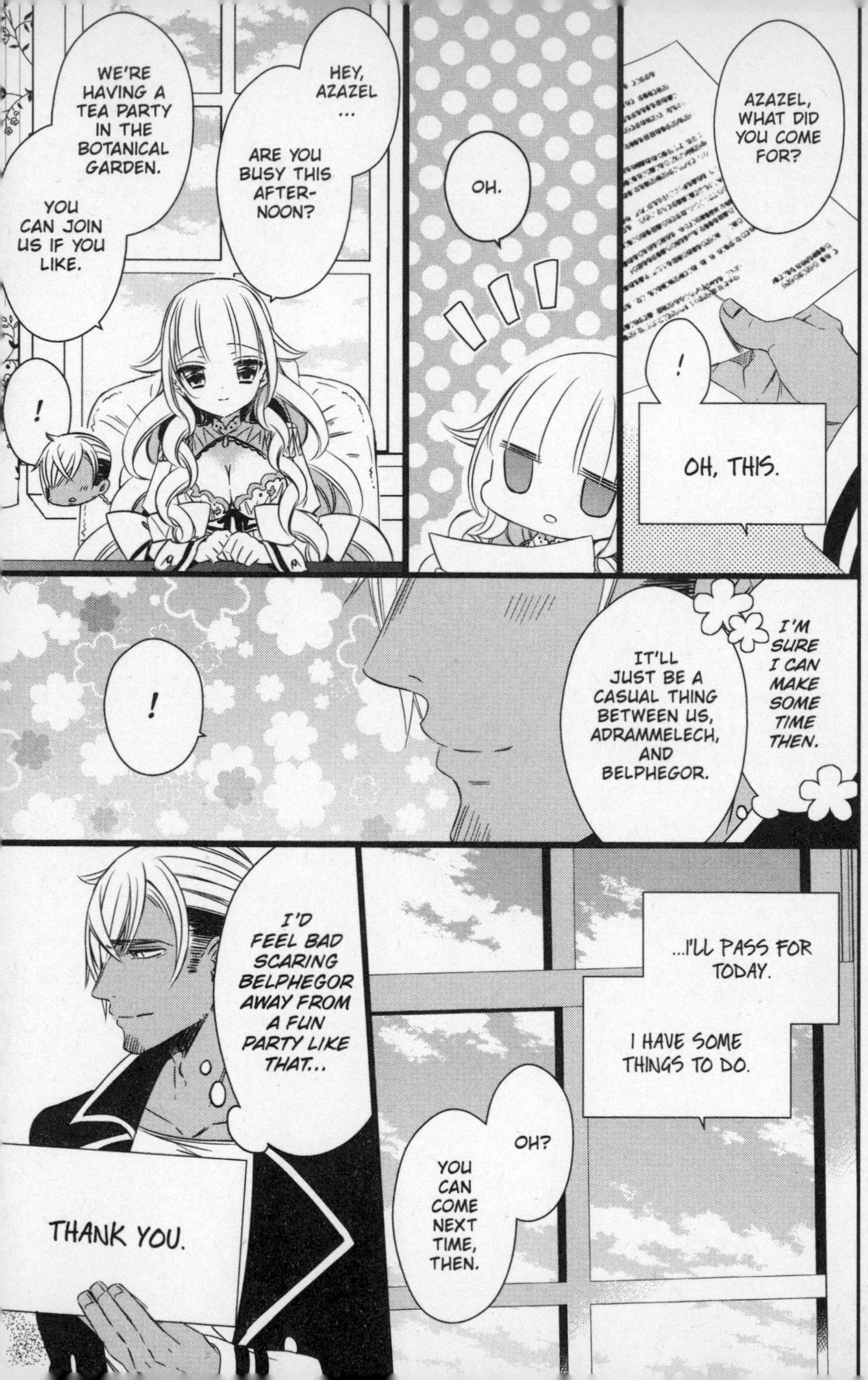
AZAZEL, WHAT DID YOU COME FOR?
!
OH, THIS.
OH.
HEY, AZAZEL ...
ARE YOU BUSY THIS AFTER-NOON?
WE'RE HAVING A TEA PARTY IN THE BOTANICAL GARDEN.
YOU CAN JOIN US IF YOU LIKE.
!
I'M SURE I CAN MAKE SOME TIME THEN.
IT'LL JUST BE A CASUAL THING BETWEEN US, ADRAMMELECH, AND BELPHEGOR.
!
...I'LL PASS FOR TODAY.
I HAVE SOME THINGS TO DO.
OH?
YOU CAN COME NEXT TIME, THEN.
I'D FEEL BAD SCARING BELPHEGOR AWAY FROM A FUN PARTY LIKE THAT...
THANK YOU.

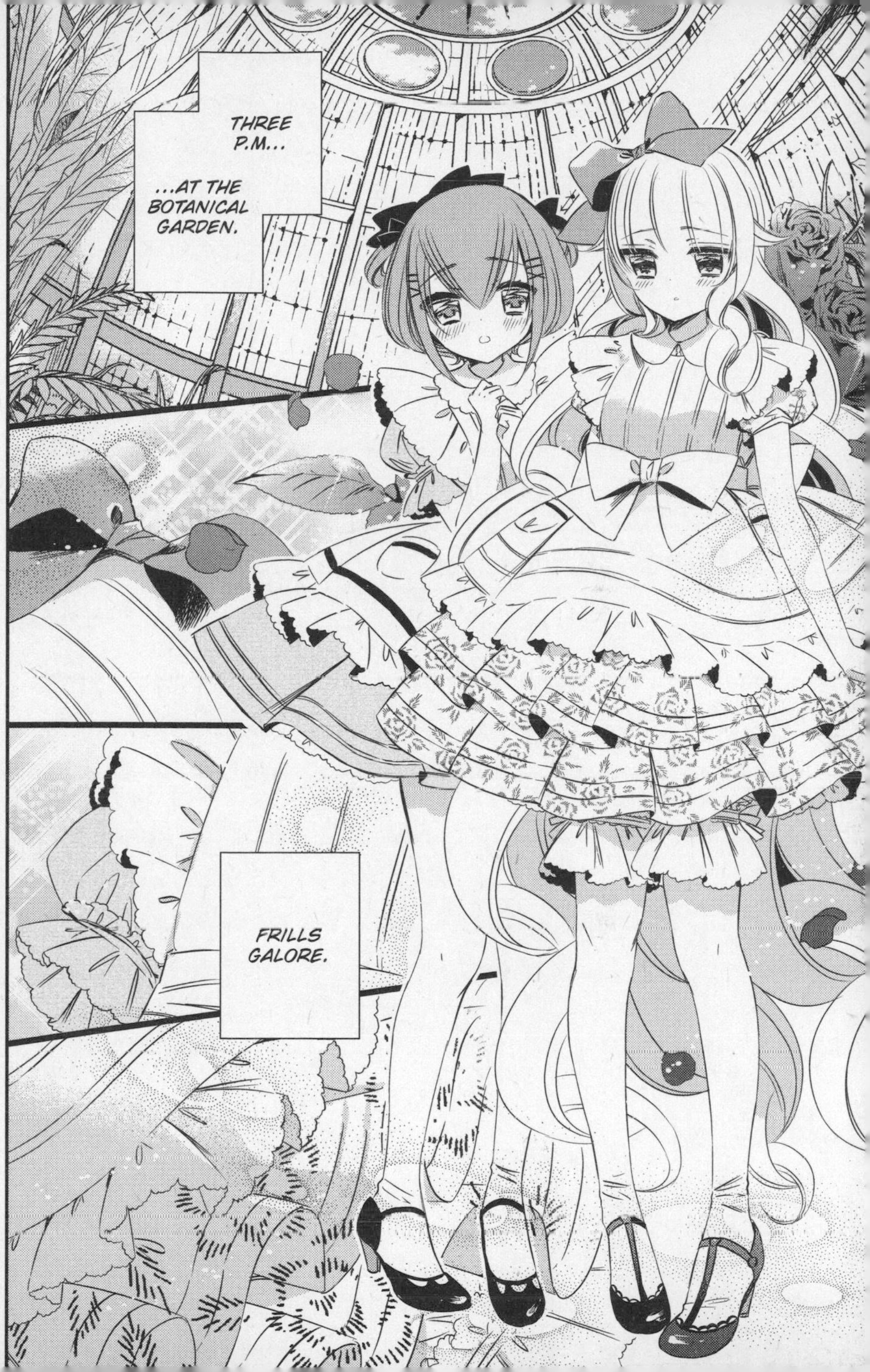
THREE P.M...
...AT THE BOTANICAL GARDEN.
FRILLS GALORE.

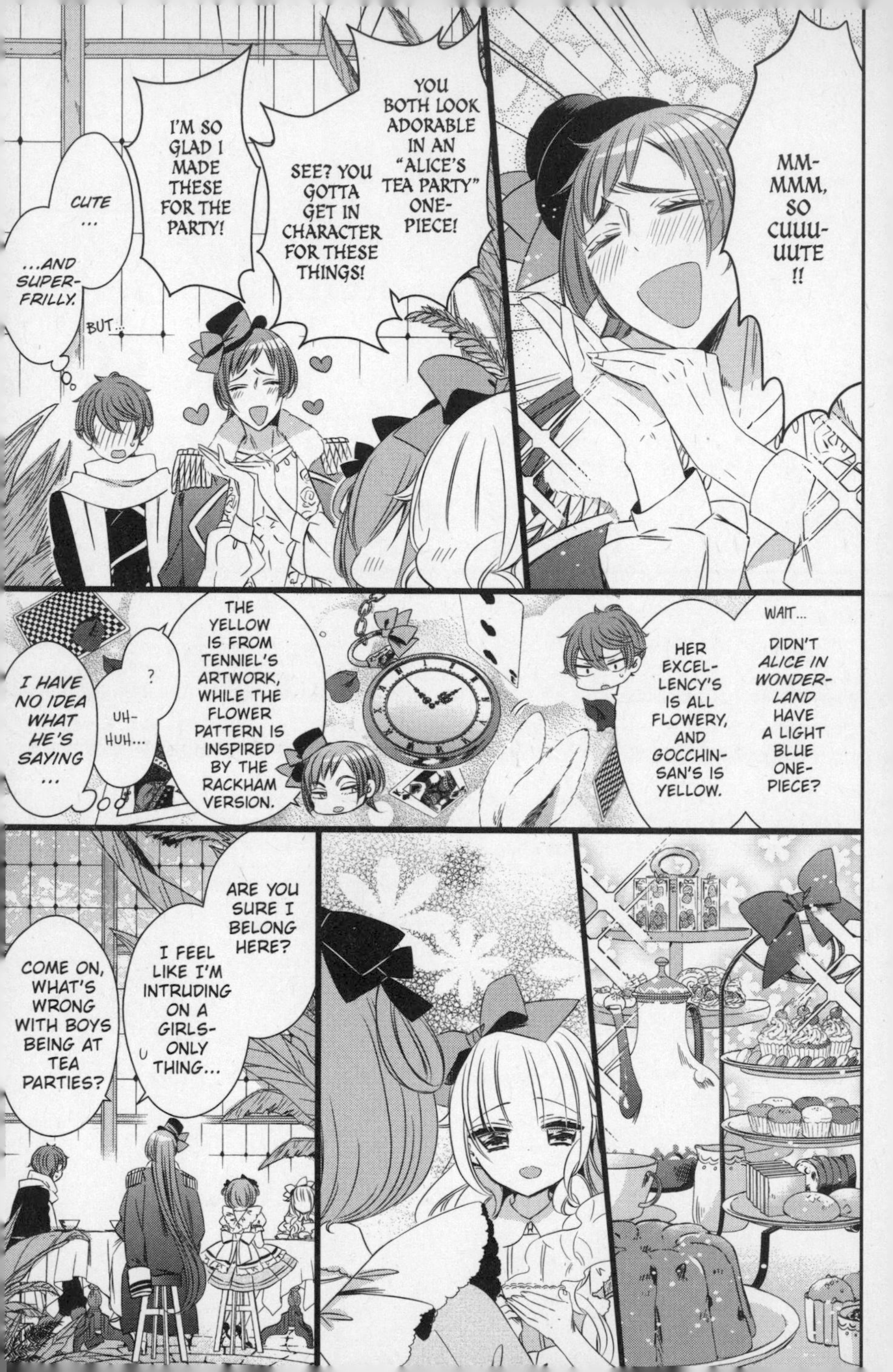
MM-MMM, SO CUUUU-UUTE!!
YOU BOTH LOOK ADORABLE IN AN "ALICE'S TEA PARTY" ONE-PIECE!
SEE? YOU GOTTA GET IN CHARACTER FOR THESE THINGS!
I'M SO GLAD I MADE THESE FOR THE PARTY!
CUTE...
...AND SUPER-FRILLY.
BUT...
WAIT...
DIDN'T ALICE IN WONDERLAND HAVE A LIGHT BLUE ONE-PIECE?
HER EXCELLENCY'S IS ALL FLOWERY, AND GOCCHIN-SAN'S IS YELLOW.
THE YELLOW IS FROM TENNIEL'S ARTWORK, WHILE THE FLOWER PATTERN IS INSPIRED BY THE RACKHAM VERSION.
?
UH-HUH...
I HAVE NO IDEA WHAT HE'S SAYING...
ARE YOU SURE I BELONG HERE?
I FEEL LIKE I'M INTRUDING ON A GIRLS-ONLY THING...
U
COME ON, WHAT'S WRONG WITH BOYS BEING AT TEA PARTIES?

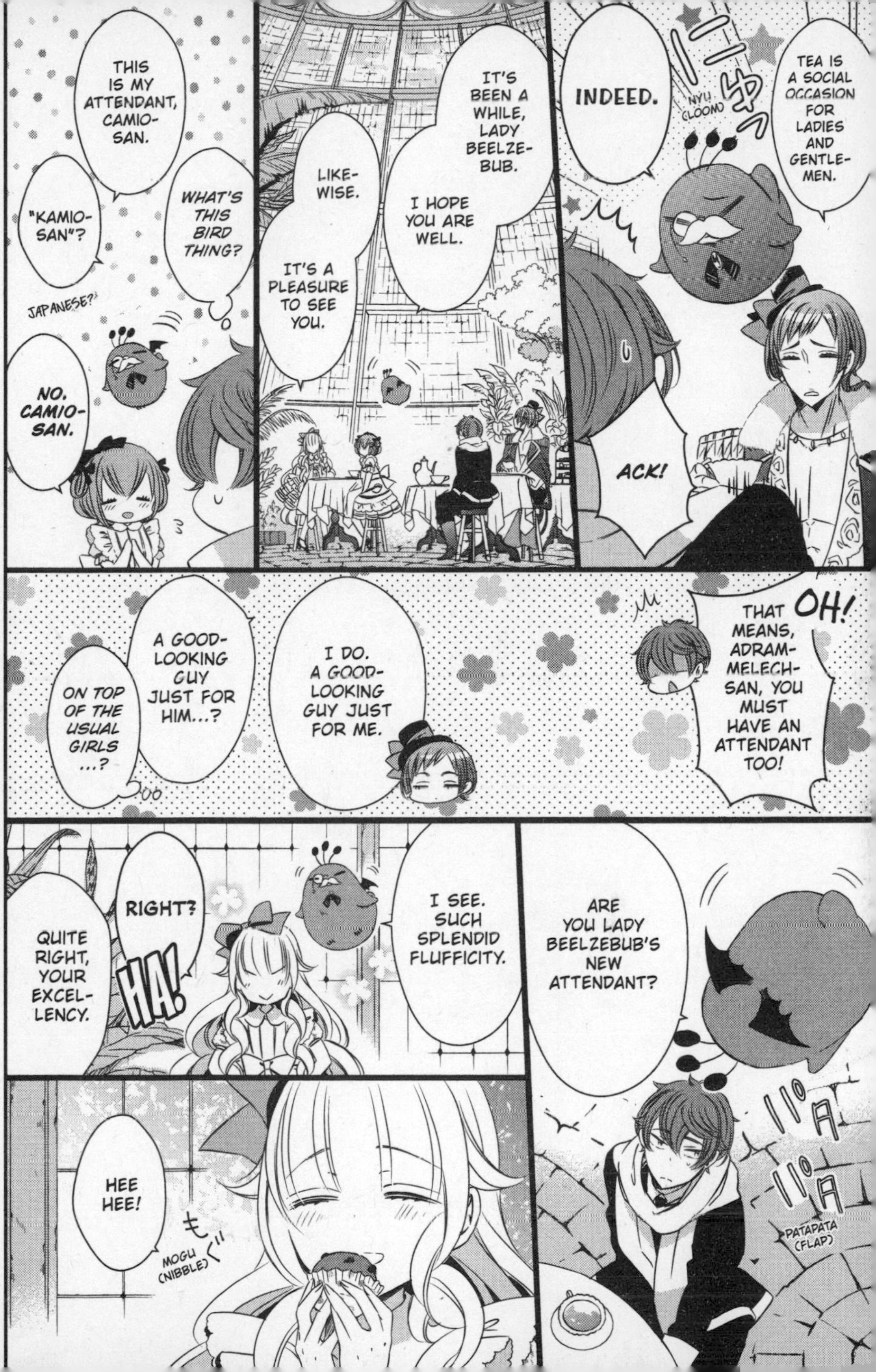
TEA IS A SOCIAL OCCASION FOR LADIES AND GENTLEMEN.
NYU (LOOM)
INDEED.
ACK!
IT'S BEEN A WHILE, LADY BEELZEBUB.
I HOPE YOU ARE WELL.
LIKE-WISE.
IT'S A PLEASURE TO SEE YOU.
THIS IS MY ATTENDANT, CAMIO-SAN.
WHAT'S THIS BIRD THING?
"KAMIO-SAN"?
JAPANESE?
NO. CAMIO-SAN.
OH!
THAT MEANS, ADRAMMELECH-SAN, YOU MUST HAVE AN ATTENDANT TOO!
I DO. A GOOD-LOOKING GUY JUST FOR ME.
A GOOD-LOOKING GUY JUST FOR HIM...?
ON TOP OF THE USUAL GIRLS...?
ARE YOU LADY BEELZEBUB'S NEW ATTENDANT?
PATAPATA (FLAP)
I SEE. SUCH SPLENDID FLUFFICITY.
RIGHT?
HA!
QUITE RIGHT, YOUR EXCELLENCY.
HEE HEE!
MOGU (NIBBLE)

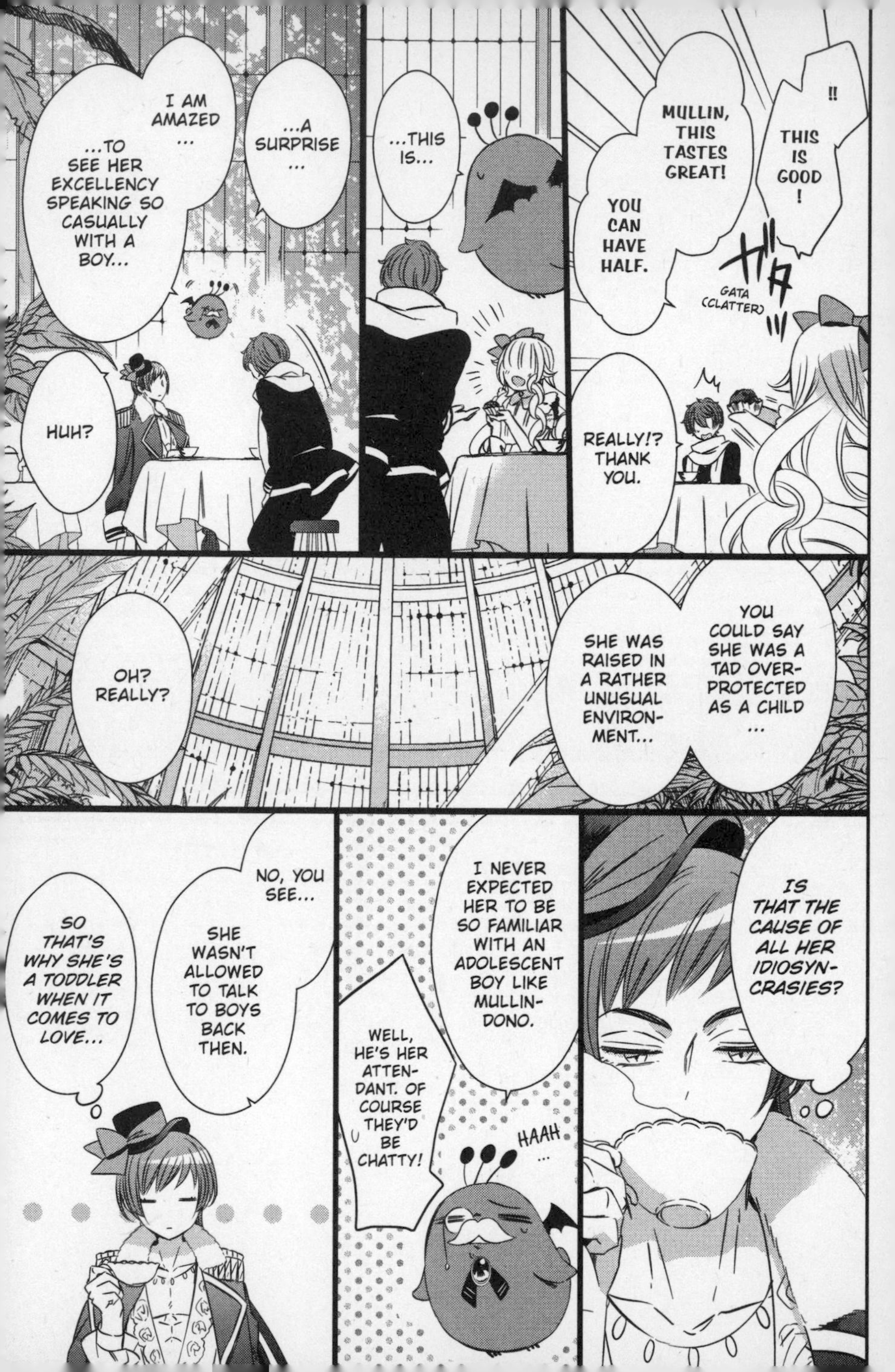
!! THIS IS GOOD!
MULLIN, THIS TASTES GREAT! YOU CAN HAVE HALF.
GATA (CLATTER)
REALLY!? THANK YOU.
...THIS IS...
...A SURPRISE...
I AM AMAZED... ...TO SEE HER EXCELLENCY SPEAKING SO CASUALLY WITH A BOY...
HUH?
YOU COULD SAY SHE WAS A TAD OVER-PROTECTED AS A CHILD...
SHE WAS RAISED IN A RATHER UNUSUAL ENVIRONMENT...
OH? REALLY?
IS THAT THE CAUSE OF ALL HER IDIOSYN-CRASIES?
I NEVER EXPECTED HER TO BE SO FAMILIAR WITH AN ADOLESCENT BOY LIKE MULLIN-DONO.
HAAH...
WELL, HE'S HER ATTEN-DANT. OF COURSE THEY'D BE CHATTY!
NO, YOU SEE... SHE WASN'T ALLOWED TO TALK TO BOYS BACK THEN.
SO THAT'S WHY SHE'S A TODDLER WHEN IT COMES TO LOVE...

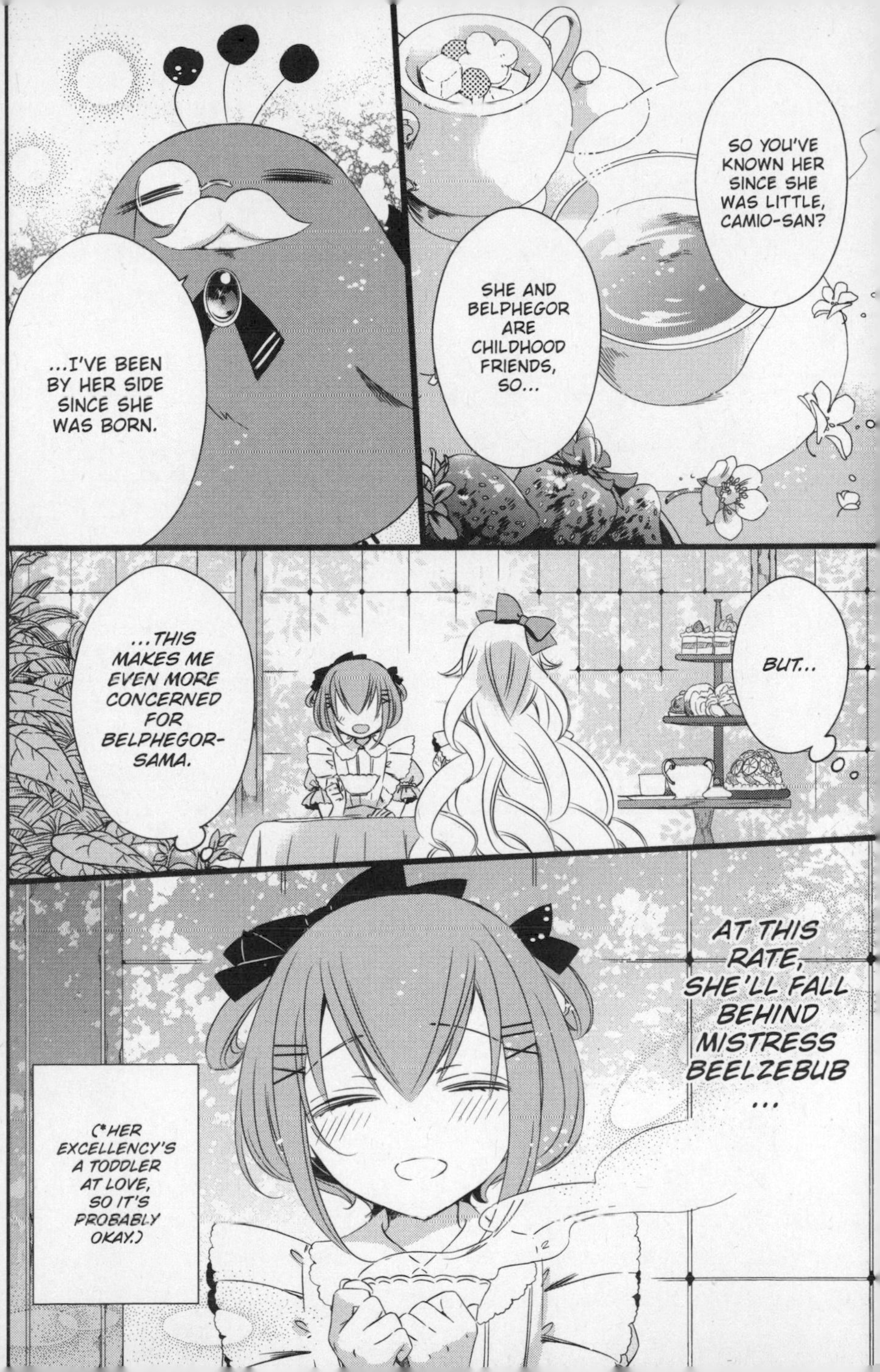
SO YOU'VE KNOWN HER SINCE SHE WAS LITTLE, CAMIO-SAN?
SHE AND BELPHEGOR ARE CHILDHOOD FRIENDS, SO...
...I'VE BEEN BY HER SIDE SINCE SHE WAS BORN.
BUT...
...THIS MAKES ME EVEN MORE CONCERNED FOR BELPHEGOR-SAMA.
AT THIS RATE, SHE'LL FALL BEHIND MISTRESS BEELZEBUB ...
(*HER EXCELLENCY'S A TODDLER AT LOVE, SO IT'S PROBABLY OKAY.)

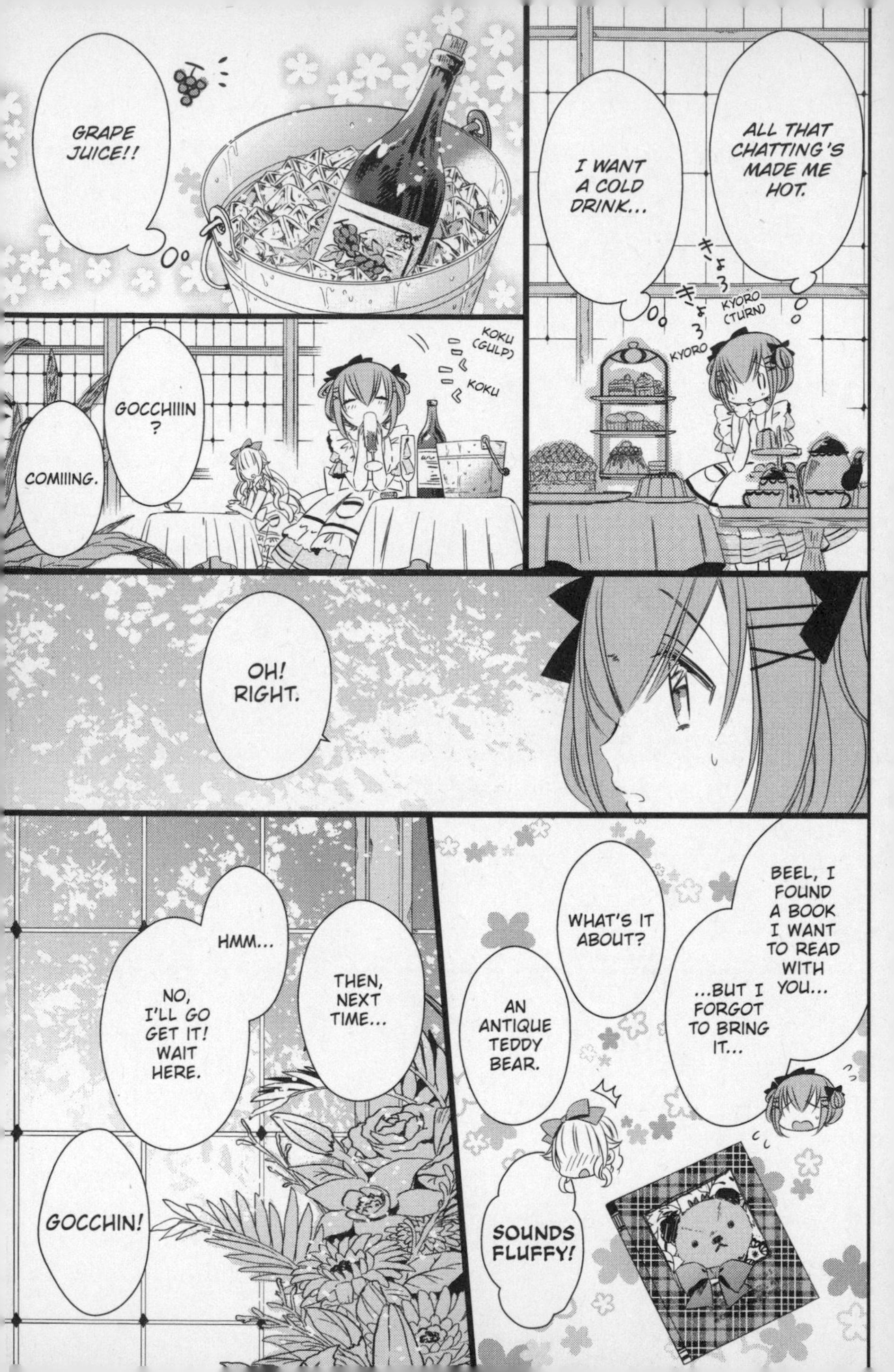
ALL THAT CHATTING'S MADE ME HOT.
I WANT A COLD DRINK...
KYORO (TURN)
KYORO
GRAPE JUICE!!
KOKU (GULP)
KOKU
GOCCHIIIN?
COMIIING.
OH! RIGHT.
BEEL, I FOUND A BOOK I WANT TO READ WITH YOU...
...BUT I FORGOT TO BRING IT...
WHAT'S IT ABOUT?
AN ANTIQUE TEDDY BEAR.
SOUNDS FLUFFY!
THEN, NEXT TIME...
HMM...
NO, I'LL GO GET IT! WAIT HERE.
GOCCHIN!

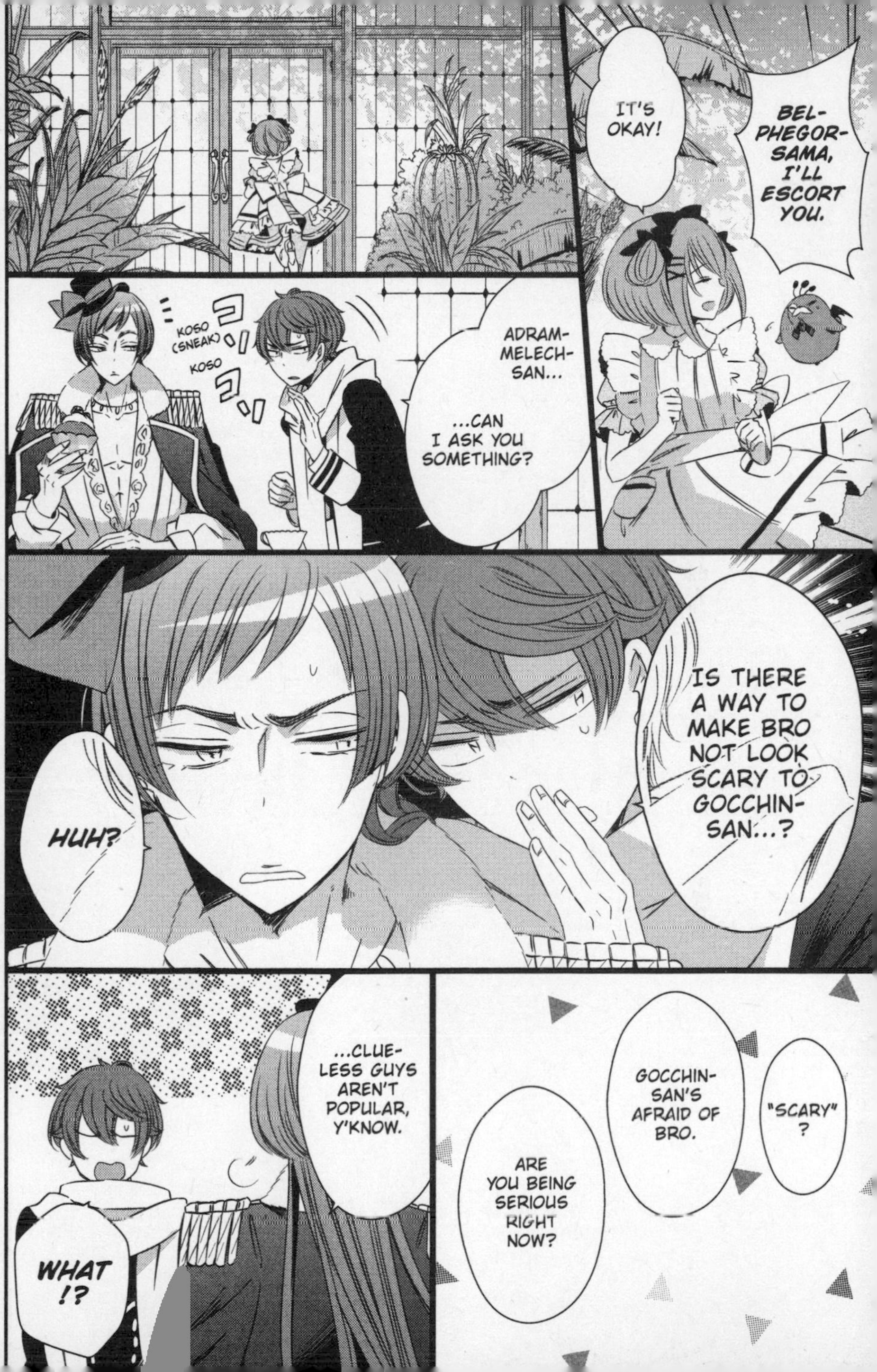
BEL-PHEGOR-SAMA, I'LL ESCORT YOU.
IT'S OKAY!
ADRAM-MELECH-SAN...
...CAN I ASK YOU SOMETHING?
KOSO (SNEAK) KOSO
IS THERE A WAY TO MAKE BRO NOT LOOK SCARY TO GOCCHIN-SAN...?
HUH?
"SCARY"?
GOCCHIN-SAN'S AFRAID OF BRO.
ARE YOU BEING SERIOUS RIGHT NOW?
...CLUE-LESS GUYS AREN'T POPULAR, Y'KNOW.
WHAT!?

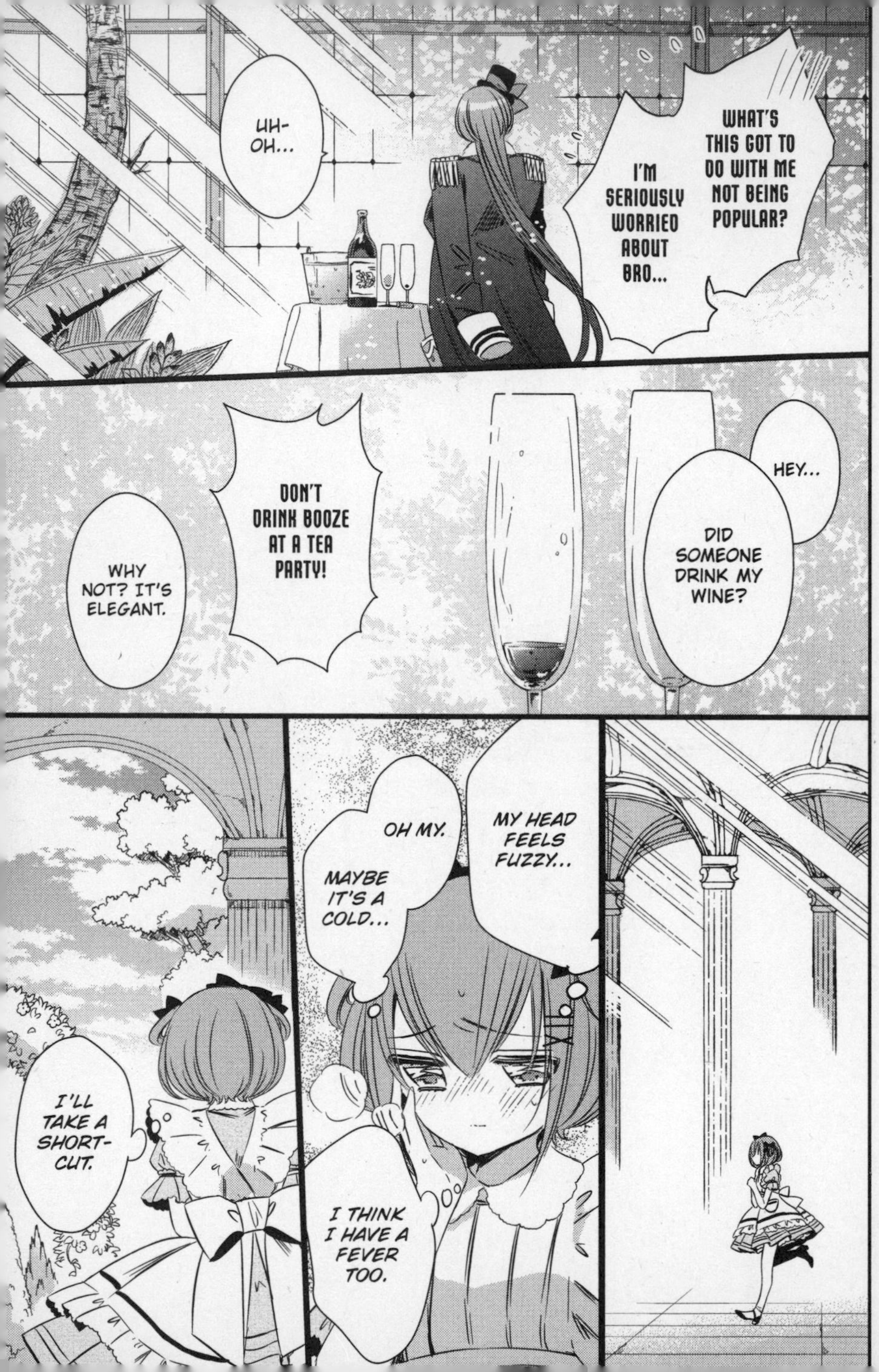
WHAT'S THIS GOT TO DO WITH ME NOT BEING POPULAR?
I'M SERIOUSLY WORRIED ABOUT BRO...
UH-OH...
HEY...
DID SOMEONE DRINK MY WINE?
DON'T DRINK BOOZE AT A TEA PARTY!
WHY NOT? IT'S ELEGANT.
MY HEAD FEELS FUZZY...
OH MY.
MAYBE IT'S A COLD...
I THINK I HAVE A FEVER TOO.
I'LL TAKE A SHORT-CUT.

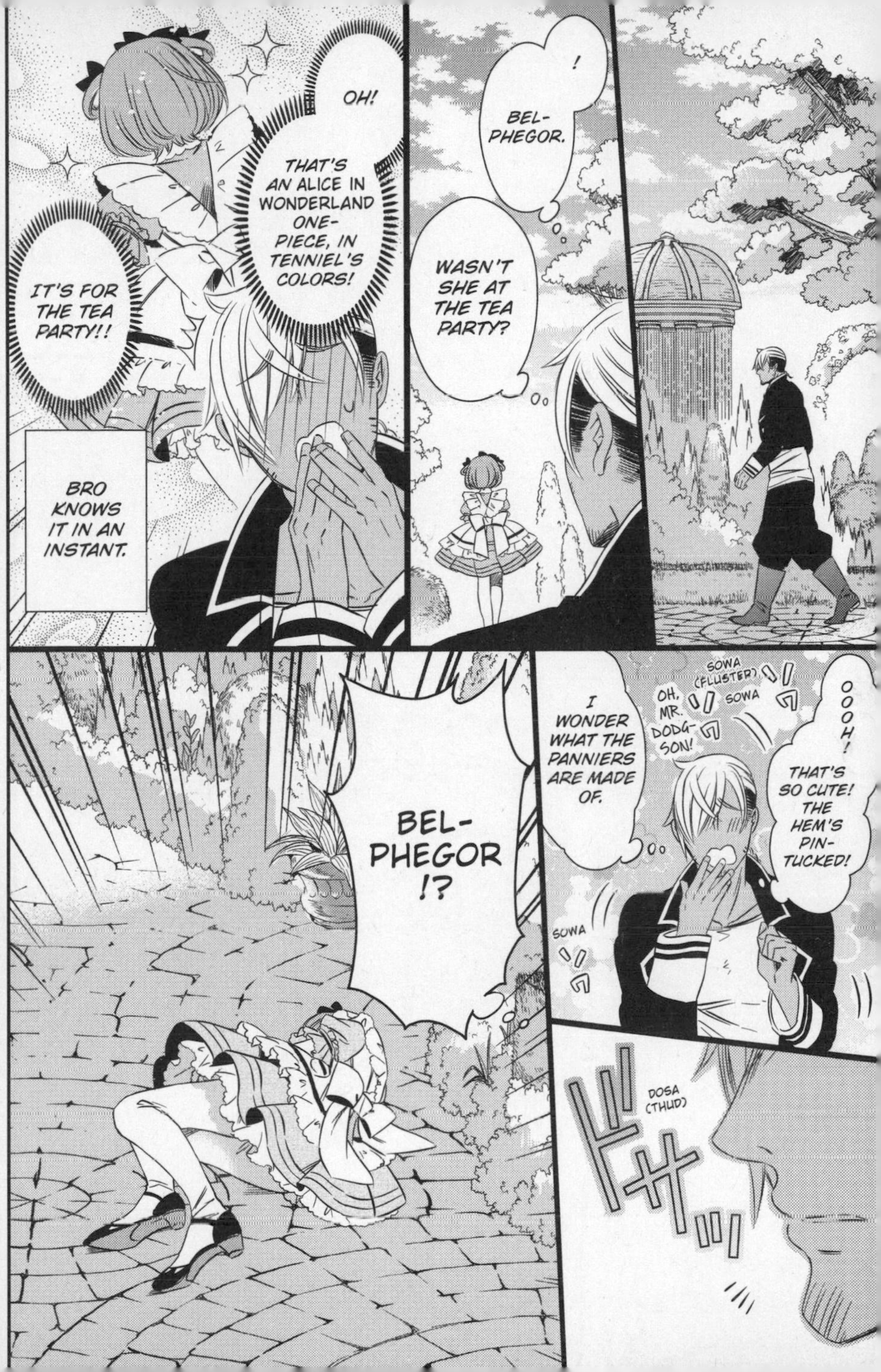
!
BEL-PHEGOR.
WASN'T SHE AT THE TEA PARTY?
OH!
THAT'S AN ALICE IN WONDERLAND ONE-PIECE, IN TENNIEL'S COLORS!
IT'S FOR THE TEA PARTY!!
BRO KNOWS IT IN AN INSTANT.
OOOH!
THAT'S SO CUTE! THE HEM'S PIN-TUCKED!
SOWA (FLUSTER)
SOWA
OH, MR. DODGSON!
I WONDER WHAT THE PANNIERS ARE MADE OF.
SOWA
DOSA (THUD)
BEL-PHEGOR!?

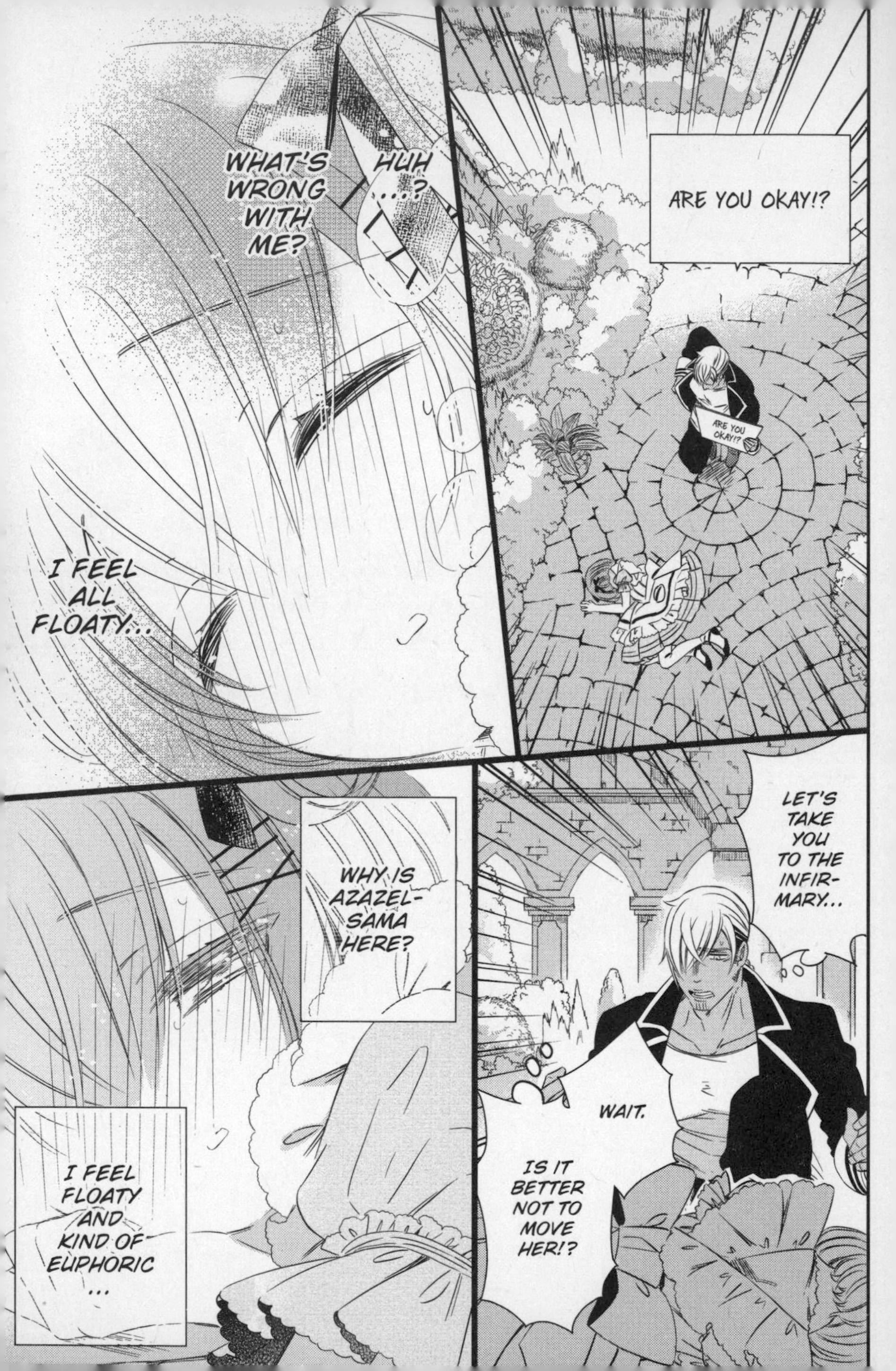

ARE YOU OKAY!?
ARE YOU OKAY!?
HUH ...?
WHAT'S WRONG WITH ME?
I FEEL ALL FLOATY...
LET'S TAKE YOU TO THE INFIR-MARY...
WAIT.
IS IT BETTER NOT TO MOVE HER!?
WHY IS AZAZEL-SAMA HERE?
I FEEL FLOATY AND KIND OF EUPHORIC ...

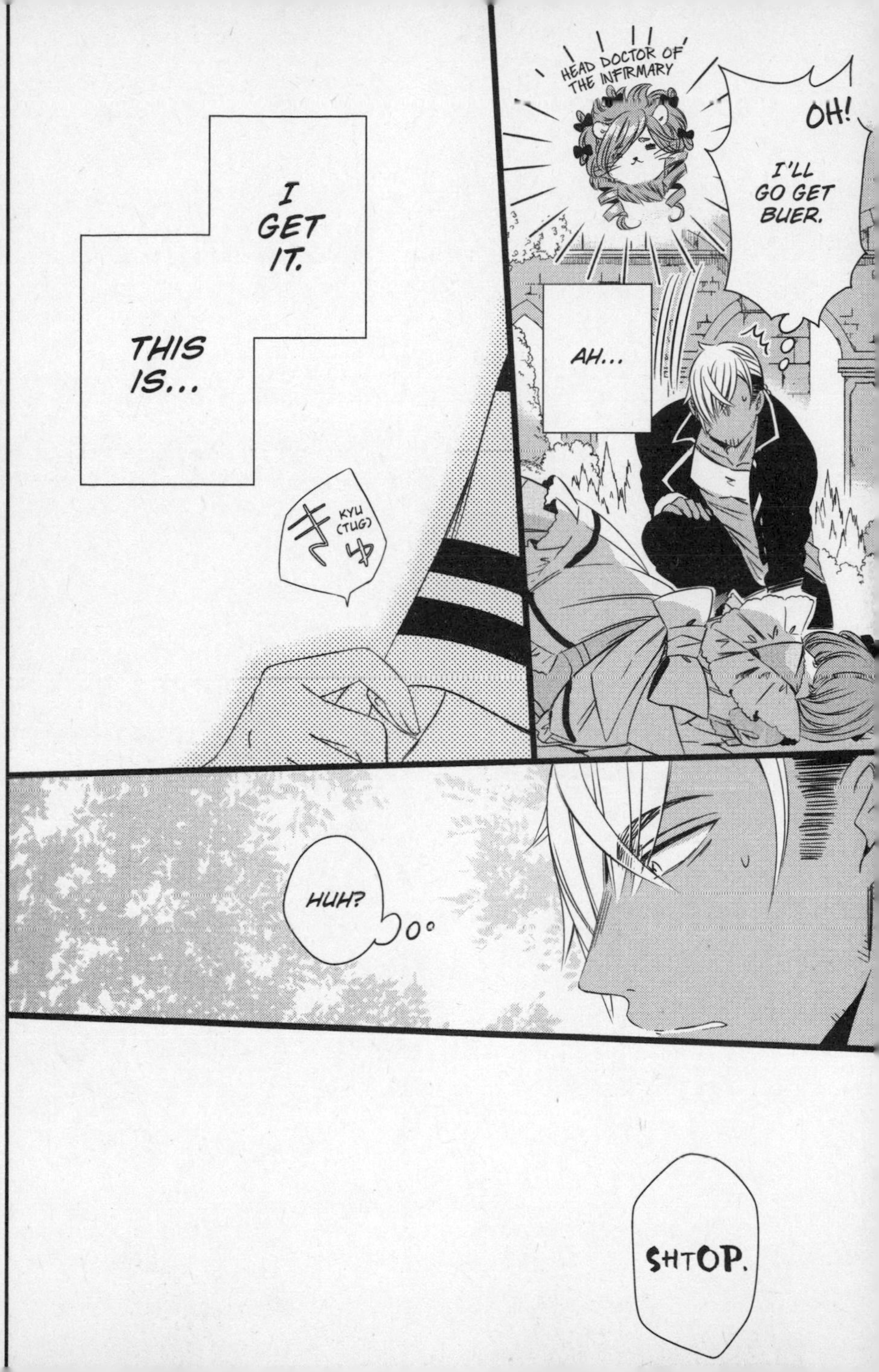
OH!
I'LL GO GET BUER.
HEAD DOCTOR OF THE INFIRMARY
AH...
I GET IT.
THIS IS...
きゅ KYU (TUG)
HUH?
SHTOP.

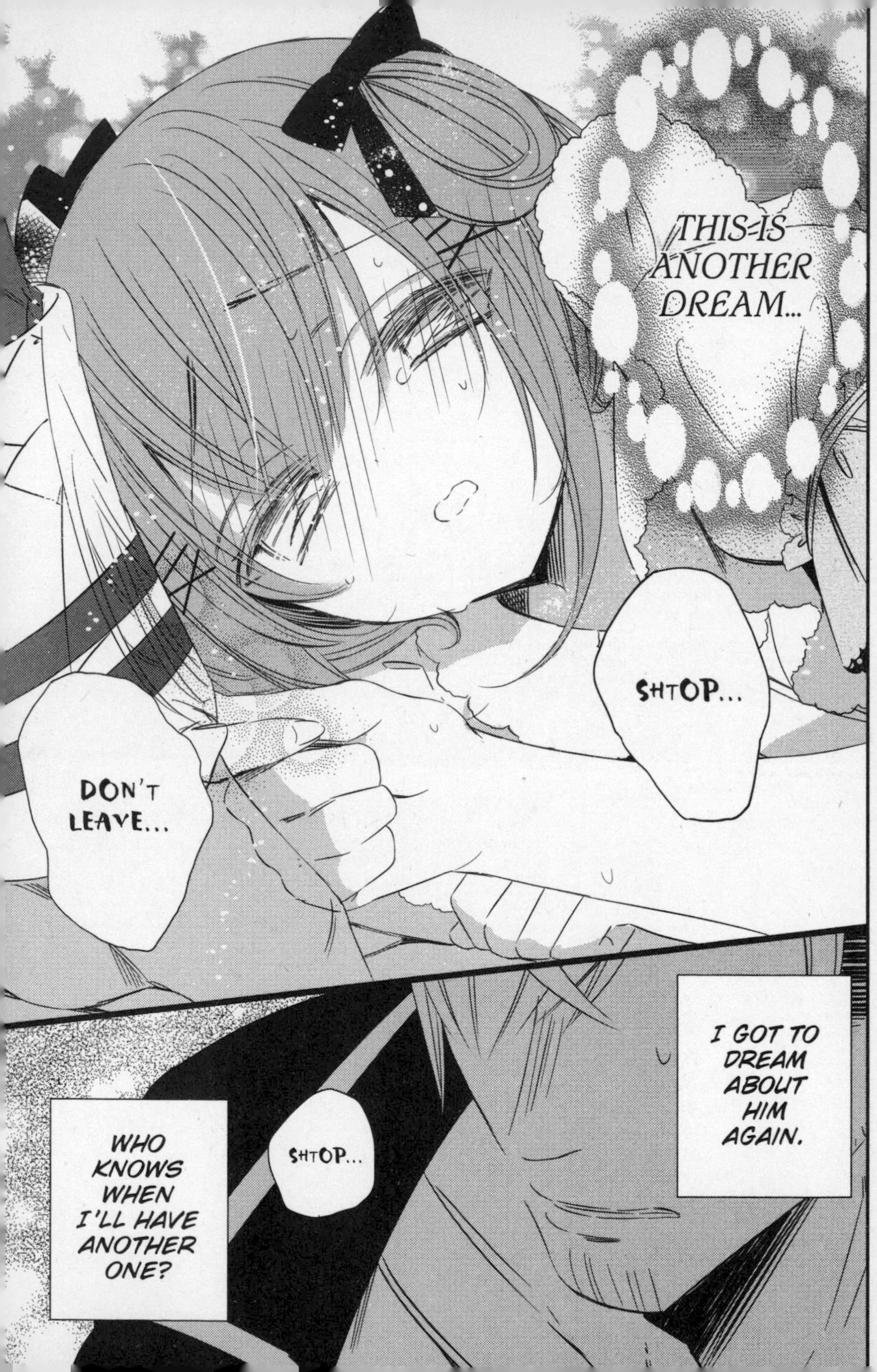
THIS IS ANOTHER DREAM...
SHTOP...
DON'T LEAVE...
I GOT TO DREAM ABOUT HIM AGAIN.
SHTOP...
WHO KNOWS WHEN I'LL HAVE ANOTHER ONE?

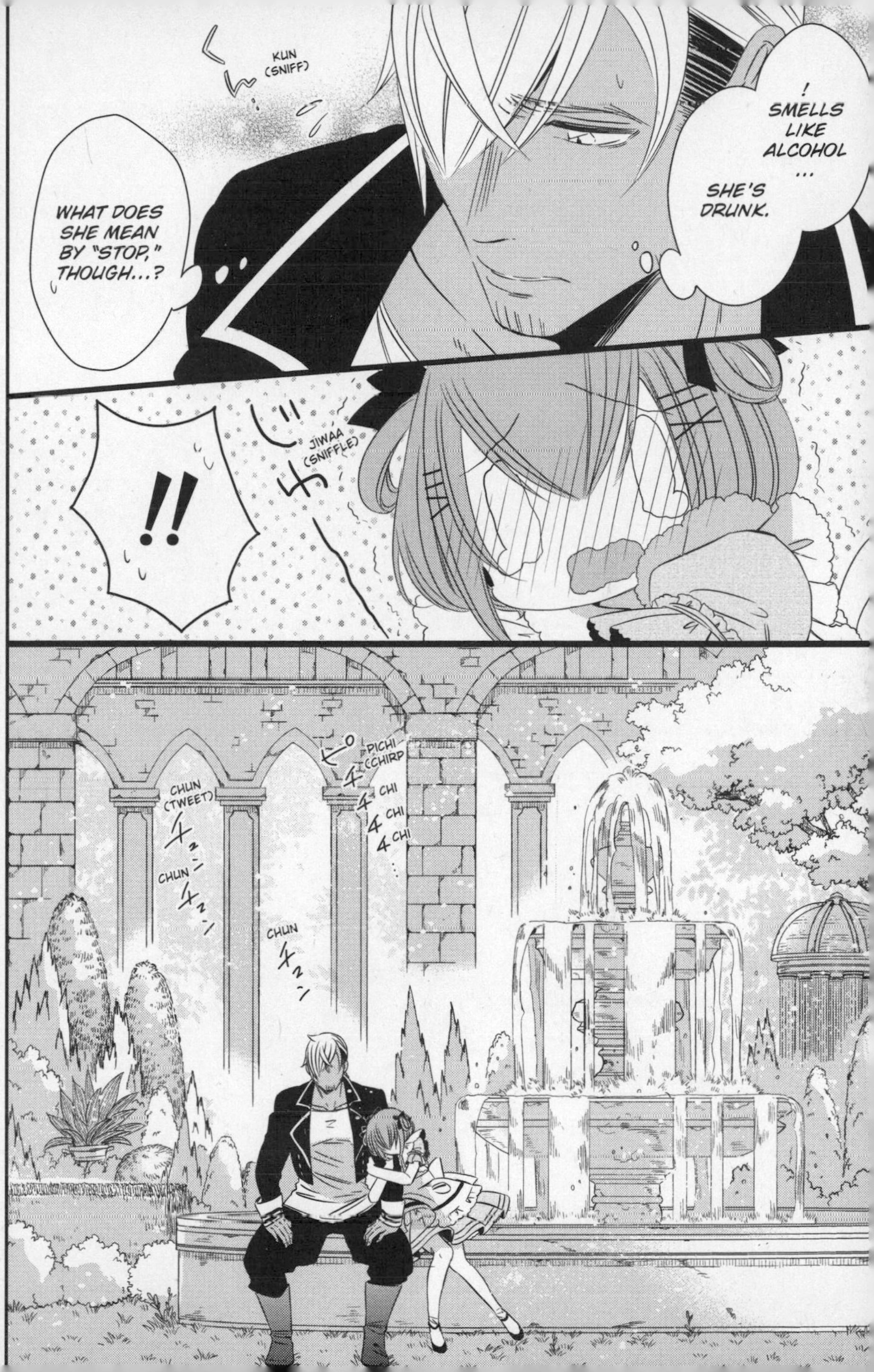

! SMELLS LIKE ALCOHOL ... SHE'S DRUNK.
KUN (SNIFF)
WHAT DOES SHE MEAN BY "STOP," THOUGH...?
JIWAA (SNIFFLE)
!!
PICHI (CHIRP)
CHI
CHI
CHI
CHUN (TWEET)
CHUN
CHUN

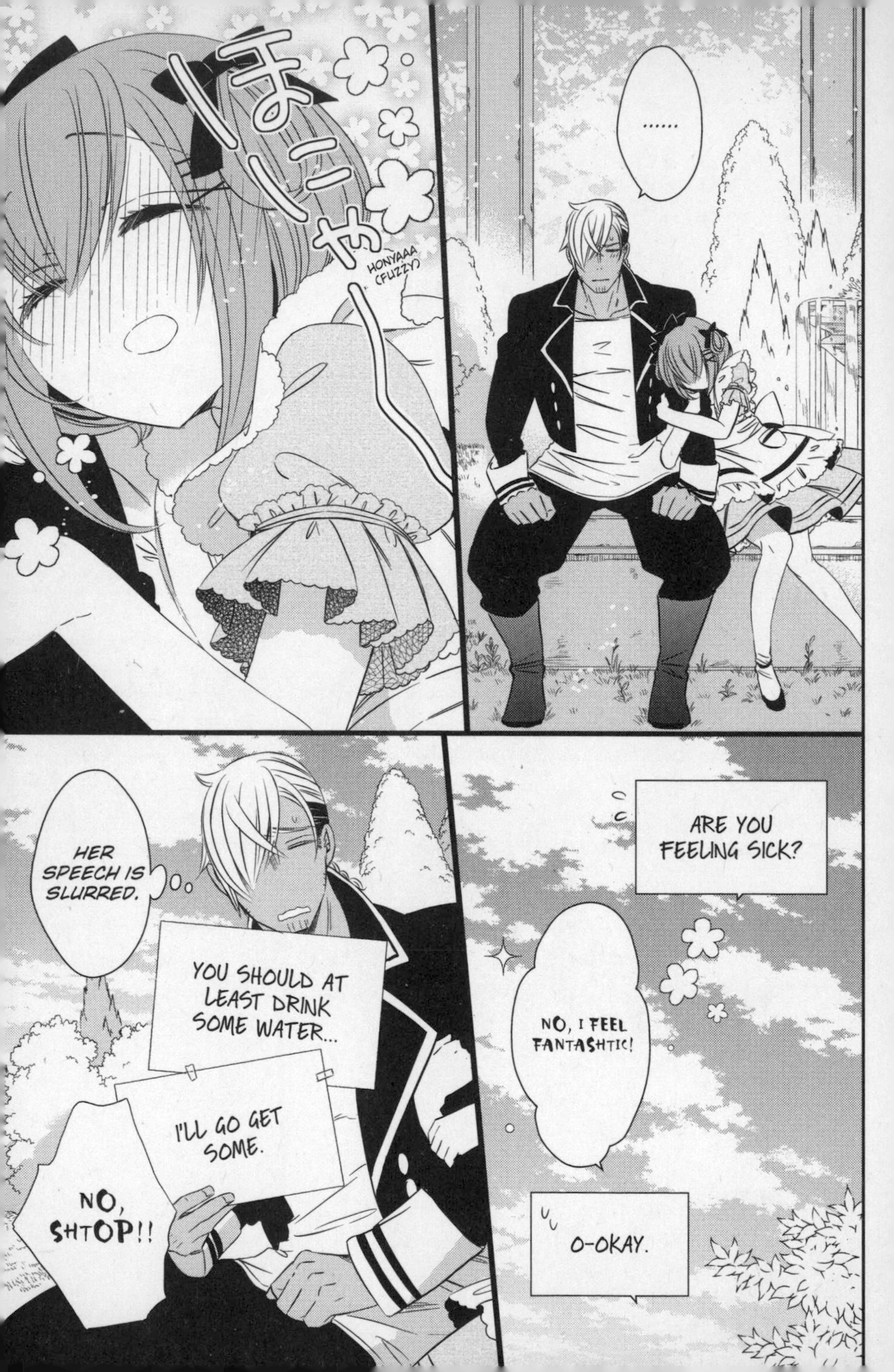
......
ほにゃ
HONYAAA (FUZZY)
ARE YOU FEELING SICK?
NO, I FEEL FANTASHTIC!
O-OKAY.
HER SPEECH IS SLURRED.
YOU SHOULD AT LEAST DRINK SOME WATER...
I'LL GO GET SOME.
NO, SHTOP!!

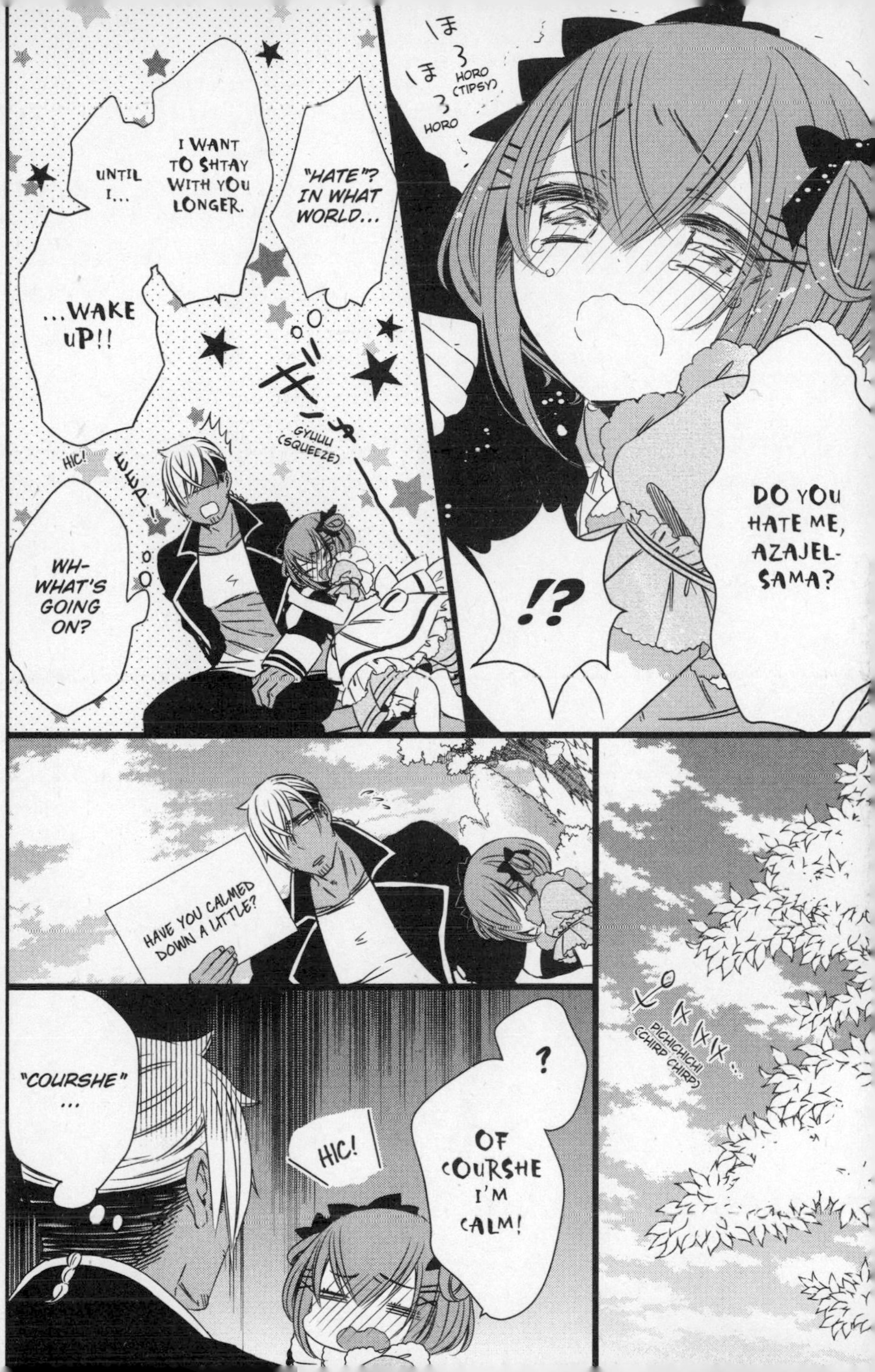
ほろ
HORO (TIPSY)
ほろ
HORO
DO YOU HATE ME, AZAJEL-SAMA?
!?
"HATE"? IN WHAT WORLD...
I WANT TO SHTAY WITH YOU LONGER.
UNTIL I...
...WAKE UP!!
GYUUU (SQUEEZE)
EEP!!
HIC!
WH-WHAT'S GOING ON?
PICHICHICHI (CHIRP CHIRP)
HAVE YOU CALMED DOWN A LITTLE?
?
OF COURSHE I'M CALM!
HIC!
"COURSHE"...

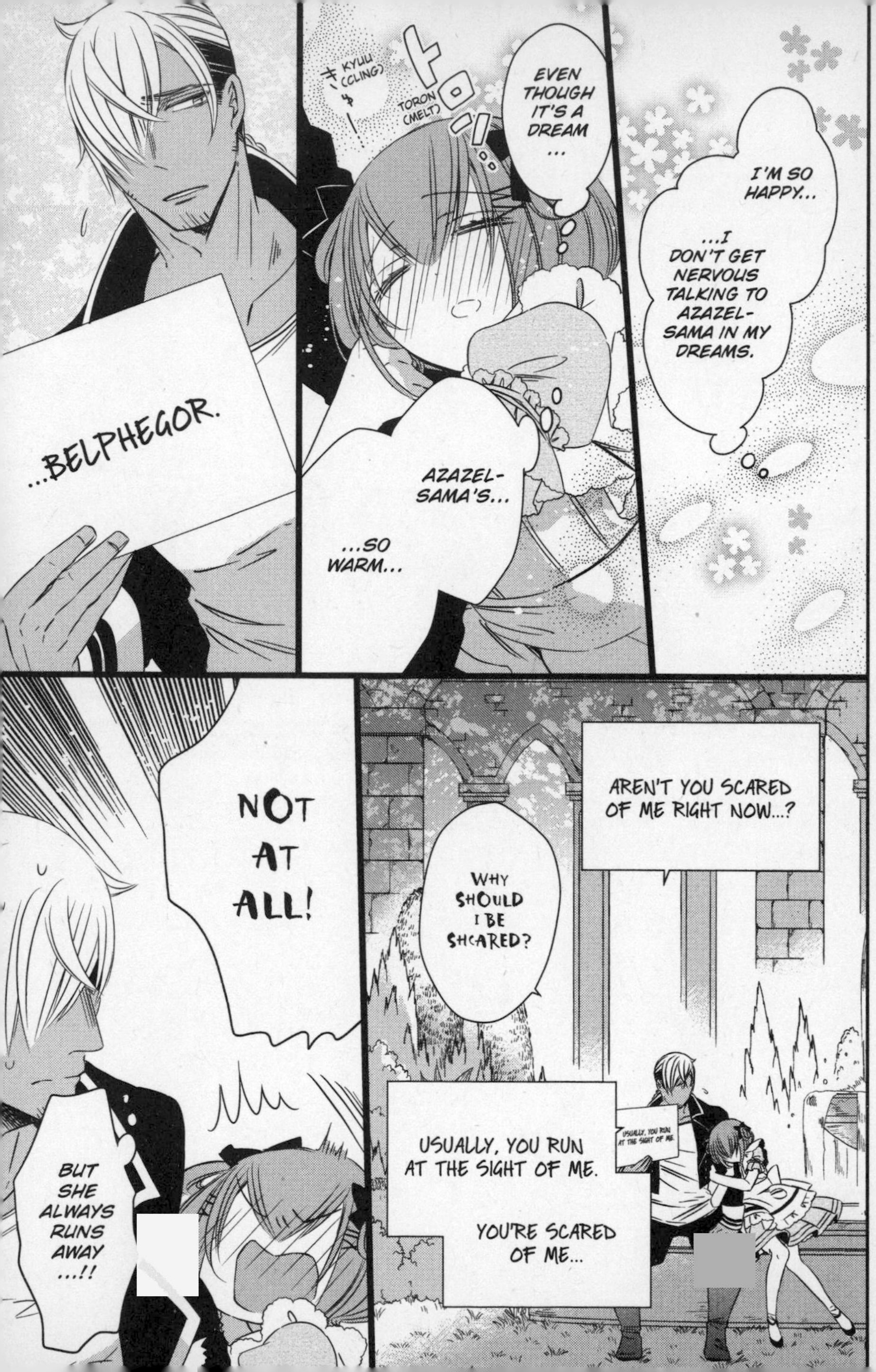
I'M SO HAPPY...
...I DON'T GET NERVOUS TALKING TO AZAZEL-SAMA IN MY DREAMS.
EVEN THOUGH IT'S A DREAM ...
KYUU (CLING)
TORON (MELT)
AZAZEL-SAMA'S...
...SO WARM...
...BELPHEGOR.
AREN'T YOU SCARED OF ME RIGHT NOW...?
WHY SHOULD I BE SHCARED?
USUALLY, YOU RUN AT THE SIGHT OF ME.
YOU'RE SCARED OF ME...
USUALLY, YOU RUN AT THE SIGHT OF ME.
NOT AT ALL!
BUT SHE ALWAYS RUNS AWAY ...!!

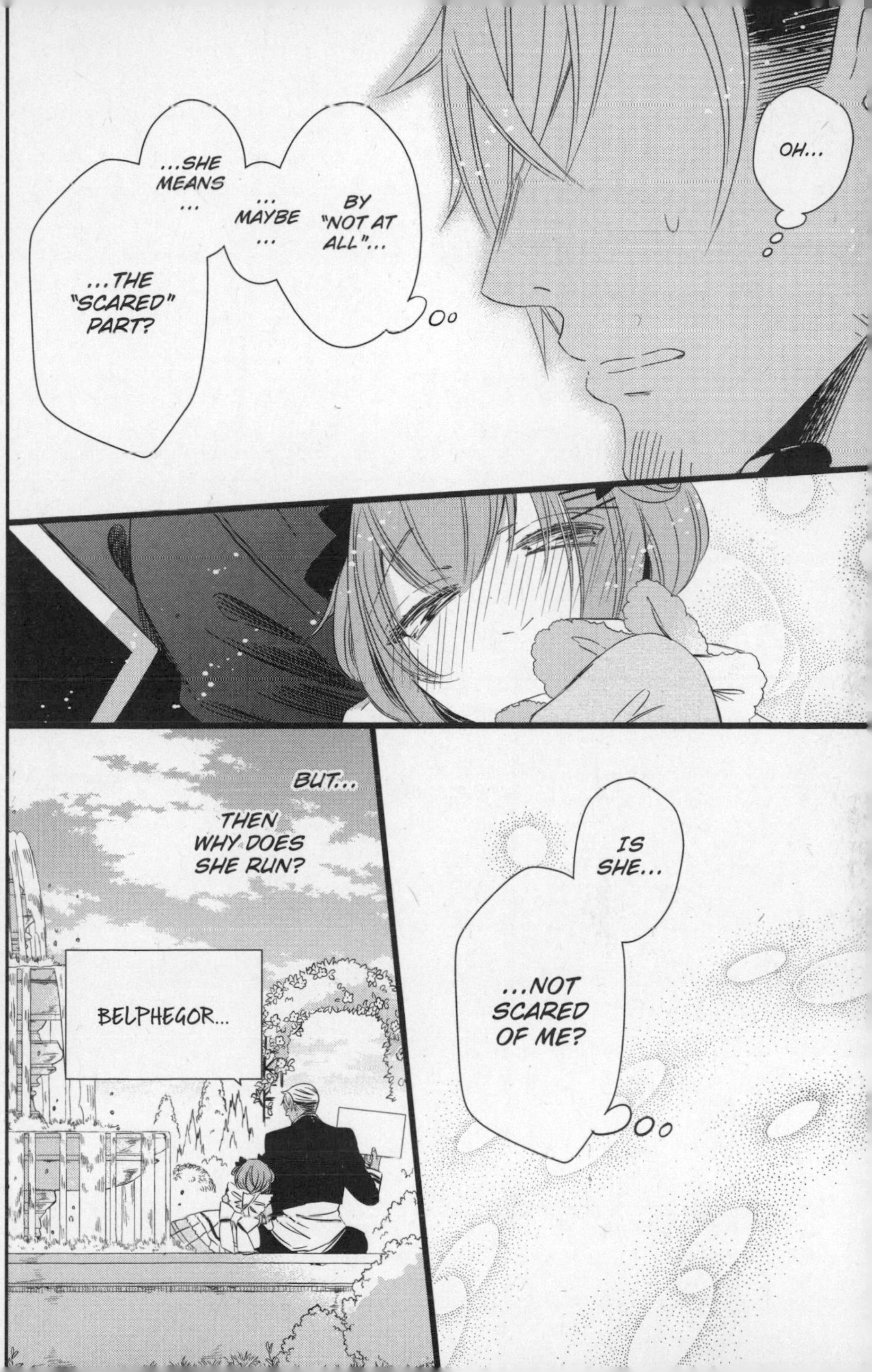
OH...
BY "NOT AT ALL"...
...MAYBE...
...SHE MEANS...
...THE "SCARED" PART?
IS SHE...
...NOT SCARED OF ME?
BUT...
THEN WHY DOES SHE RUN?
BELPHEGOR...

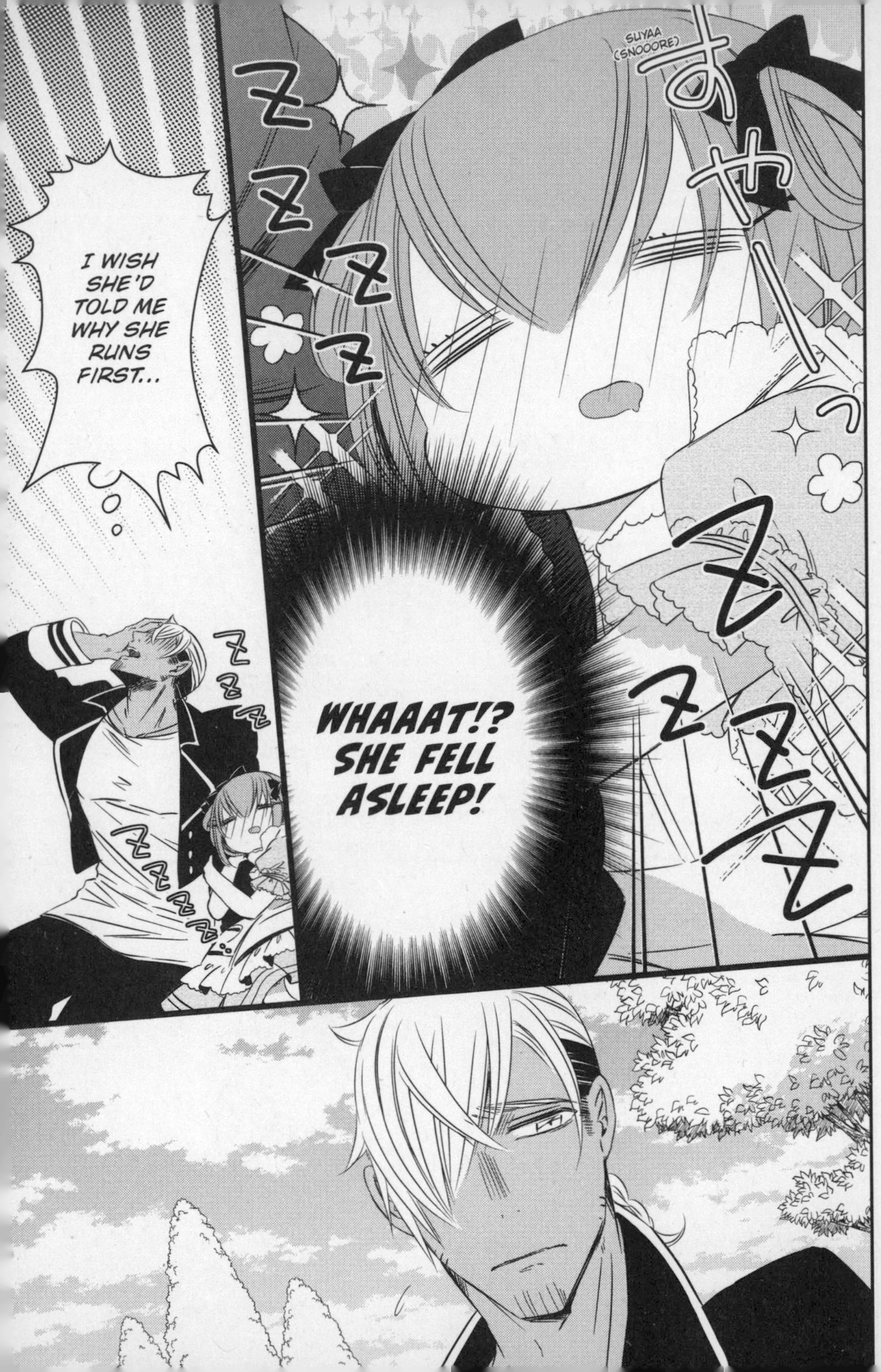
SUYAA (SNOOORE)
WHAAAT!? SHE FELL ASLEEP!
I WISH SHE'D TOLD ME WHY SHE RUNS FIRST...

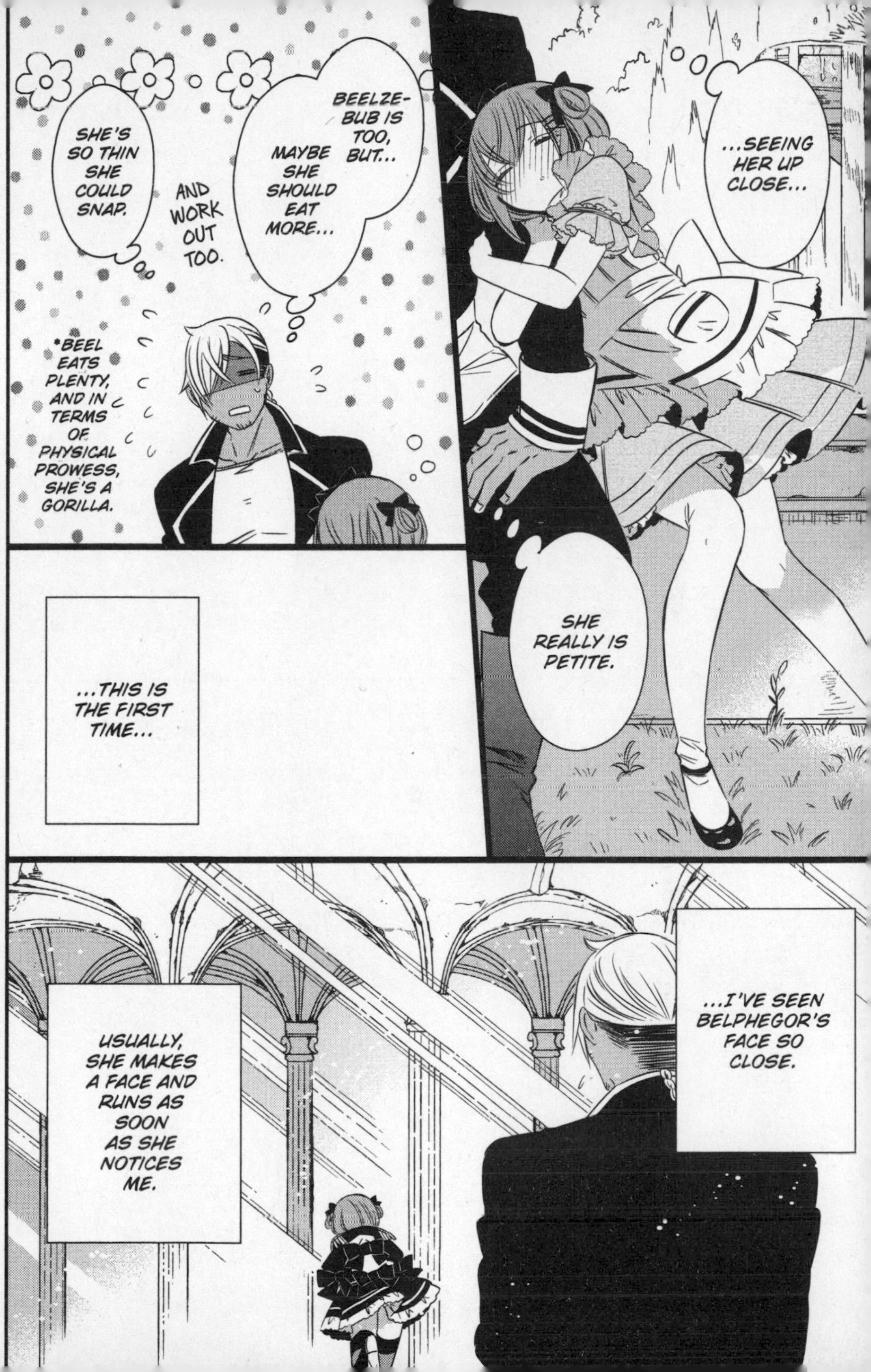
...SEEING HER UP CLOSE...
SHE REALLY IS PETITE.
BEELZE-BUB IS TOO, BUT...
MAYBE SHE SHOULD EAT MORE...
AND WORK OUT TOO.
SHE'S SO THIN SHE COULD SNAP.
*BEEL EATS PLENTY, AND IN TERMS OF PHYSICAL PROWESS, SHE'S A GORILLA.
...THIS IS THE FIRST TIME...
...I'VE SEEN BELPHEGOR'S FACE SO CLOSE.
USUALLY, SHE MAKES A FACE AND RUNS AS SOON AS SHE NOTICES ME.

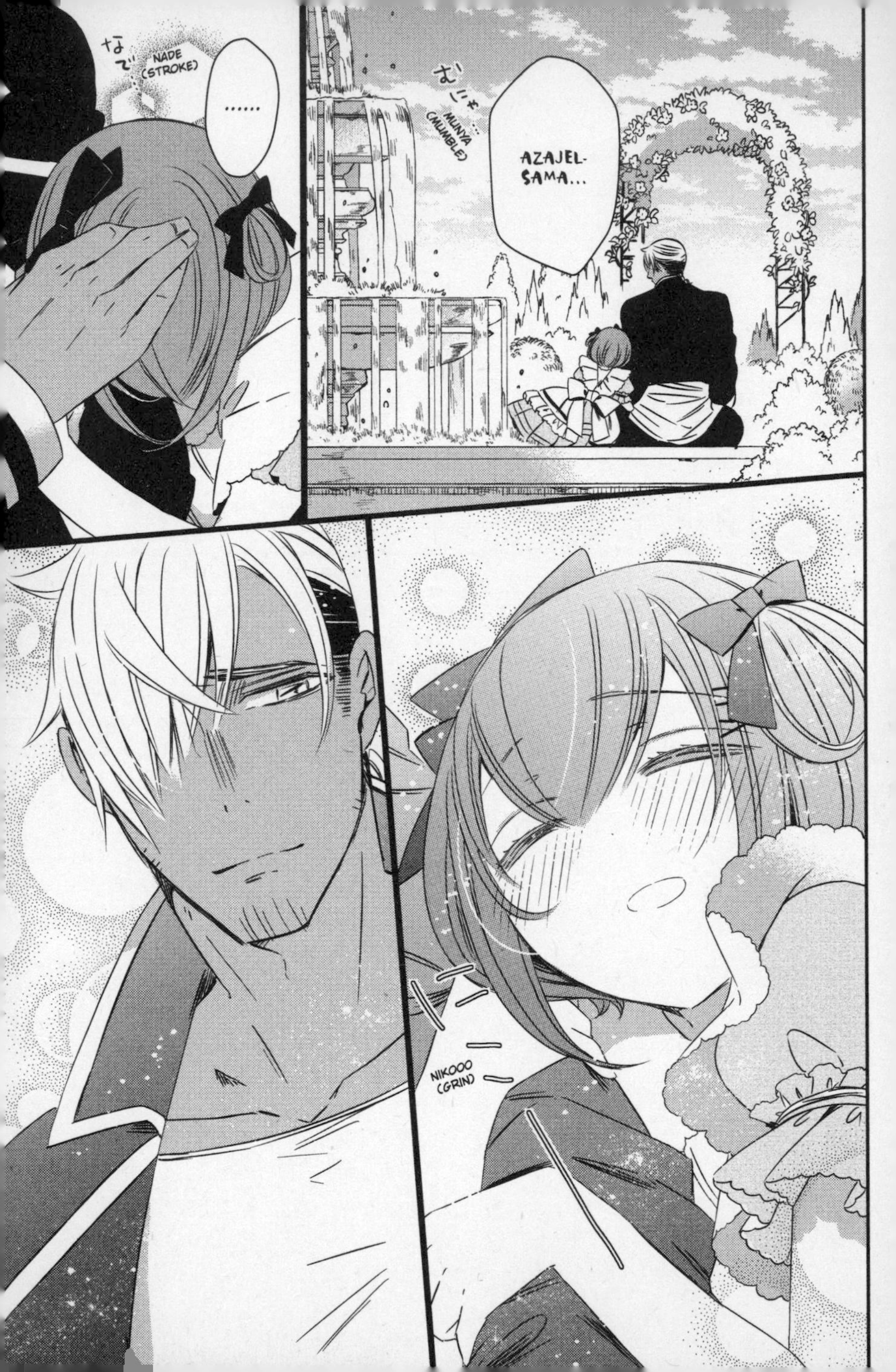
AZAJEL-SAMA...
むにゃ…
MUNYA (MUMBLE)
......
なで…
NADE (STROKE)
NIKOOO (GRIN)

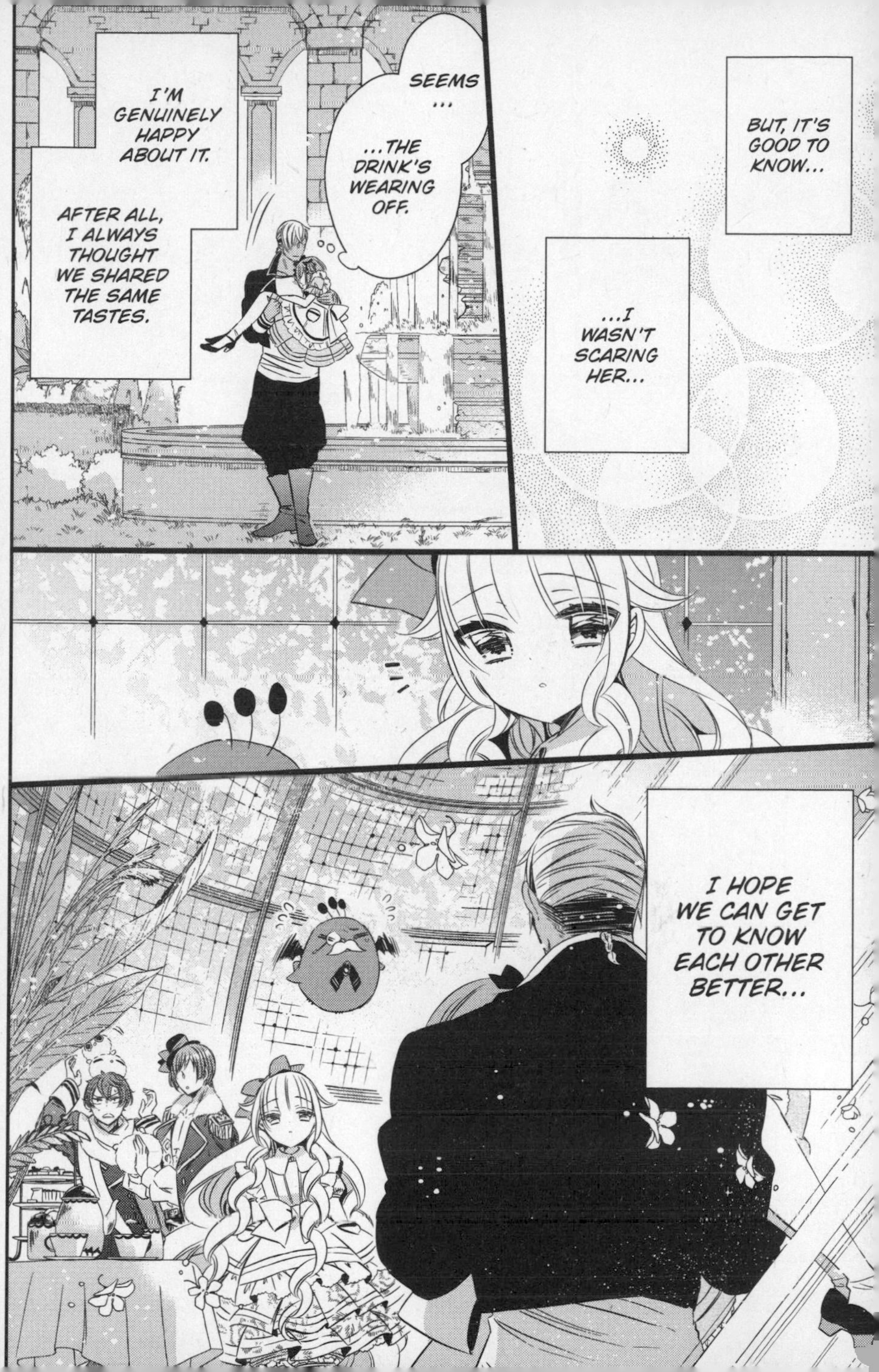
BUT, IT'S GOOD TO KNOW...
...I WASN'T SCARING HER...
SEEMS...
...THE DRINK'S WEARING OFF.
I'M GENUINELY HAPPY ABOUT IT.
AFTER ALL, I ALWAYS THOUGHT WE SHARED THE SAME TASTES.
I HOPE WE CAN GET TO KNOW EACH OTHER BETTER...

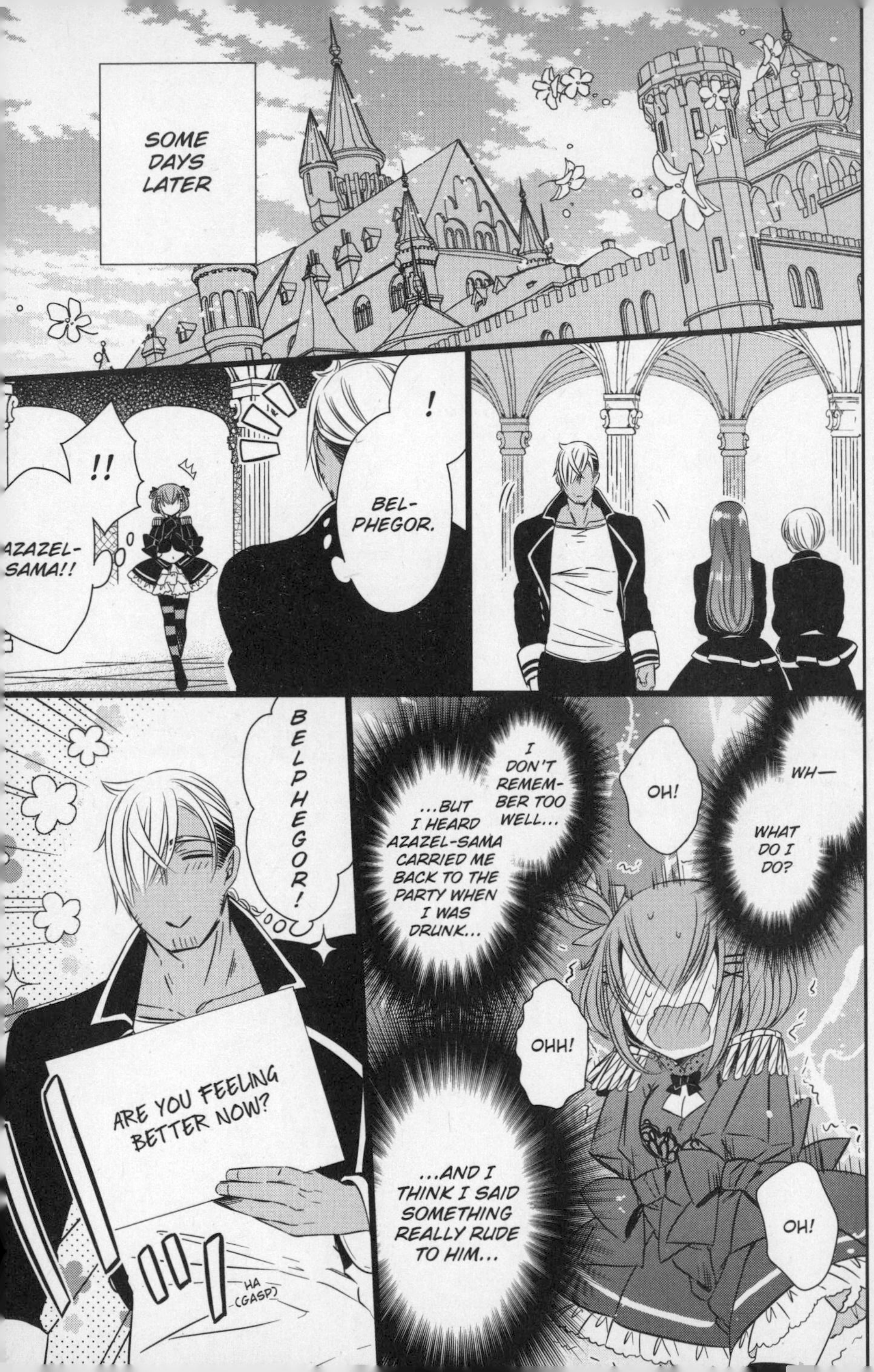
SOME DAYS LATER
!
BEL-PHEGOR.
!!
AZAZEL-SAMA!!
WH—
WHAT DO I DO?
OH!
I DON'T REMEMBER TOO WELL...
...BUT I HEARD AZAZEL-SAMA CARRIED ME BACK TO THE PARTY WHEN I WAS DRUNK...
OHH!
...AND I THINK I SAID SOMETHING REALLY RUDE TO HIM...
OH!
BELPHEGOR!
ARE YOU FEELING BETTER NOW?
HA (GASP)

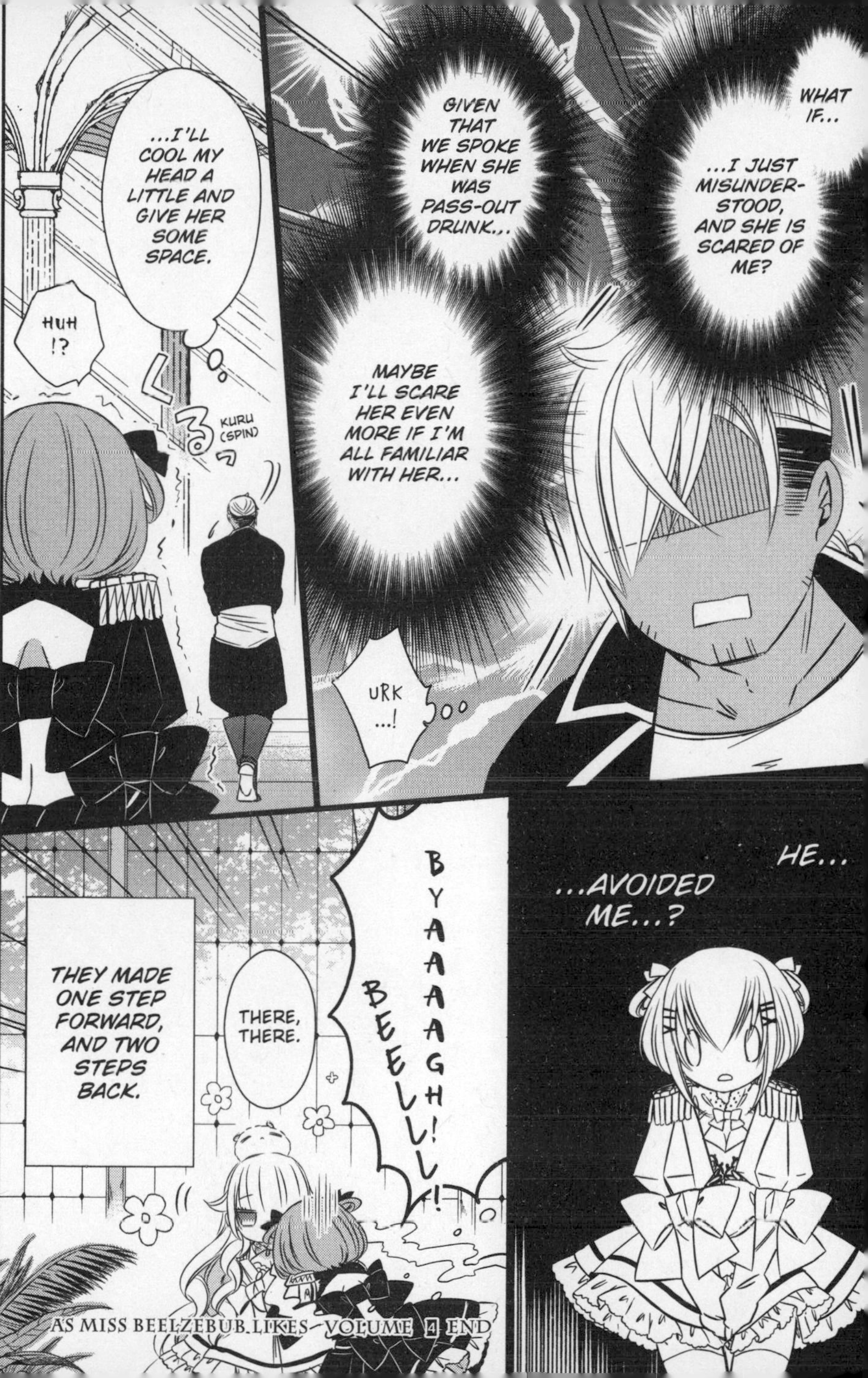
WHAT IF...
...I JUST MISUNDERSTOOD, AND SHE IS SCARED OF ME?
GIVEN THAT WE SPOKE WHEN SHE WAS PASS-OUT DRUNK...
MAYBE I'LL SCARE HER EVEN MORE IF I'M ALL FAMILIAR WITH HER...
URK ...!
...I'LL COOL MY HEAD A LITTLE AND GIVE HER SOME SPACE.
KURU (SPIN)
HUH !?
HE...
...AVOIDED ME...?
BYAAAAAGH!
BEELLLL!
THERE, THERE.
THEY MADE ONE STEP FORWARD, AND TWO STEPS BACK.
AS MISS BEELZEBUB LIKES VOLUME 4 END

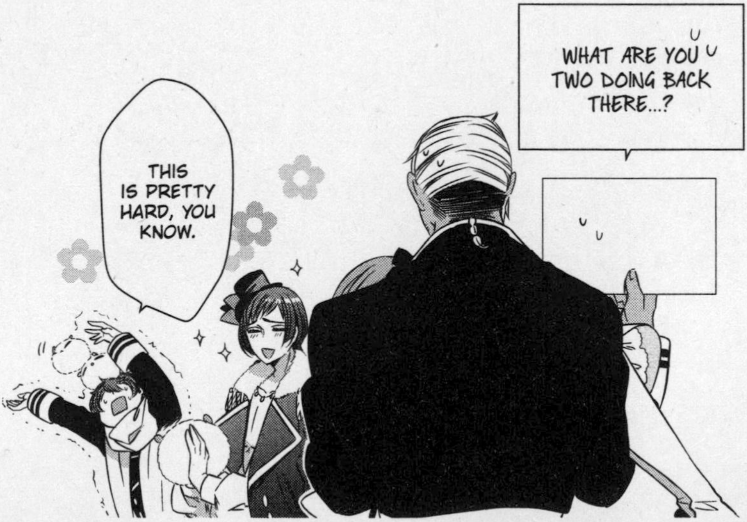
WHAT ARE YOU TWO DOING BACK THERE...?
THIS IS PRETTY HARD, YOU KNOW.

As Miss Beelzebub Likes

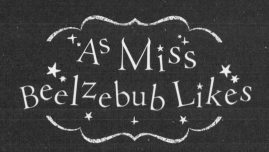

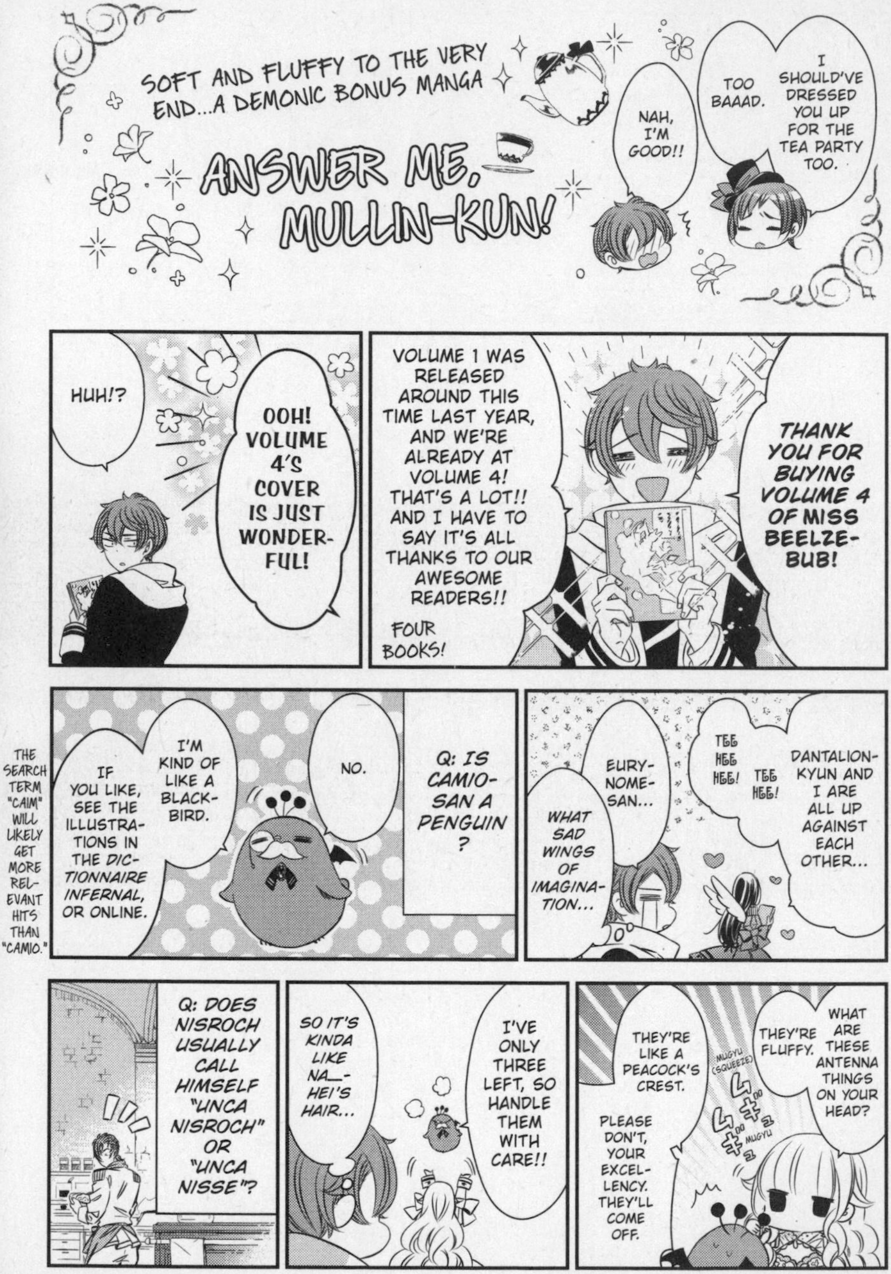
SOFT AND FLUFFY TO THE VERY END...A DEMONIC BONUS MANGA
ANSWER ME, MULLIN-KUN!
I SHOULD'VE DRESSED YOU UP FOR THE TEA PARTY TOO.
TOO BAAAD.
NAH, I'M GOOD!!
THANK YOU FOR BUYING VOLUME 4 OF MISS BEELZEBUB!
VOLUME 1 WAS RELEASED AROUND THIS TIME LAST YEAR, AND WE'RE ALREADY AT VOLUME 4! THAT'S A LOT!! AND I HAVE TO SAY IT'S ALL THANKS TO OUR AWESOME READERS!!
FOUR BOOKS!
OOH! VOLUME 4'S COVER IS JUST WONDERFUL!
HUH!?
DANTALION-KYUN AND I ARE ALL UP AGAINST EACH OTHER...
TEE HEE HEE!
TEE HEE!
EURYNOME-SAN...
WHAT SAD WINGS OF IMAGINATION...
Q: IS CAMIO-SAN A PENGUIN?
NO.
I'M KIND OF LIKE A BLACKBIRD.
IF YOU LIKE, SEE THE ILLUSTRATIONS IN THE *DICTIONNAIRE INFERNAL*, OR ONLINE.
THE SEARCH TERM "CAIM" WILL LIKELY GET MORE RELEVANT HITS THAN "CAMIO."
WHAT ARE THESE ANTENNA THINGS ON YOUR HEAD?
THEY'RE FLUFFY.
MUGYU (SQUEEZE)
MUGYU
THEY'RE LIKE A PEACOCK'S CREST.
PLEASE DON'T, YOUR EXCELLENCY. THEY'LL COME OFF.
I'VE ONLY THREE LEFT, SO HANDLE THEM WITH CARE!!
SO IT'S KINDA LIKE NA_-HEI'S HAIR...
Q: DOES NISROCH USUALLY CALL HIMSELF "UNCA NISROCH" OR "UNCA NISSE"?

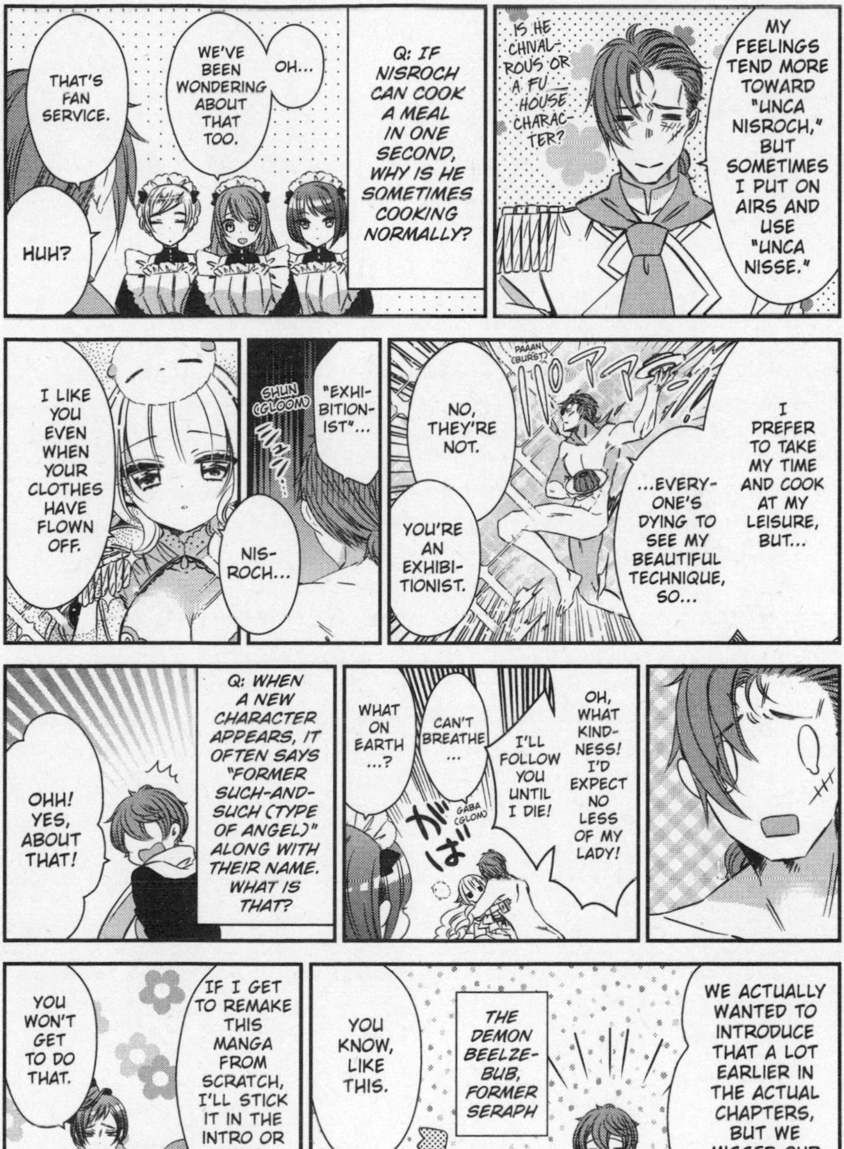
MY FEELINGS TEND MORE TOWARD "UNCA NISROCH," BUT SOMETIMES I PUT ON AIRS AND USE "UNCA NISSE."
IS HE CHIVALROUS OR A FU_ HOUSE CHARACTER?
Q: IF NISROCH CAN COOK A MEAL IN ONE SECOND, WHY IS HE SOMETIMES COOKING NORMALLY?
OH...
WE'VE BEEN WONDERING ABOUT THAT TOO.
THAT'S FAN SERVICE.
HUH?
I PREFER TO TAKE MY TIME AND COOK AT MY LEISURE, BUT...
...EVERYONE'S DYING TO SEE MY BEAUTIFUL TECHNIQUE, SO...
PAAAN (BURST)
NO, THEY'RE NOT.
YOU'RE AN EXHIBITIONIST.
"EXHIBITIONIST"...
SHUN (GLOOM)
NISROCH...
I LIKE YOU EVEN WHEN YOUR CLOTHES HAVE FLOWN OFF.
OH, WHAT KINDNESS! I'D EXPECT NO LESS OF MY LADY!
I'LL FOLLOW YOU UNTIL I DIE!
CAN'T BREATHE...
WHAT ON EARTH...?
GABA (GLOM)
Q: WHEN A NEW CHARACTER APPEARS, IT OFTEN SAYS "FORMER SUCH-AND-SUCH (TYPE OF ANGEL)" ALONG WITH THEIR NAME. WHAT IS THAT?
OHH! YES, ABOUT THAT!
WE ACTUALLY WANTED TO INTRODUCE THAT A LOT EARLIER IN THE ACTUAL CHAPTERS, BUT WE MISSED OUR CHANCE, SO LET ME EXPLAIN IT HERE!
THE DEMON BEELZEBUB, FORMER SERAPH
YOU KNOW, LIKE THIS.
IF I GET TO REMAKE THIS MANGA FROM SCRATCH, I'LL STICK IT IN THE INTRO OR SOMETHING.
YOU WON'T GET TO DO THAT.
MATOBA

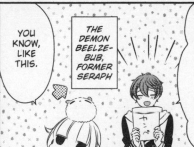

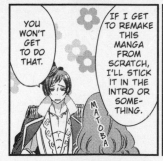

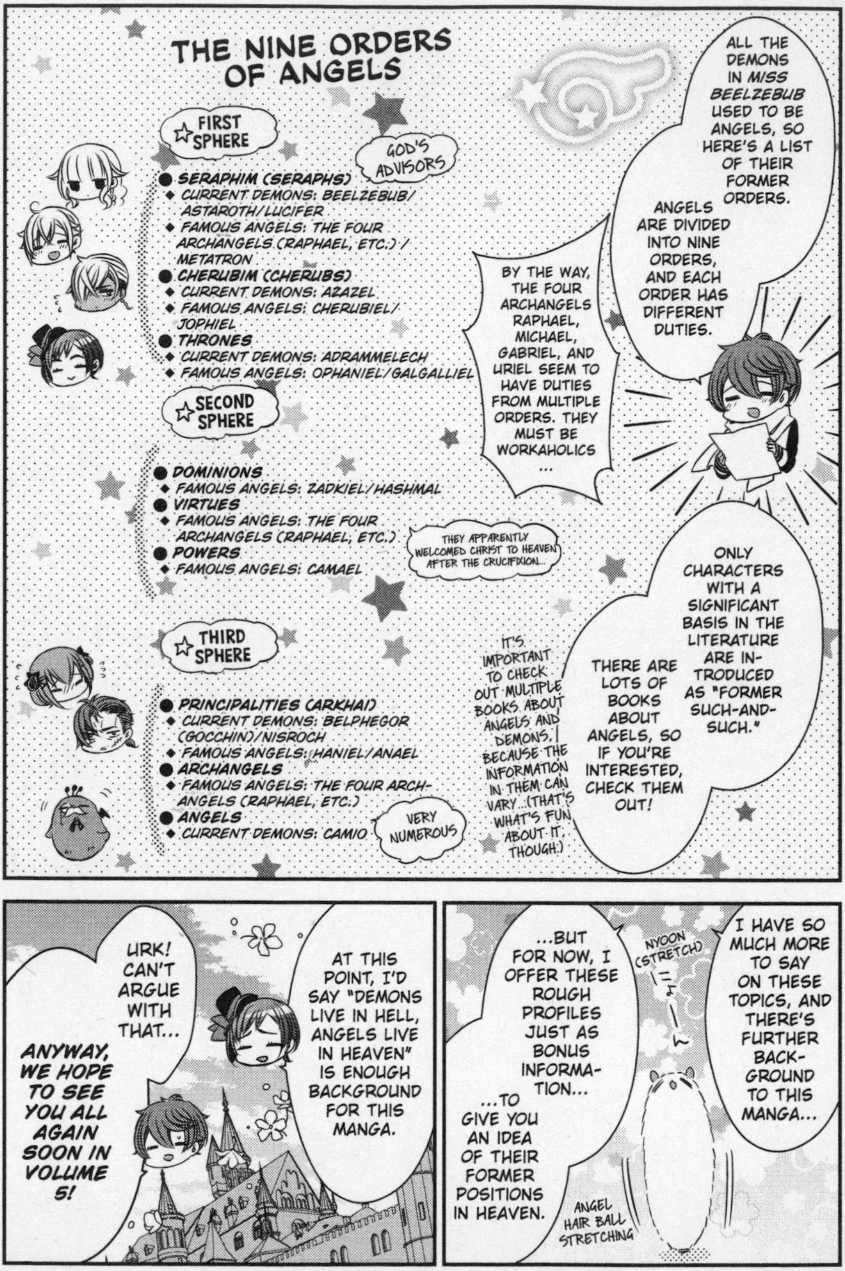

THE NINE ORDERS OF ANGELS
ALL THE DEMONS IN MISS BEELZEBUB USED TO BE ANGELS, SO HERE'S A LIST OF THEIR FORMER ORDERS.
ANGELS ARE DIVIDED INTO NINE ORDERS, AND EACH ORDER HAS DIFFERENT DUTIES.
BY THE WAY, THE FOUR ARCHANGELS RAPHAEL, MICHAEL, GABRIEL, AND URIEL SEEM TO HAVE DUTIES FROM MULTIPLE ORDERS. THEY MUST BE WORKAHOLICS ...
FIRST SPHERE
GOD'S ADVISORS
SERAPHIM (SERAPHS)
CURRENT DEMONS: BEELZEBUB/ ASTAROTH/LUCIFER
FAMOUS ANGELS: THE FOUR ARCHANGELS (RAPHAEL, ETC.)/ METATRON
CHERUBIM (CHERUBS)
CURRENT DEMONS: AZAZEL
FAMOUS ANGELS: CHERUBIEL/ JOPHIEL
THRONES
CURRENT DEMONS: ADRAMMELECH
FAMOUS ANGELS: OPHANIEL/GALGALLIEL
SECOND SPHERE
DOMINIONS
FAMOUS ANGELS: ZADKIEL/HASHMAL
VIRTUES
FAMOUS ANGELS: THE FOUR ARCHANGELS (RAPHAEL, ETC.)
THEY APPARENTLY WELCOMED CHRIST TO HEAVEN AFTER THE CRUCIFIXION...
POWERS
FAMOUS ANGELS: CAMAEL
THIRD SPHERE
PRINCIPALITIES (ARKHAI)
CURRENT DEMONS: BELPHEGOR (GOCCHIN)/NISROCH
FAMOUS ANGELS: HANIEL/ANAEL
ARCHANGELS
FAMOUS ANGELS: THE FOUR ARCH-ANGELS (RAPHAEL, ETC.)
ANGELS
CURRENT DEMONS: CAMIO
VERY NUMEROUS
ONLY CHARACTERS WITH A SIGNIFICANT BASIS IN THE LITERATURE ARE INTRODUCED AS "FORMER SUCH-AND-SUCH."
THERE ARE LOTS OF BOOKS ABOUT ANGELS, SO IF YOU'RE INTERESTED, CHECK THEM OUT!
IT'S IMPORTANT TO CHECK OUT MULTIPLE BOOKS ABOUT ANGELS AND DEMONS, BECAUSE THE INFORMATION IN THEM CAN VARY... (THAT'S WHAT'S FUN ABOUT IT, THOUGH.)
I HAVE SO MUCH MORE TO SAY ON THESE TOPICS, AND THERE'S FURTHER BACK-GROUND TO THIS MANGA...
NYOON (STRETCH)
...BUT FOR NOW, I OFFER THESE ROUGH PROFILES JUST AS BONUS INFORMA-TION...
...TO GIVE YOU AN IDEA OF THEIR FORMER POSITIONS IN HEAVEN.
ANGEL HAIR BALL STRETCHING
AT THIS POINT, I'D SAY "DEMONS LIVE IN HELL, ANGELS LIVE IN HEAVEN" IS ENOUGH BACKGROUND FOR THIS MANGA.
URK! CAN'T ARGUE WITH THAT...
ANYWAY, WE HOPE TO SEE YOU ALL AGAIN SOON IN VOLUME 5!

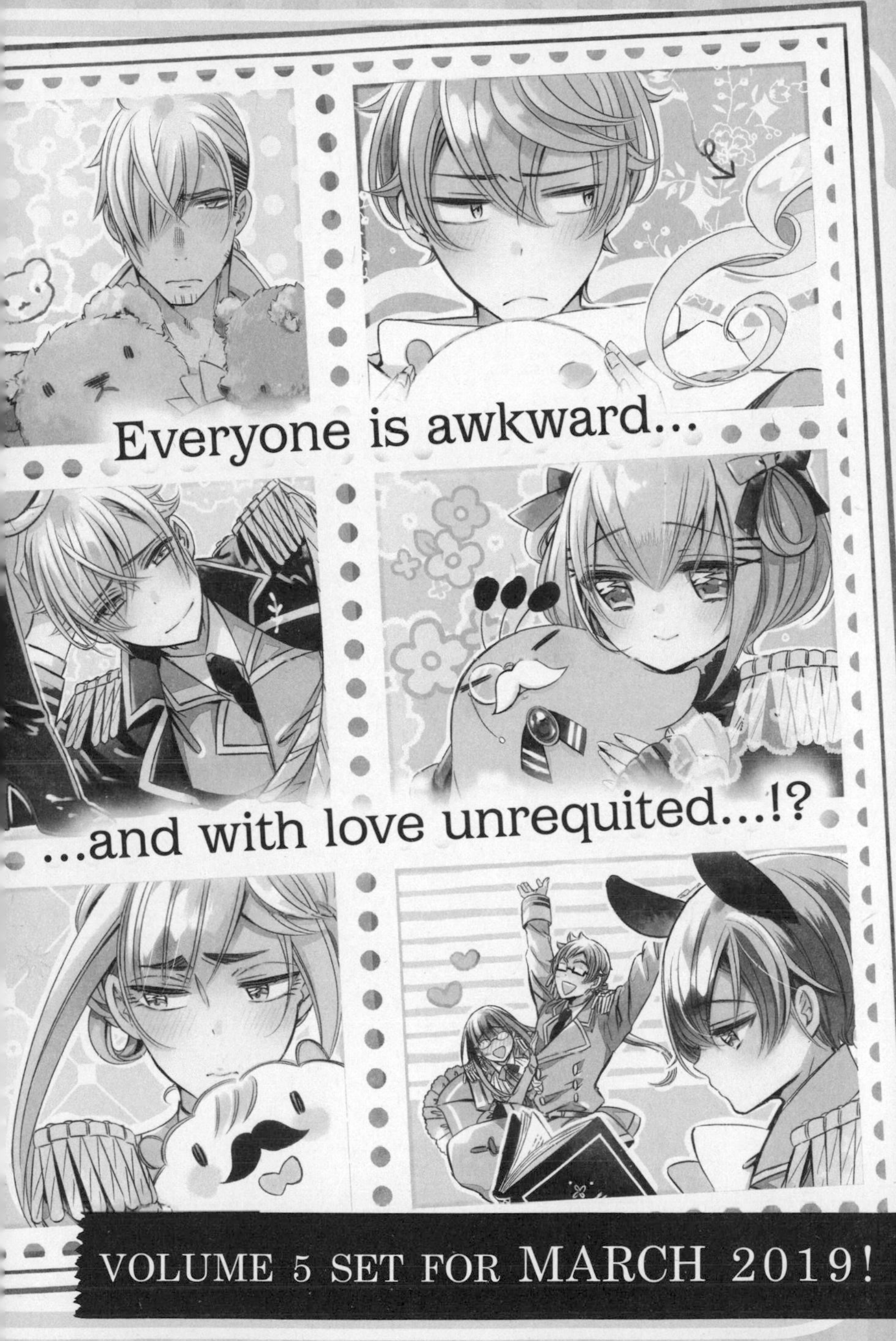
Everyone is awkward...
...and with love unrequited...!?
VOLUME 5 SET FOR MARCH 2019!

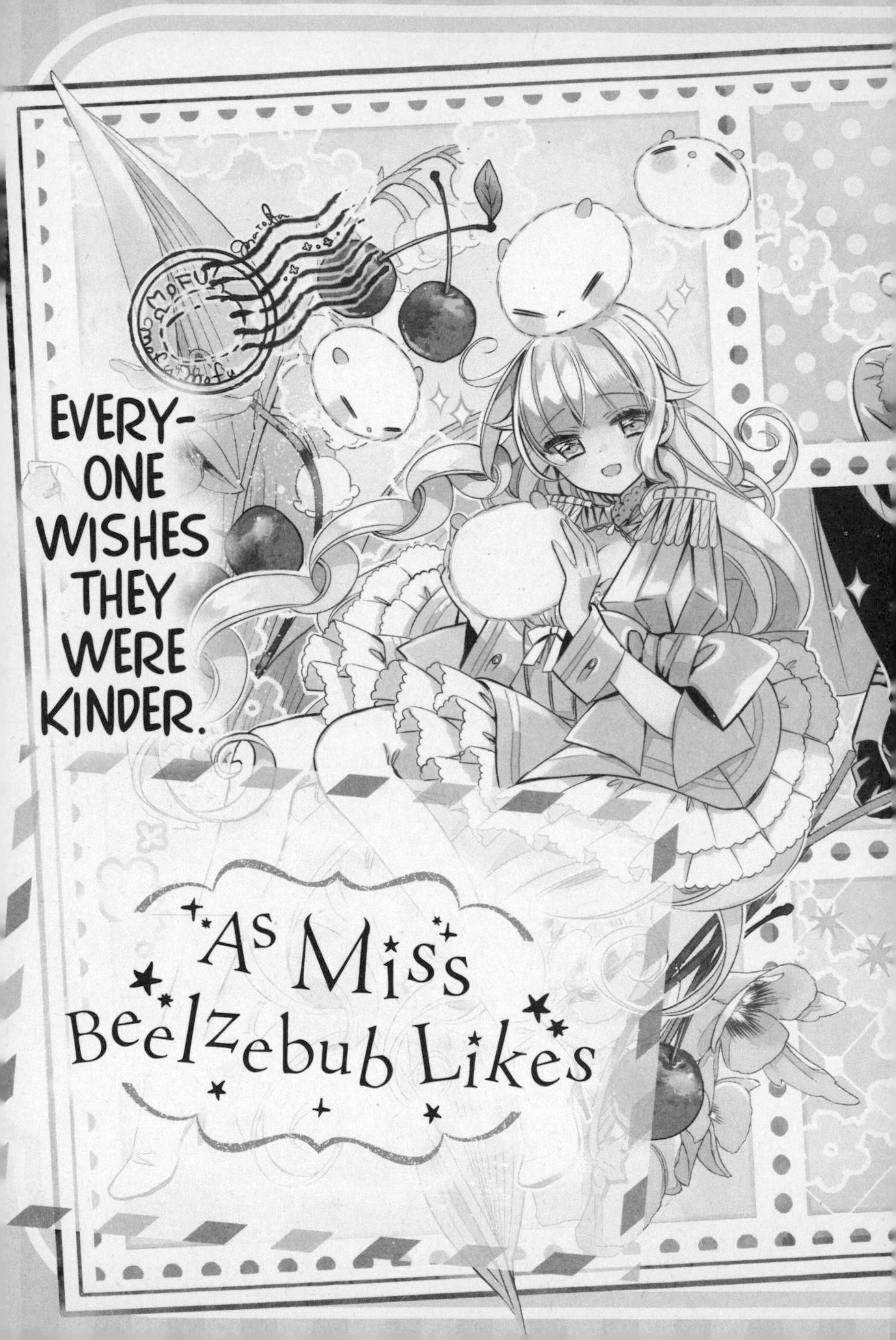
EVERY-ONE WISHES THEY WERE KINDER.
As Miss Beelzebub Likes

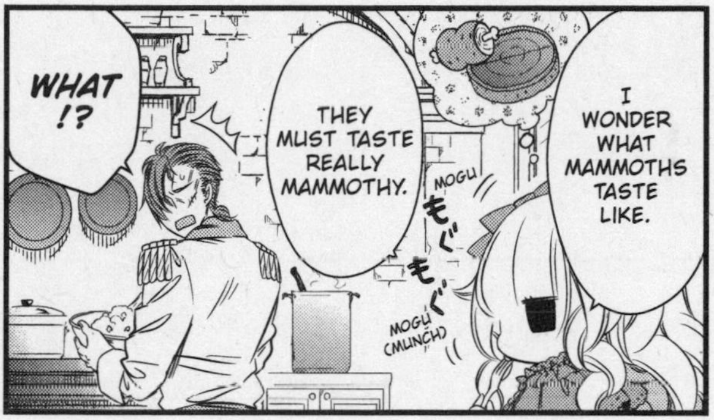
I WONDER WHAT MAMMOTHS TASTE LIKE.
THEY MUST TASTE REALLY MAMMOTHY.
MOGU もぐ
もぐ MOGU (MUNCH)
WHAT!?

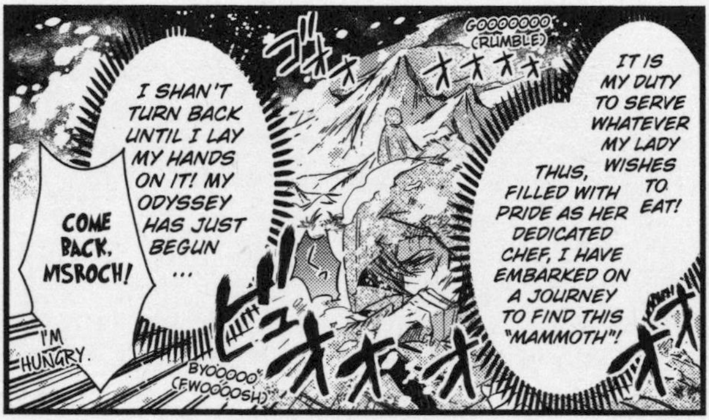
IT IS MY DUTY TO SERVE WHATEVER MY LADY WISHES TO EAT!
THUS, FILLED WITH PRIDE AS HER DEDICATED CHEF, I HAVE EMBARKED ON A JOURNEY TO FIND THIS "MAMMOTH"!
GOOOOOOO (RUMBLE)
I SHAN'T TURN BACK UNTIL I LAY MY HANDS ON IT! MY ODYSSEY HAS JUST BEGUN …
BYOOOOO (FWOOOOSH)
COME BACK, MISROCH!
I'M HUNGRY.

Translation Notes

COMMON HONORIFICS

no honorific: Indicates familiarity or closeness; if used without permission or reason, addressing someone in this manner would constitute an insult.

san: The Japanese equivalent of Mr./Mrs./Miss. If a situation calls for politeness, this is the fail-safe honorific.

-sama: Conveys great respect; may also indicate that the social status of the speaker is lower than that of the addressee.

-shi: An impersonal honorific used in formal speech or writing, e.g. legal documents.

-dono: Roughly equivalent to "master" or "milord."

-kun: Used most often when referring to boys, this indicates affection or familiarity. Occasionally used by older men among their peers, but it may also be used by anyone referring to a person of lower standing.

-chan: An affectionate honorific indicating familiarity used mostly in reference to girls; also used in reference to cute persons or animals of either gender.

-tan: A cutesy version of *-chan*.

-(o)nii/(o)nee: Meaning "big brother"/ "big sister," it can also refer to those older but relatively close in age to the speaker. It is typically followed by *-san*, *-chan*, or *-sama*.

-senpai: An honorific for one's senior classmate, colleague, etc., although not as senior or respected as a *sensei* (teacher).

PAGE 7

Big G (Jaian in the Japanese version) is a character from the manga *Doraemon* who always bullies others to get his way.

PAGE 13

Ginza is an expensive entertainment and shopping district of Tokyo.

Yakitori is grilled chicken on a skewer seasoned with either salt or sauce.

Hand salons in Japan don't just do your nails. They depilate, remove spots, etc. to treat your whole hand.

PAGE 14

Kanda is a district of Tokyo famous for its secondhand bookstores.

"End-of-century, mohawked hidebu-abeshi" is a reference to the types of common thugs that appear in the manga *First of the North Star*. When the hero uses his martial arts to literally explode their bodies, these mohawked goons will commonly make meaningless exclamations of horror such as "Hidebu!" and "Abeshi!"

Acheron is one of the five rivers of the Greek underworld.

Tonkotsu ramen is a type of ramen (egg noodle dish) with pork bone broth.

PAGE 19

Soba is Japanese buckwheat noodles.

Shinshuu is an old province of Japan that is now Nagano Prefecture, which is famous for its *soba*.

PAGE 27

Manjuu is a traditional Japanese confection made of flour, rice powder, and buckwheat, usually with an *anko* (red bean paste) filling.

PAGE 28

The First Demon Beelzebub is a reference to the 1974 manga *Hajime Ningen Gyatoruzu*. The fake logo even resembles the *Gyatoruzu* logo.

PAGE 33

Ajikko is a reference to the cooking manga *Mister Ajikko*.

PAGE 38

Oden is a Japanese one-pot dish consisting of soy-flavored broth and various ingredients such as daikon radish, konjac, fish cakes, and boiled eggs.

PAGE 40
Ai___tsu! is a reference to *Aikatsu!*, an idol-themed arcade game that uses trading cards.

PAGE 43
Coco _chi is a reference to CoCo ICHIBANYA, a Japanese curry restaurant chain.

Chilled tofu, or *hiyayakko*, is a Japanese dish consisting of tofu served chilled with soy sauce and toppings such as chopped green onion, ginger, and dried bonito flakes.

PAGE 53
Shiitake is a kind of mushroom native to East Asia.

PAGE 54
In Japan, children are taught that there's a **proper order** to eating, where you cycle through three elements of the meal so that you get even amounts of every food. It's called "triangle eating" in Japan due to the fact that you eat in a three-part pattern.

PAGE 67
Daifuku is a round mochi (glutinous rice cake) with a filling.

PAGE 76
Weekly Demon's Self is a reference to *Josei Jishin*, a women's weekly magazine in Japan.

PAGE 77
In Japanese, the word for "cute" can also mean "have affection for."

PAGE 81
Usa-chan is basically a cute way of saying "bunny" in Japanese.

PAGE 84
Mullin's **comeback** is originally a joke about *manzai*, a form of Japanese comedy where one person plays a foolish straight man (*boke*) and another gives retorts about the other's nonsensical statements (*tsukkomi*). Mullin is basically playing both roles in his head.

PAGE 87
Nii-ni is a cute way of saying *nii-san* (big brother).

PAGE 113
John **Tenniel** was the original illustrator for Lewis Carroll's *Alice's Adventures in Wonderland* (1865).

Arthur **Rackham** illustrated the later 1907 edition of *Alice's Adventures in Wonderland*.

PAGE 121
Charles Lutwidge **Dodgson** is the real name of author Lewis Carroll.

PAGE 137
Na___hei is Namihei from the family comedy manga and anime *Sazae-san*. His distinguishing characteristic is a lone hair on his bald head.

PAGE 138
Fu___ House is a reference to the American TV sitcom *Full House*, which was quite popular when it aired in Japan. In the Japanese version of *Miss Beelzebub*, Nisroch calls himself "*oitan*," which is what Michelle Tanner calls Uncle Jesse in the Japanese version of *Full House*.

As Miss Beel

mato

volume 4

Translation: Lisa Coffman
Lettering: Lorina Mapa

This book is a work of fiction. Names, characters, places, and incidents are the product of the author's imagination or are used fictitiously. Any resemblance to actual events, locales, or persons, living or dead, is coincidental.

BEELZEBUB-JO NO OKINIMESU MAMA. Vol. 4
©2017 matoba/SQUARE ENIX CO., LTD.
First published in Japan in 2017 by SQUARE ENIX CO., LTD. English translation rights arranged with SQUARE ENIX CO., LTD. and Yen Press, LLC through Tuttle-Mori Agency, Inc., Tokyo.

English translation ©2018 by SQUARE ENIX CO., LTD.

Yen Press, LLC supports the right to free expression and the value of copyright. The purpose of copyright is to encourage writers and artists to produce the creative works that enrich our culture.

The scanning, uploading, and distribution of this book without permission is a theft of the author's intellectual property. If you would like permission to use material from the book (other than for review purposes), please contact the publisher. Thank you for your support of the author's rights.

Yen Press
1290 Avenue of the Americas
New York, NY 10104

Visit us at yenpress.com
facebook.com/yenpress ★ yenpress.tumblr.com
twitter.com/yenpress instagram.com/yenpress

First Yen Press Edition: December 2018

Yen Press is an imprint of Yen Press, LLC.
The Yen Press name and logo are trademarks of Yen Press, LLC.

The publisher is not responsible for websites (or their content) that are not owned by the publisher.

Library of Congress Control Number: 2017963582

ISBNs: 978-0-316-44778-2 (paperback)
978-0-316-44779-9 (ebook)

10 9 8 7 6 5 4 3 2 1

WOR

Printed in the United States of America